WITH JUSTICE FOR ONE

A JUDGE'S DEATH SENTENCE

To Chris —

Life isn't always fair.

But life is always good!

Ray

ABOUT THE FRONT COVER

Dayton, Ohio Attorney Laurence A. Lasky sent me a fraudulent court order postmarked October 18, 1994, and used "World Peace through LAW" stamps. The nineteen-year-old stamps on the envelope were as unconventional as its contents.

First day cover of World Peace through LAW stamp

The back of the envelope of the first day cover reads:

WORLD PEACE THROUGH LAW

Issued as a prelude to the Seventh World Law Conference of the World Peace through Law Center held at Washington, D.C., October 12-17, 1975, the new stamp focused attention on the Center's efforts for World Peace. International law is the body of legal rules which apply to relations between sovereign nations. In theory, international law can prevent a nation's resort to arms against another. Subject to interpretation and implementation by an independent judicial authority such as the International Court of Justice at The Hague, such law is potentially enforceable through sanctions as well. Since earliest times forms of international law have existed without total success in maintaining peace. The Center seeks to meet this challenge.

WITH JUSTICE FOR ONE

A JUDGE'S DEATH SENTENCE

HORACE RAY METZ

ProAm Publishing Company
3601 Alexandria Pike, #9
Cold Spring, KY 41076

WITH JUSTICE FOR ONE
A Judge's Death Sentence

All Rights Reserved © 2012 by
Horace Ray Metz

ProAm Publishing Co.

For information:
ProAm Publishing Co.
3601 Alexandria Pike, #9
Cold Spring, KY 41076

raymetz@live.com

Cover designed by Loni Reeder

ISBN: 978-0-9845757-3-2

Printed in the United States of America

To my dearest Ann, who steadfastly exemplifies

Tammy Wynette's *"Stand by Your Man"*

Other books by the author:

God Is My Co-Counsel – My Search for Peace in the Valley

God Is My Co-Counsel – The Rules of the Game

INTRODUCTION

Sexually abused at age nineteen by Sherrill Wilkes, a University of Cincinnati professor, a crime worse than the assault was an ensuing cover-up; orchestrated by Cornelius Wandmacher, associate dean of the College of Engineering. I was left to struggle alone; with the immense harm caused me.

I lived in a prison of the psyche for decades. There had been no trial; no judge; and no jury fair. In this prison there were no walls of stone or razor wire; no warden; no prison guards; and no parole board. There were no other inmates. There was no visitation.

A life sentence was served in stark, lonely solitary confinement; with dark secrets from the past buried deep within the soul. Life was viewed from a prison window. The *good life* remained elusive; so close – and yet – so far away.

In darker moments throughout the decades, while under the influence of alcohol; I could have murdered Wandmacher. Momentary insanity would pass.

Thirty-five years after the cover-up, fate provided a surrogate; who would not be as fortunate as Wandmacher had been. After acknowledging my innocence, Judge James J. Gilvary sentenced me to an Ohio prison; in order to cover-up criminal activity within the judicial system in Dayton. Déjà vu!

Using the Biblical Paul as a role model, *With Justice for One* is the story of my escape from a prison of the psyche. Shakespearian in genre, it is the inspiring story of *A Judge's Death Sentence,* told as I lived it.

Ralph Waldo Emerson wrote:

> He has seen but half the universe who
> never has been shown the house of pain.

My *house of pain* is now a museum. A private prison has become a public venue. Visitors may observe life through this former prisoner's window; as if on a tour of Alcatraz.

The reader is invited into the seclusion of the mind, the intimacy of the heart, and the depths of the soul. *To each of you* who enters therein, *from all of me,* may God bless your life as He has mine.

–Horace Ray Metz

FREEDOM OF THE PRESS

It is widely understood that the First Amendment guarantees freedom of the press. Often overlooked is that this *freedom* is virtually absolute.

As the First Amendment guarantees the freedom of religion, including the freedom not to worship, or even believe in God; freedom of the press guarantees that same absolute - the freedom of newspapers to be unresponsive to any particular story, regardless of any perceived societal benefit to the community they serve.

The choices of what stories to cover; and how to cover them, are subjective discretions. The *right to choose* when/how to cover stories must always be protected. This brings me to the *Dayton Daily News*.

Though my ordeal within the judicial system was well-known to reporters, the newspaper chose to ignore my story, *in toto.* And while it is my personal belief that the greater Dayton community would have been better served had that not been the case; I expressed support, to acquaintances at the newspaper.

Though the criminal activity I stumbled onto, and the criminal activity undertaken against me was never reported; the mere *possibility* that it *could* happen was instrumental in reaching a just conclusion. It is likely concern was ever-present in the minds of oppressors; that the *Dayton Daily News* might respond differently.

While many reasons may exist for failing to cover my story, there is no call here for an after-the-fact justification; no call for an explanation of editorial decisions. At the same time, perception creates a problem for me.

Wherever Third World Justice is invoked, control of the press is instrumental in succeeding - over time. Aside from my case, the manner in which some stories were covered by the *Dayton Daily News* suggests undue influence. Given that, seeking permission to quote is reluctantly forsaken. Instead, permission to quote is *assumed* with gratitude; invoking the *fair use* doctrine, and the *greater needs* of the community to know.

Contents

THE RULES OF THE GAME

Law is the highest reason, implanted in nature, which commands what ought to be done and forbids the opposite. This reason, when firmly fixed and fully developed in the human mind, is Law.

True law is right reason in agreement with Nature; it is of universal application, unchanging and everlasting; it summons to duty by its commands, and averts from wrongdoing by its prohibitions.

It is a sin to try to alter this law, nor is it allowable to attempt to repeal any part of it, and it is impossible to abolish it entirely. We cannot be freed from its obligations by Senate or People, and we need not look outside ourselves for an expounder or interpreter of it.

And there will not be different laws at Rome and at Athens, or different laws now and in the future, but one eternal and unchangeable law will be valid for all nations and for all times, and there will be one master and one ruler, that is God, over us all, for He is the author of this law, its promulgator, and its enforcing judge.

Whoever is disobedient is fleeing from himself and denying his human nature, and by reason of this very fact he will suffer the worst penalties.

- Cicero (106 – 43 B.C.)

CHAPTER ONE

Judge Killer

It was four o'clock count and mail had just been handed out. I sat on my bunk; and opened Saturday's *Dayton Daily News.*

As was customary, I read the editorial page first, and then flipped to the metro section, where I kept tabs on my friends in Dayton.

During the twenty-six months I had been in prison, I often wondered what my reaction would be; when I learned Gilvary had died. But no matter how I imagined it, nothing could have prepared me for the stark finality of the headline on the front page of the Metro section of the *Dayton Daily News,* dated May 22, 1999:

Judge James J. Gilvary dead at age 69

"My judge died!" I blurted out, to no one in particular, breaking the mandatory silence of count time.

"There's a son-of-a-bitch that's in hell," came an immediate retort.

Initial shock quickly wore off. It was news I had expected. Staring at the headline in quiet contemplation, I thanked God the perverted judge would never abuse again.

Then I read the flattering obituary article written by reporter Rob Modic, comparing it to the man I knew. Not surprisingly, convicts sent to prison by Gilvary were not interviewed.

When count cleared, we were free to move about and talk until released for dinner. Rick Granger stopped by my bunk on his way back from the restroom.

The self-avowed atheist grinned down at me and said bemusedly, "Maybe there is a god after all."

I looked up at Granger and softly replied, "My friend, there's a lesson here for you, if you can see it. Judge Gilvary violated his oath of office, egregiously and repeatedly; an oath taken to God. It's one thing to be in *contempt of court* and quite another to be in *contempt of God.*"

"What'd he die from?" Granger asked.

"The article doesn't say, but that's beside the point."

"What do you mean?" Granger wanted to know.

"God doesn't use bullets," I observed with a smile, "I was only the warden. God handled the execution."

Granger, uneasy with the scope of the conversation, moved on back towards his bunk. I reflected on my prison acquaintance; a man without faith, lost and all alone - *The Lone Granger.*

A young man on a bunk next to mine said, "Mr. Metz, I hope you never get pissed off at me!"

"Not a chance," I assured.

Prisoners lived in an angry and hostile environment, with a pervasive underlying lack of personal identity caused, in some measure, by decidedly un-American inequities within the judicial system. In summation, a culture and code of *us-against-them* exists.

Fifty-five years old when I entered prison, many younger inmates looked to me for guidance. It was provided them. The occasion called for a proclamation of one kind or another.

Gilvary's sense of humor was mentioned in his obituary. Perhaps, from heaven, he would laugh along with me. If so, it would be the first laugh we shared.

"Listen up, eight-bay. This is a time of personal sorrow for me, having just learned my judge is dead," I began factitiously while standing beside my bunk.

"Yeah, right!" yelled someone behind me.

"I said listen up – not speak up!" I continued in a stern, slightly raised voice. "Now hear me out; this is important to me. This is a time to reflect on my dead judge and what he stood for. It's a time to reach out, to make some kind of gesture no matter how small or insignificant, as a token in honor of his-honor.

"You see, men, my judge suffered from Anal Anxiety – he pretended to be the perfect asshole, and it finally killed him.

"Simply saying *shit happens* doesn't seem adequate. So from now on, instead of taking a *shit*, I'm going to take a *gilvary*.

"I'd like for you men to join me in showing proper respect for my judge. I know most of you have no love of judges. But out of respect for the dead, I'm asking each of you to take one *gilvary* instead of a *shit* – in remembrance of the dumb ass that put me here.

"I'm asking each of you, just this once, to *give-a-shit* for a judge! Will you do that for me? Are you with me, men?"

It was a momentous occasion. I sat down to laughter and a shaking of heads in wonderment at my ability to find so perfect a way to express my respect.

When we were released for dinner, I skipped the meal in the cafeteria. I went to the cinder track on the yard, and walked in quiet contemplation over Judge Gilvary's death.

I slowly walked the cinder track for three hours. Dusk approached and a loud speaker announced the yard was closed. Inmates went inside for the night.

An inmate serving what amounted to a life sentence saw me, and proclaimed in a loud voice overheard by all, "There's *Judge Killer!*"

The nickname stuck with me throughout the rest of my time in prison; giving me unsolicited notoriety. This is the story of how I earned that nickname. This is the story of *Justice for One.*

CHAPTER TWO

The Dead Man's Hand

The following morning, another inmate confronted me. "So Gilvary's dead; so what? What have you proved? I'll tell you what you proved; you ain't proved shit! You're still stuck in prison, Judge Killer!"

There was no compunction to attempt to explain the truth. Granger had looked at me with a blank stare, unable to comprehend, the day before; as he was told, *"I was only the warden. God handled the execution."*

I simply shrugged and agreed with the know-it-all inmate. There were plenty of those; among the 2,200 I shared a home with in Pickaway Correctional Institution, just south of Columbus.

I thought back to when we met. August 26, 1996 was Judge Gilvary's unlucky day. He was appointed to my criminal case at 11:52 a.m. Wasting no time; he personalized matters immediately. And the first thing on his agenda was an attempt to revoke my personal recognizance bond.

Late in the afternoon, I received a telephone call. A legal secretary from Attorney John P. Kolesar's office informed me I was commanded to appear in the chambers of Judge James J. Gilvary at ten o'clock the following morning.

Kolesar would meet me there. And she had no idea of why we were meeting Gilvary, since Judge Barbara P. Gorman had recently been assigned the case; who had replaced Judge Dennis J. Langer.

In places with Third World Justice, such as was found in Dayton, appalling abuses of the system were routine. From experience gleaned while dealing with my foes, I could conceptualize what was planned.

In criminal cases, orders compelling prosecutors and a defendant's counsel to meet in chambers, or in open court, would have been scheduled in writing. An entry would become a part of the official case record.

This meeting was scheduled via *oral* command. It was bogus. If I failed to appear as commanded, my personal recognizance bond would be revoked. And I would be off the streets; no longer a threat to ethically challenged officers of the court.

On the morning of August 27, 1996, I made the journey from Cold Spring, Kentucky - fifteen minutes south of Cincinnati - to Dayton, Ohio. As was my practice, I arrived at the Montgomery County Courts Building early, providing for half an hour of quiet reflection over coffee in the basement snack shop.

Everything I had experienced in life prepared me to go to battle with Judge James J. Gilvary. All I had endured in life provided the motivation to do so. *He has no idea of what lay ahead,* I thought somberly.

In worldly terms, we were opposites in life experiences. Gilvary held the prestige and power of a judge. I was a gadfly with a checkered past; representing myself pro se. In the secular world; I stood the proverbial snowball's chance in hell. But there was an equalizer.

In spiritual terms, *I walked the walk.* Officers of the court took an oath of office; it was an oath taken to God. Gilvary's Achilles heel would be his willingness to desecrate his oath. If this were not so, he would never have become embroiled in my case.

Before even meeting him; I knew Gilvary *talked the talk.* So in the spiritual world, it was he who had the proverbial snowball's chance in hell.

In conceptualizing the battle looming with Judge Gilvary, I envisioned the two trials being conducted simultaneously. In the secular world, Gilvary would decide my fate. And in the spiritual world, God would decide Gilvary's fate!

Leaving the basement snack shop, I took the elevator to the third floor and Gilvary's chambers. I took a
seat and waited for Kolesar. He was late as usual.

Attorney John P. Kolesar had been assigned as my
legal advisor; supposedly to assist me in representing
myself. That was the superficial reason given. But his
actual mission was to act as a double-agent; and as a
snitch for my foes within the judicial system.

Having been licensed less than a year, the mousey
young attorney was out of his element in the rough
and tumble world of criminal law. I thought he was
better suited for fixing parking tickets for nuns - who
did not drive.

Being my legal advisor caused John-boy considerable consternation. His fellow officers of the court were
out to get me, by hook-or-crook, and I was just as determined to take them down. And while his oath to
practice included allegiance to his client; his *In God
We Trust* payments came from dependency on the
good will of judges.

There was a definite upside. Since being chosen to
act as a double-agent the previous spring, Kolesar's
court-appointed case load had increased dramatically;
very, very dramatically. The young fool told me so
himself.

It was a quid pro quo. By helping my unscrupulous
foes, Kolesar was generously compensated by them.
And so, he was a busy young beaver, at the beck and
call of ethically challenged judges; haplessly scurrying
from case to case, courtroom to courtroom.

Outwardly, it gave him a sense of self-importance.
But secretly, he knew the underlying reasons for his
sudden prosperity. And inwardly it created a sense of
guilt and shame. Soon after leaving the idealism of law
school, he sold his soul for a few pieces of silver.

At the same time, John-boy had not done so long
enough to become a jaded cynic. But that was where
he was headed.

Understanding that, Kolesar would become essential to me, when the timing was right. Two could play the double-agent game. And I held an advantage. My egotistical foes would be aware of his role for them; but could never suspect I would use him, just as they did.

We waited as the judge cleared his docket, calling defense attorneys and prosecutors into his chambers for three or four cases. A lowly pro se defendant, and his young court appointed legal eagle were at the rear of the pecking order.

Being at the back of the line gave me a chance to observe; to take in the lay of the land. I had no interest in learning about Gilvary from others. Everyone presents a public persona. I wanted to make close up and personal, unbiased observations about this newest threat. Any information gleaned about my newest opponent could prove invaluable.

Kolesar informed me in a guarded voice that Gilvary was now our judge. *No shit, John-boy,* I thought. It was time to play mind games with Kolesar. It helped pass the time; keeping the annoyance factor in check.

"Why is he our judge, John?"

Kolesar's most accurate answer came forth, as if a reflex, "I don't know."

"There must be a reason, John. You're the lawyer. What do you think?"

"Nobody wants to stay on your case very long, Mr. Metz."

"It's because they have been outrageously crooked, and I keep catching them. You're not crooked are you, John?"

A nervous laugh was followed by, "No."

"Good, 'cause if I catch you pulling any fast ones, you're outta-here!" I said with a laugh.

Two judges had come and gone, like gypsies in the night, and so had prosecutors. Much to his consternation, Kolesar was the only one forced to stick it out.

Kolesar became uncomfortably quiet; once I brought up the question of his integrity. I wanted to play some more.

"John, what happens when we run out of judges? Do they have to dismiss?"

"We're not going to run out of judges," Kolesar answered without assuring me.

"Well hell, John, there's only eleven of 'em. Gilvary is the *third* one in a month,"

"I don't know what's going on," Kolesar confessed.

It was the most intelligent thing he said to me, since his unsolicited appointment to "assist" in my defense. O.J. had his *dream team;* I had Dayton's version of Pee-wee Herman.

Finally, Kolesar and I were the only ones left waiting to be seen. Gilvary came out of his inner sanctum and asked, "Are you Mr. Metz?"

"Yes, Your Honor."

Gilvary attempted to look puzzled as he mused, "I don't know *who* scheduled you to come in this morning, but your presence here isn't needed. You are free to go."

"Thank you, Your Honor," I said politely.

You're a lying, no good son-of-a-bitch! I thought to myself as Kolesar and I departed.

I had taken a day off work, and had driven 140 miles roundtrip for this charade. But I learned many things.

Gilvary was in his sixties. Body language told me he was adequately impressed with himself.

For all his superficial smugness, I detected an underlying uneasy demeanor. He had involved himself in something so sleazy; I had to wonder *why* he would be willing to do it. He masked disappointment that I appeared as commanded; but his intent was confirmed, via the same body language.

Gilvary seemed unsure of himself. For my reputation preceded me; and thirteen judges had preceded him.

As we waited for the elevator to the lobby, I asked, "Well, John?"

"Well what?" John-boy asked in his clueless fashion.

"*Who* called you?"

"Called me for what?"

"Damn it! I just took a day off work and drove seventy miles to get here. All I heard was Gilvary's bullshit. *Who* told you about the so-called meeting?"

"Ah - I received a message. It was from someone in the prosecutor's office."

"I see. John, did you see any prosecutor's present in chambers, who are involved in our case?"

"No."

"Why not, John?"

Advisor Kolesar gave his favorite response, a hesitant, "I don't know."

A correct answer: *Because they weren't there.*

Leaving Kolesar after finishing in Gilvary's chambers, I went to the University of Dayton, and the law library. By now it was familiar turf.

I sat in the law library, amongst the innocence; the idealism of students aspiring to learn the intricacies and nuances of the law, and thought of the reality of the world many faced.

Kolesar was a year removed from them. Three years of law school had prepared him to be a shill for the system. It was a depressing thought. I shook it off.

I began by preparing a plan for spending precious time in legal research. I studied a transfer form served on me when the case was transferred from Langer to Gorman, time-stamped on July 29, 1996. It read:

> This case, originally assigned to Judge ___LANGER___, is transferred pursuant to local rule, to Judge __GORMAN.__

As we waited in Judge Gilvary's chambers, double-agent Kolesar had handed me a document. I put it away. Now as I looked at it, I became puzzled. It was a Request for Disqualification from Gorman. It read:

> See attached letter – I talked to Judge Langer about this case after I read the letter. He said there appears to be strong feelings by the defendant against Larry Lasky – who will possibly be called as a witness in this case. Since I was a classmate of Larry's in law school, a co-employee in the prosecutor's office & a friend, I believe it should be transferred to another judge. Dennis & I believe it should be transferred to someone who hasn't worked in the prosecutor's office.

It was obvious Gorman wanted me to believe she was looking out for my interests. But! She confessed to God and country that she was *"a friend"* of Larry Lasky. And that told me volumes about her. Nothing that came out of her mouth - or from her pen - had any credibility. Including the b.s. found on the form I possessed.

What puzzled me was that Langer provided me with the Transfer Form, and Gorman had not. But Gorman provided me a Request for Disqualification, and Langer had not. I concluded both time-stamped forms were necessary to transfer a case from one judge to another. The reason Gorman offered one, but not the other; was self-evident. It provided *planted* contrived information - meant for my eyes. But the other form, like Langer sent me, was to be kept from me. For it read:

> This case, originally assigned to...

The case could not have been *originally* assigned to Judge Gorman <u>and</u> to Judge Langer. I reflected on the two originally assigned judges, in the context of:[1]

> There's only one Mona Lisa
> One Leaning Tower of Pisa
> One Paris and there's only one you

---

[1] Lyrics from "Only One You"; released by T.G. Sheppard in 1981. The renowned artist has a God-given ability to write a classic in an hour. The story of his career is truly remarkable.

Immersed in thought, I processed matters further. *But in State of Ohio vs. Horace Raymond Metz there are two originally assigned judges! Is there any limit to how many times a case could be reassigned?*

I searched the Ohio Revised Code and found the law providing for a change of venue from one county to another, when substantial conflicts of interest existed. A change of venue was unquestionably called for.

But if my foes intended to follow O.R.C., the bogus criminal case would never have been *created.* So that would never happen. Too many people had gone to a lot of trouble, in assuring that justice *did not* prevail.

Finally it hit me. The search for the answer lay right in front of me! The wording on the transfer forms were pre-typed, reading [emphasis added as they appeared to leap from the page]:

...is transferred **pursuant to local rule**, to...

I concluded *local rule provided for only one transfer!* This was confirmed upon reviewing the Montgomery County Local Rules of Court. I finally hit pay dirt, under Rule 1.10 Rules of Construction and Rule 1.19 The Assignment System:

IV. Effective Date.
These rules **shall** take effect on July 1, 1993. They govern **all** proceedings in actions brought on or after July 1, 1993.
Rule 1.19 The Assignment System
III(C) Transfer Of Assigned Cases To A New Judge
If the case is transferred from the originally assigned judge to a new judge, **the** new judge **shall** hear **all** motions and proceedings to the case. [Emphasis added.]

Next I referenced a legal dictionary. Pertaining to law, ***the*** is exclusive; ***shall*** is a mandate; and ***all*** means every. I listed the ABCs of the case:

A   **the** originally assigned judge - Dennis J. Langer
B   to **the** new judge - Barbara P. Gorman
C   James J. Gilvary

Local Rule 1.19 III(C was ironclad. My case *could not* be transferred to Gilvary - pursuant to explicit local rule! What if he illegally sent me to prison?

Next I referenced the kidnapping section of the Ohio Revised Code. § 2905.01 read in pertinent part:

> (A) No person, by force, threat, or deception...shall remove another from the place where he is found or restrain the liberty of the other person, for any of the following purposes:
> (2) To facilitate the commission of any felony or flight there-after...
> (B) No person, by force, threat, or deception...shall knowingly
> (1) Remove another from the place where the other person is found;
> (2) Restrain another of his liberty;
> (3) Hold another in a condition of involuntary servitude.
> (C) Whoever violates this section is guilty of kidnapping, a felony of the first degree.

Ohio Revised Code language was explicit; *no person* describes with exacting precision who the law applies too: *everyone!* Without having jurisdiction in my case, Gilvary attempted to have me jailed by revocation of my Personal Recognizance bond. He did so to cover up the crimes of others.

The ploy was audaciously clever. But at the same time, it was exceedingly dumb. For whether Gilvary kidnapped me with a gun - or his gavel - was moot.

If Gilvary succeeded in having me arrested, he would have been guilty of kidnapping. Arguably, even making me appear in his chambers, under implicit threat of arrest, was kidnapping.

As discovered in January 2010, pursuant to Local Rule, the computer program utilized by the clerk of courts would accommodate only *one transfer!* Barbara P. Gorman has always been listed as my judge.

Nothing Judge Gilvary did - or ever would do - could have any legal basis! Aside from later discoveries, the magnitude of what I knew was unsettling.

Gorman was simply having Gilvary do her dirty work.

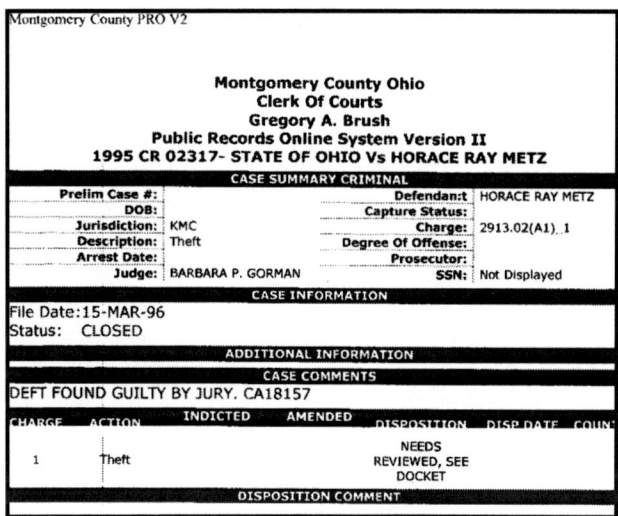

Taken from Internet - in January 2010
Ohio v. Metz Case Summary - **Judge: Gorman**

The complexion of the game had taken a drastic turn. We were playing Ohio's version of *Texas Holdem!* Believing the high-stakes game was rigged, no matter our hands; Judge Gilvary committed to going *all in.*

The most gratifying thing I gained from this night's work in the University of Dayton law library was: *The cards on the table* became Local Rule 1.19 III(C). Hole cards gave me a *royal flush,* while Gilvary's hole cards gave him *aces and eights.*

Table stakes were identified and reduced to writing; in the University of Dayton's law library, the same day Gilvary and I met:

HIGH-STAKES POKER

Perhaps the renowned Russian novelist Dostoevsky would have been impressed with Metz's bet: twelve years of his life on the table with nothing in "his hand" except his faith in God and his belief in his country – against the power of a vengeful state and the tyranny of an out-of-control judiciary. Metz's sanity could be questioned. Metz was certain that it would be. He was holding a *royal flush* against *aces and eights*.

Gilvary took an oath to God and country. If he kidnapped me, would the spiritual dynamics involved be enough to kill him? It was an intriguing secular question; far beyond the scope of Local Rule.

It mattered not to me. If spiritual dynamics failed; I resolved to kill him from prison - using my pen! One thing was clear; that was a nonnegotiable certainty.

Aces and eights were *The Dead Man's Hand.*[2]

---

[2] When Wild Bill Hickok was shot and killed at the poker table on June 25, 1876 in Deadwood, South Dakota, his last hand was black *aces and eights* (with a queen kicker). Thus they became known as *The Dead Man's Hand.* Living in Cincinnati, Hickok's widow learned of his death in a local newspaper. She was persuaded not to take the legendary gunfighter's remains back East. In a trial that was rigged; his killer, Jack McCall was found "not guilty." Later, a deputy U.S. marshall heard a drunken McCall brag that he had "put one over" on the Deadwood jury. He had; for he shot Hickok in the back of the head, with a barroom full of witnesses! Asked why he shot Hickok in the back of the head; instead of confronting him, McCall responded, "I didn't want to commit suicide." Because of his drunken braggadocio; McCall was arrested and tried in federal court for first degree murder. The defense claimed double jeopardy. The government claimed McCall's first trial had no legal standing, in an extra-legal court in an outlaw town; and the judge agreed with prosecutors. Found guilty; McCall was hanged on March 1, 1877. (See *Wild Bill Hickok* by Richard O'Connor; ©1959.)

CHAPTER THREE

Déjà Vu

It was after ten o'clock when I left the University of Dayton, and headed home to Cold Spring, Kentucky. Lost in somber reflection while driving the speed limit, it had been a long day and I was extremely weary.

Going down I-75 from Dayton to Cincinnati, I approached the Tylersville Road exit, near Mason and West Chester. Off to the left, the blinking lights atop the two towers at the Voice of America Relay Station facility could be seen.

Acting on impulse, and forgetting being tired, I took the exit, turned left and crossed over I-75. Approximately a mile from I-75, I turned left on Butler Warren County Line Road. On the east side of the Voice of America property, I was back on sacred grounds.

Just north; off Tylersville Road, I turned right onto a new street named Tyler Court. The homes there had been built while I was in the residential water conditioning business. I had had six customers out of the twenty or so homeowners who lived there.

I drove slowly down the winding dead-end street; turning around in the cul-de-sac and drove slowly back up it - to the stop sign at Butler Warren County Line Road. Turning north in the darkness, I stopped at the spot where a sexual attack had occurred, decades before. And as I sat there, in the quiet of night, I took a trip down memory lane:

The Professor

I graduated from Beavercreek High School with six majors; and was accepted into the 1960 freshman engineering class at University of Cincinnati. My goal was to become an electrical engineer, and then a radio astronomer. My dream was to explore God's vast universe; to places beyond visual comprehension. The idea was to enhance man's understanding of the universe, and his place in it.

Fate is a funny thing. Two weeks after graduating high school, I went home from summer baseball practice and played basketball in our driveway with brothers Jerry and Tom. It was something we had done hundreds of times. Tom stepped in front of me as I drove for a lay-up, and I vaulted over his knee, landing hard in the gravel.

Both bones in my left arm were shattered, and I was in Miami Valley Hospital for a week. A plate was placed on one bone and a steel rod was placed inside the other, through my elbow almost to my wrist.

The cast was removed from my arm before college began. Dr. David Heller informed me he would remove the rod from my arm at Thanksgiving break.

At Thanksgiving break I went to Miami Valley Hospital as an outpatient, where Dr. Heller attempted to remove the rod from my arm. After making an incision in my elbow, the doctor tried to unscrew the rod via a flange on the end. The rod snapped off about a quarter-inch into the bone.

The surgeon had never experienced anything like this before. He said the rod would be removed at Easter break, when the plate was removed from the other bone.

Returning to campus after Thanksgiving, I developed a bone infection in my elbow. The incision would not heal because the broken rod agitated it. I visited the school dispensary almost daily.

As the spring of 1961 approached, I was told by school doctors it was unlikely the rod could ever be removed from my arm. The prognosis was dire: the bone infection could not heal with the rod agitating it; and amputation at the elbow was proposed as a likely solution. For the first time in my life, I experienced raw unadulterated fear.

Health problems placed me at a competitive disadvantage, in a very difficult engineering school. I shared my concerns with Associate Dean Cornelius Wandmacher, who referred me to Professor Sherrill Wilkes, the counselor for engineering students.

I did not know Wilkes, an English professor. I shared my concerns with him over several meetings; I feared losing my arm and I feared flunking out of school. My dream of becoming a radio astronomer was in jeopardy.

Wilkes had an almost magical way of renewing my self-confidence. He led me to *believe* the arm problem would be resolved at Spring break; and after that the Dean's List was the goal.

Freshman engineering students had final exams before leaving campus for two weeks. I would take six exams – one per day beginning on Saturday.

Professor Wilkes suggested I use his office to study for the first exam, pointing out the dorm would be noisy on a Friday night. His office would be quiet. I readily agreed.

Wilkes had to go to Dayton, Ohio, and locked me in the engineering building on Friday evening. He returned after eleven o'clock.

I was excited, as studying had gone well. I was ready for the exam, and felt an immense sense of gratitude for all Professor Wilkes had done for me.

He asked if I were hungry and suggested a late-night snack. I was famished and agreed. He knew just the place – the Sugar 'n' Spice Restaurant out on Reading Road. I remember we each had a ham and Swiss sandwich, fries and a strawberry shake. In effect, it was *the last supper*.

Upon leaving the Sugar 'n' Spice, Wilkes headed away from campus. When questioned, he said he made a "wrong turn" coming out of the parking lot, having been distracted by our conversation. He would go out to Tylersville Road, cut over to I-75, and return to campus that way.

Wilkes was going miles out of the way. My senses were on high alert. I sensed something sinister was taking place, though I could not phantom what it was. Weighing my options, there did not seem to be any. We were far from campus; it was late, and in a few hours I had a final exam to take.

I carefully observed where Wilkes drove. He went out Reading Road to Butler-Warren County Line Road and headed north. He crossed Tylersville Road, went about a mile and turned around. Before getting back to Tylersville, he stopped the car on the side of the road, next to the Voice of America Relay Station facility.

Professor Wilkes told me I needed a form of acupuncture therapy. Fearing what might happen should I refuse to go along, I followed his instructions, lowering my pants and underwear to lie across his lap.

I felt revulsion as Wilkes ran his hands over my buttocks, saying, "Oh, a nice hairy one!" His depravity filled me with terror; with humiliation. I felt a strong instinct to resist, but did not know what to do.

Wilkes began his "treatment" by jabbing me with needles held in both hands. It hurt and I asked him to stop.

Ignoring my pleas for him to stop, he seemed to lose any sense of rationality, as he began jabbing me faster and faster, harder and harder. The pain became intense. Survival instincts took over as I tried to avoid panicking.

Wilkes continued to abuse me, continued to ignore my pleas to stop. Finally I blurted in pain, "Professor Wilkes, please stop. My arm is bleeding on your seat!"

Though not true, this seemed to snap Wilkes out of his trance-like assault, and he stopped the abuse. He told me to pull up my underwear and pants, as he placed the needles in a fancy case that held many others.

He got out of the car and went to the rear. I thought he was urinating, but he was taking too long.

As I waited, I "accidently" hit the brake pedal and in the illumination created by the brake light, I could see Professor Wilkes in a side-view mirror. The pervert was masturbating, apparently having difficulty reaching orgasm.

The assault was a life-changing experience. In the quiet of night, next to the Voice of America Relay Station, where a message of hope, a message of freedom was beamed across the heavens, mine was taken from me.

I sat alone in the darkness, remembering the long-ago past; while comparing it to the present mess. I conceptualized:

In the legal arena, the pen is a weapon of choice. The battles of wits are akin to gunfights on Main Street, in the Old West.

There is mythology about Old West gunfights. They are remembered in romantic nostalgia as fair fights for the most part, where the *good guy* prevailed more often than not. Reality was; the fastest gun usually prevailed. He was *good* - with a gun!

Mythology exists in modern courtrooms too. In modern-day legal skirmishes, the unscrupulous lawyer uses the pen unconscionably; with the mindset of a criminal thug wielding an AK-47.

I used this insight in dealing with lawyers. My approach was to make an immediate and unrelenting counterattack whenever confronted, as if I were defending myself in the back alley of a ghetto.

I liked to reference the power of the pen, quoting from *Richelieu; Or the Conspiracy* written by Edward Bulwer-Lytton in 1839:

True, This!
Beneath the rule of men entirely great,
The pen is mightier than the sword. Behold
The arch-enchanters wand! – itself is nothing! –
But taking sorcery from the master-hand
To paralyse the Caesars, and to strike
The loud earth breathless! – Take away the sword
States can be saved without it.

I continued the trip down memory lane:

The Cover-Up

On the way back to campus, Professor Wilkes attempted to assure me that the "treatment" had not been sexual in nature. Survival instincts were still on high alert; my only objective was to get back to campus alive, and escape the madman.

Concerned about how Wilkes might react if he realized how distraught I was, I managed a subdued composure. Wilkes mistook my silence for agreement; for weakness, and said we would use the same plan when preparing for five other exams. I should meet him at his office Sunday evening.

"Great idea," I assured him.

In this hour of darkness, there was only one place to turn. It was about one-thirty in the morning when I slipped into my room and retrieved my Bible. I walked the quiet campus, clutching God's word to my breast as I sobbed in despair, searching for guidance.

I decided to entrust a classmate I believed to be discrete, whose roommate had gone home for the weekend. I woke him up about 3:00 a.m., and told him I needed a friend to confide in; and thought of him. I requested he not ask what had happened, and never mention my visit to anyone. He assured me of his silence and I showed him my mutilated buttocks.

Observing his shocked face, I simply said something terrible happened, and one day I might need a witness to my physical condition. I would depend on his silence unless he was called upon, and counted on his honesty should that day come. He silently nodded his agreement.

Leaving my acquaintance, I went into the nearby Burnet Woods, where I spent the rest of the night. Sitting on a park bench under a street light, in my hour of anguish and despair, I opened my Bible. My eyes fell on Proverbs 24:10:[3]

If thou faint in the day of adversity, thy strength *is* small.

I read the verse over and over, through tear stained eyes. As I focused on the verse, a sense of calm came over me. I sensed that God was with me. I sought His direction.

With all the doubts, and all the fears tormenting my soul; one thing became crystal clear. I had to report Professor Wilkes.

No matter what Wilkes had done to help me prior to that night; no matter that he was a popular professor with seventeen years tenure at UC; no matter who might not believe me, I had a *moral obligation* to see that Wilkes did not abuse again. I had a *moral obligation* to see that Wilkes received the mental health help he needed. Though the victim, I experienced a sense of responsibility *for* Professor Wilkes.

What if he attacked another who was not as lucky as I? What might he do to such a person? What lengths might he go too, to assure a victim's silence? For that matter, how did I know I was safe? How would I avoid further encounters with

---

[3] King James Version.

him? A resolve grew within me. I would not *faint in the day of adversity!*

Daybreak found me wandering around the campus again, waiting for direction; for some intuitive inkling of what to do next. And then I remembered.

I thought of a former African missionary and the college-age Sunday night Bible study I attended. We recently had had a clothing drive on campus to gather donations to send to African missionaries. In order to set up donation boxes around campus, I obtained permission from a Dean James Sculley.

I went to Sculley's office, and for some unremembered reason, he was in that Saturday morning. I finally got my story out and showed Sculley the physical evidence.

I skipped the part about confiding in another student. I need not have been concerned about being believed, as the shock at seeing my physical condition was self-evident.

Dean Sculley told me he had never encountered anything remotely like this. He needed time to assemble some of his colleagues. He would take care of my missing the final exam that morning. I was instructed to return in the afternoon, and advised to avoid other students in the meantime.

After coffee at a restaurant, I returned to Burnet Woods until it was time to return to Sculley's office; deeply relieved I found someone to confide in. Six to eight university officials were there when I returned. Associate Dean Wandmacher was among them.

Some things had already been decided. Wilkes would not be confronted in the following week, as he was English professor for half of the engineering freshmen. It would be too disruptive of final exams. He would be dealt with during Spring break. I was told to avoid him during the week.

But I was to meet Professor Wilkes at his office Sunday evening, for another "treatment," I reminded. How was I to handle this? Simply do not go, came the collective wisdom.

And if I saw him on campus, I should avoid him. If he approached me, I was told not to get into a situation where I was alone with him. I would take my exams as scheduled, making up the one missed.

I was asked not to divulge anything about the incident to other students, and I agreed. Again, I failed to mention one had already been confided in.

Then I was asked how my parents might react, and the group was told I could not know. It was agreed it would be "best" not to confide in them. And in return for my cooperation, the group would collectively do anything possible to assist me in attaining my education.

It was arranged for me to meet with Associate Dean Wandmacher each day, so he could monitor my activity. I left the meeting believing my prayers had been answered; a bond had been established. I vowed my silence to a group of university officials I did not know, but whom I trusted; and in return they vowed to help me.

Wilkes knew I ate meals in the cafeteria. He confronted me Monday morning, wanting to know why I had not kept our scheduled appointment the evening before. I promised to meet him in his office that evening.

It was very, very unnerving, being face-to-face with the perverted professor. After finishing breakfast, I had to take a final exam. I flunked it.

Twice more, Professor Wilkes cornered me in the cafeteria in the mornings that week. Twice more I agreed to meet him in his office; and stood him up. Wilkes was more and more insistent that we meet privately. And Wandmacher would just shrug it off.

Wandmacher failed to comprehend the turmoil Wilkes's predatory acts caused within me; though we met daily. Even though, I failed five final exams.

I went home for Spring break an emotional basket case. I had not told my parents of concerns my arm might have to be amputated at the elbow. I did not share what had happened with Wilkes, or that I failed the five final exams. Instead, I attempted to put up a brave front of normality.

I prayed as never before; promised God that if it be His will that I lose my arm, I could accept it. If He had another plan for my life, other than being a radio astronomer, so be it. My faith was in the only Source I knew.

With God's help, I would not fail in life. I might lose an arm, and I might fail in college, but my faith in Almighty God assured me I would not fail in life. For I came from somewhere; and one day I would go somewhere. In the meantime, my life had meaning and purpose.

II Corinthians 5:7 became my mantra:

For we walk by faith, not by sight.

I entered Miami Valley Hospital on Sunday, in preparation for surgery the following morning. Normally, Dr. Heller would have conferred with me before operating, explaining what would take place and offering assurances. He avoided me. This told me he was not certain the broken rod could be removed.

The broken rod had been an aberration; was not the fine surgeon's fault. I prayed that God would consider Dr. Heller's well-being; how failure would affect his life and career. I prayed for God to put His hand on the surgeon's shoulder as he faced fear of the unknown.

The operation was a success and miraculously the rod was removed. Dr. Heller acted as if it had not been that big a deal. We both knew better. I understood the fear the fine surgeon experienced. I knew we had both mercifully won a big victory, and I believed the credit belonged to Almighty God! My arm would heal.

Upon returning to campus following Spring break, I was summoned to Dean Sculley's office. Professor Wilkes had been terminated. The official story was; he decided to retire.

When Wilkes had been confronted, he broke down and admitted he had a "problem." His explanation included that years before his fiancé had been killed in an auto-train wreck, and he had not been the same since. Wilkes had relocated out-of-state, and I need not be concerned about him anymore.

Though I had not failed any courses, the final exams brought some averages down to an "E" level, between passing and failure. I would have to repeat those courses during the next two terms, as well as carry the normal schedule. This meant 23½ credit hours the first term, followed by 24½ credit hours.

Wilkes had been extremely active; and was popular on campus. He was praised as one of the better professors, as students expressed disappointment that he had left.

There was a great deal of speculation as to *why* he had suddenly decided to retire. Some students, knowing I had been counseled by him, asked if I knew something more about his departure. I denied knowing anything.

There were unseemly whispered rumors about Professor Wilkes. And I wondered in anguish: *How many know the truth about him? Could they figure it out: I had ratted on him!* Interaction with students was difficult; exacerbating my fragile mental state.

I experienced an enormous sense of guilt, and came to believe I had been *responsible* for Wilkes' sudden demise. While my arm was healing physically, my mental state was deteriorating rapidly.

Half way through the first term, I went to see Dean Wandmacher and attempted to explain my feelings to him. He arranged for me to see a school psychologist, with the explicit understanding I would say *nothing* about the abuse incident.

I was to tell the psychologist I had been very worried about my arm; and that concern affected my class work. Of course, the psychologist could be of no help.

After meeting with me several times, and administering tests such as the Rorschach Inkblot Test, I was informed I was not crazy. The psychologist found me normal, though a little too serious. He recommended I lighten up, and perhaps have an occasional beer with the guys. As a teetotaler, I felt even more isolated; and so very, very alone, after seeing the psychologist.

But I made it through the first term, with better grades. The 24½ credits in the next term involved 41 hours in class and labs per week. It was a heavy load for a normal student. I was far, far from normal.

I felt a profound sense of sadness, of depression and detachment; as though experiencing a mental breakdown. My plight exemplified, being *alone in a crowd* – on a campus where I no longer belonged.

Finally I informed Dean Wandmacher I needed to withdraw from school for awhile; in order to regain my health. I wanted to return in one year, picking up my studies where I was at the present time.

Wandmacher attempted to dissuade me, pointing out my grades were improving. Nothing would matter if I had a nervous breakdown, I reminded. How would we explain that? My mental state was in chaos, and I simply had to get away from campus. It was a matter that could not, *and would not,* be postponed. It was agreed. I would leave school and resume my studies in a year. And so, I withdrew from UC in the summer of 1961.

As the time approached to return to school, I wrote Dean Wandmacher. In my letter I informed him of my excellent work history, listed the fifty nonfiction books I had read, and described my preparation for the courses I would have to take. I had a co-op job arranged. I was ready to resume my studies as we had agreed.

I heard nothing from Dean Wandmacher, and intuitively knew what had probably happened. A review committee approved readmissions. Unless Wandmacher spoke up in my behalf – with the truth – the committee had no basis to readmit me. Once again, Wandmacher betrayed me. After the time passed for me to return to UC, I received a letter welcoming me to the freshman class in September. They expected me to start all over!

$2,000 had been invested in my higher education to date. I was expected to duplicate it - for appearances. The insincere offer was simply ignored.

It was a callous slap in the face by Wandmacher, with an unspoken message: GO AWAY! I felt enormously betrayed and unwelcomed; like some kind of outcast, solely responsible for Professor Wilkes' sudden demise. I imagined the anger and scorn his former colleagues directed to me. And I went away.

Once again, while suffering in silence, I believed I had let my dear parents down. I experienced intense feelings of shame and remorse, and slid into an even deeper depression.

Finally the sense of Wandmacher's betrayal tormented me to the point; Mother confronted me in the spring of 1963. She demanded to know what had happened to me in college that troubled me so. Mom assumed I had gotten my girlfriend pregnant. Shocked at her suspicions, I told her the truth.

UNIVERSITY OF CINCINNATI
COLLEGE OF ENGINEERING
CINCINNATI 21, OHIO

May 3, 1961

Mrs. Horace Metz
R.R. #1
Waynesville, Ohio

Dear Mrs. Metz:

——I have had the opportunity to get to know Ray fairly well during— the two weeks just preceding spring vacation when I had a number of conferences with him.

In these conferences he freely admitted that he had not made the best use of his time during the early part of the year but felt that he was now in a position to improve his study habits and hopefully his scholastic record.

In these interviews I could sense also that his arm had been giving him considerable concern and that he was looking forward to the hospitalization during the spring vacation with the hope that this would ease this condition.

We discussed fully his program for the summer term and the fact that he may still have some remaining work to make up next year. During the last week which was a critical one for him, he visited my office every day and I found that he fulfilled all of the obligations which were put to him successfully. He passed mathematics and statics although the grades in these were only minimum passing grades. Ray did demonstrate an ability to pull himself up at the last minute.

I am pleased to note that he has registered for the summer term and I will be pleased to counsel further with him. It would seem that while his problems at the moment are numerous he has now shown an ability to deal with them and overcome these difficulties. It may take some time but I think there is reason to believe he can be fairly successful in getting back to good standing during the summer and next year.

Sincerely yours,

Cornelius Wandmacher
Associate Dean

CW:jpr

cc: Mr. Horace R. Metz
Freshman Advisor
Professor Knapp

Cover-up letter from Associate Dean Wandmacher

I never saw Mother so angry. Unknown to me, she had contacted University of Cincinnati officials after that fateful Spring break, wanting to know what happened to her son while in college; that upset him so terribly. She showed me a cover-up letter received from Dean Wandmacher, written May 3, 1961. Though the letter indicates I received a copy, I had never seen it before. The extent of Wandmacher's deception from the beginning was summarized in his words:

> In these interviews I could sense also that his arm had been giving him considerable concern and that he was looking forward to the hospitalization during the spring vacation with the hope that this would ease this condition.

Soon after writing to Mom, this was precisely the posture Wandmacher coerced me into taking with the school psychologist! It was one thing not to voluntarily disclose Professor Wilkes sexual assault on me. It was quite another to deliberately mislead about it to cover-up. For Mother had asked: *WHY?*

Later I inadvertently learned; Professor Wilkes went to a university in Tennessee. And I learned he continued to abuse; again and again.

Guilt, shame, and remorse became shadows that accompanied depression; endured in silence. I had done *nothing* to prevent the cover-up of a predator.

The present was compared to a distant past, as I sat alone in the darkness, next to the Voice of America facility. I was not in my parked car in the darkness of night, because of the acts of Attorney Larry Lasky. Nor was I back at the Voice of America facility because of a long-ago sexual attack by Professor Sherrill Wilkes.

I was there because of Judge James J. Gilvary. And I was there because of the long-ago cover-up by Associate Dean Cornelius Wandmacher; whose actions had sentenced me to a prison of the psyche!

Through the decades; my biggest regret was *permitting him to escape any accountability for his deceit; for*

*putting the university's reputation ahead of my best in-
terests; and the interests of students Wilkes continued
to abuse elsewhere.*

During the tumultuous decades to follow; I regretted
Wandmacher was never held accountable. And during
moments of intense pain, while under the influence of
alcohol; I sometimes had thoughts of murdering him.

Now fate gave me another chance to confront a chill-
ingly callous cover-up. And dynamics were compelling:

Lasky (1994) was to Wilkes (1961)
as
Gilvary (1996) was to Wandmacher (1961)

In the darkness, the still of the night; I vowed again:

*If Judge James J. Gilvary insists on having his
way with me; if he kidnaps me, and sends me to
prison with no legal or moral authority to do so, he
shall die. He will answer to God;*
*Or, he will answer to me. If I must; I will kill him
with my pen - from state's prison. But he will never
be permitted to live; to commit a rape of the psyche
of another; such as Wandmacher perpetrated on me!*

Fate is a funny thing. I was taken back to a place of
a long ago sexual attack, and the rape of my psyche.
For the party in Count One of an eight-Count Indictment lived in the first house on Tyler Court, within
three football field-lengths from where the 1961 sexual
assault occurred.

I foresaw a compelling way out of the darkness of the
past. Conceptualizing; I would escape the prison of the
psyche, by being cast into an Ohio prison.

And as I left the horrific conditions, as endured by
this abuse victim; the rapist would take my place in
his own prison of the psyche! I would become *his* warden. And Gilvary would be placed on death row.

It was *déjà vu* - with a profoundly different ending.

CHAPTER FOUR

The Trainable Retarded

Kolesar wrote me of scheduled court dates: a final pre-trial conference would take place Thursday, November 14, 1996; and the trial would begin Monday, November 25th at 1:00 p.m.

Looked solemnly at the letter, I knew there was no turning back. I was trapped and they were playing for keeps. This was the big leagues, and I was merely a bush league player – a pro se defendant.

Yes, buts were defense mechanisms; random rationalities that attempted to invade the conscious mind; to ward off the accompanying fear of what lay ahead. To alleviate my inner turmoil, work began on a strategy.

I spent an enormous amount of time doing research. Usually, I drove to University of Dayton to use the law library. I was more comfortable there. Occasionally, I used the law library at University of Cincinnati.

I would take Ann to her job at the Greater Cincinnati - Northern Kentucky Airport. She would ride the bus home. I spent day after day in research, long into the night.

Fighting for one's freedom creates its own form of dedication. But freedom for me never involved winning at trial. I was destined to lose the battle – and would go to prison – but I would go down fighting. Freedom meant escaping my prison of the psyche.

I would lose a battle, but win the war; taking Gilvary down in the process. Strategizing to assure his death became my magnificent obsession.

By falsely confessing, I could be spared being cast into prison. And without a confession; Gilvary would make sure I was found "guilty" and send me to prison. Having sent an innocent man to prison; Gilvary would fear being publicly revealed - for what he had become.

Since I would know the truth, I would hold the power that counted; in essence would become his warden. Once Gilvary cast me into prison, once he kidnapped me; I resolved to prevent him from ever doing to another, what had been done to me.

Just as I was escaping my prison of the psyche; Gilvary would be entering therein. And just as I was reclaiming my soul, he would be losing his. Being a morality play of Shakespearian proportions; *an inmate would become his judge's warden!*

Gilvary was destined to remain in his prison of the psyche, unless he confessed to kidnapping; and willingly took my place in the Ohio prison - just as he had forced me to do! Sadly for him, the same lack of character enabling him to kidnap me; would make him incapable of freeing himself. Hell would freeze over before he acquiesced. But unlike me, who endured decades in the prison of the psyche; Gilvary lacked the character, the intestinal fortitude to endure the pain - as found in lonely isolation, on his prison's death row.

So with a hypothesis as conceptualized; once Gilvary sentenced me to his secular prison, he unknowingly *sentenced himself to death.* In the end, as I envisioned: Gilvary would die; while I remained freed from a prison of the psyche. Though still serving time in the Ohio prison, haunting memories of permitting Wandmacher to escape accountability would finally be assuaged.

I looked for another way to be freed. Perhaps Judge Gilvary could be prevented from inflicting a death sentence upon himself. Perhaps by saving him from himself – I could free myself from my prison of the psyche.

It seemed a lofty; very worthy humanitarian cause. But far from being a noble undertaking; it was a much better resolution, than serving time in an Ohio prison – theoretically awaiting Gilvary's execution.

Gilvary could seek development of the character; his reputation implicitly suggested he possessed. We both stood to win. I would be freed from the past; and Gilvary would be transformed into a better man.

So my focus would not be an attempt to do the impossible; to win at trial against the power of the State of Ohio, and the tyranny of a corrupt judiciary. My objective would be to motivate Gilvary to save himself.

Alas, a massive ego stood in his way. This was problematic. I could not infer, *Send me to prison, and you really ask for it. Conduct yourself accordingly!*

A fear of public disclosure would have to carry the day. For it would be his fear that made me his warden!

The task before me was formidable. I never knew where to start researching. At times it seemed overwhelming. But I would shake it off, and plod on.

Legal matters are governed by the law and by *case precedent*. In court, the future is most often determined by the past.

Case precedent was my main focus. I stumbled onto a case that was absolutely incredible, as it applied to Judge Gilvary. It was so exciting; it provided the stimulation to continue putting in twelve to fourteen hour days. And so I did.

And it was appropriately named too, considering all the scurrilous judges I faced, and the group insanity involved. The following is from that case.

Cuyahoga County Board of Mental Retardation v. Association of Cuyahoga Teachers of the Trainable Retarded et al. (1975), 47 OApp2d 28, 1003d, 168, 351 N.E.2d 777:

The **oath of office** of a judge, required under Section 7, Article XV of the Ohio Constitution and specified in R.C. §3.23 requires that a judge will "discharge and perform all the duties incumbent on him as such judge"... **the trial judge was <u>prohibited</u> from hearing this case; that he was under a compulsory duty to disqualify himself, and that his breach of that duty rendered his subsequent actions <u>null</u> and <u>void</u>. The attempt of a trial judge to exercise his**

authority as a judge in violation of his mandatory duty is
of absolutely no effect.... The duty of the trial judge under
Section 3(C)(1)(d)(i) of the Code of Judicial Conduct, similar
to that provided under U.S.C. Section 455 (1975 Supp.) controlling **the disqualification of federal judges, is one placed
solely upon the individual judge.** [Emphasis added.]

The beauty of this case was that it gave absolute
credence to my basic supposition. Gilvary had no authority to preside in my case; Gilvary was *solely responsible* for not doing so; and every act performed by
him, from the get-go, would be outside the law!

While this was vital information, it was not information I could use! For I wondered, *What would happen if I exposed my knowledge to those who plotted to
kidnap me? Would they simply turn to violence in order
to silence me?*
I had no idea. But I viewed kidnapping perpetrated
by a judge to be an extremely desperate act. Desperate
parties with criminal intent were unpredictable.
There was never a decision to be made; I would error
on the side of caution. The judge would be permitted
to have his way with me. All I could hope for was to
dissuade. I remained pessimistic.

Kolesar telephoned me with some unsolicited advice.
And I had some for him in return.
"Mr. Metz, I've been talking to some other attorneys
about Judge Gilvary. And ah - I'm not to sure how tol-
erant he's going to be – ah - or how he's going to react
to your court filings."
"He'll react by ruling on them. What's the problem?"
"Well, Mr. Metz, what I mean is, I'm concerned about
how you make up your filings. Judge Gilvary likes
them short and to the point."
"I don't give a damn what he likes. He's free to run
his railroad anyway he wants. And I assure you, I intend to do the same with mine."

"Well – ah - I just wanted to mention it to you, since I was talking to those other attorneys, who have dealt with Judge Gilvary."

"Thank you, John."

"Ah - you're welcome. My advice would be for you to just stick to the issues you're writing about, and leave all that other stuff out. It will make a better impression, that's all."

"Right. Can I give you some advice, in return, John – strictly in the spirit of helping you out?"

"Yeah."

"You worry too much. You remind me of the story of a young attorney about to try his first murder case. He asked a veteran defense lawyer to recommend anything that could help get over his extreme nervousness. A solution was offered: Only two things; get your fee in advance, and remember you don't have to serve the sentence."

Kolesar laughed nervously as I continued on, "John, when you read my motions, just remember that I am the one who is going to serve the sentence; and you are the one who is being paid handsomely, via a lot of extra cases, for advising me."

"Okay, Mr. Metz," Kolesar said, again emitting his nervous laugh.

"One more thing, John; Gilvary ordered me to provide the court with my address. Since we've had this conversation, I think I'll put a little extra effort into it."

Reflecting on matters, I assumed Gilvary did not enjoy my repeated references to Lasky, crooked judges, or deviant prosecutors; while forced to make written decisions. He preferred a *see no evil* landscape; where *pretense of ignorance is bliss.* He did not want to risk being trapped, like appellate judges had been.

Hopefully, Gilvary would hear the voice of reason; while he had an opportunity to do so. But it was such a faint hope. For the ethically challenged judge was adrift; amongst *the trainable retarded.*

CHAPTER FIVE

Stains upon Democracy

Judge Gilvary ruled on three defense motions. A demand for grand jury transcripts was overruled; a demand for a transcript of proceedings in Kettering Municipal Court was overruled; and a demand for proper use of my mailing address was sustained.

Nothing happened involving my case in October 1996. Election Day was Tuesday, November 5th. The following day, a *Dayton Daily News* headline provided me with proof of what I intuitively knew.

A theft ring masterminded by Judge Robert E. Messham, Jr. existed in Miamisburg Municipal Court. The article by reporter Rob Modic read:

MISSING MONEY
Bookkeeper faces theft counts
A grand jury levels 2 indictments against a former Miamisburg Municipal Court worker.

A Montgomery County grand jury Tuesday indicted a former Miamisburg Municipal Court bookkeeper on two counts of theft in office stemming from more than $44,000 missing from the court's accounts.

Maria Lowman, 47, of 4873 Loxley Drive is scheduled to be arraigned Dec. 3.

She faces up to three years in prison if convicted. The money vanished between Jan. 1, 1995, and the end of July 1996.

Lowman was fired Aug. 6, two weeks after a motorist served with an arrest warrant for nonpayment of a traffic ticket complained he had paid the fine and showed a cancelled check. Other discrepancies involving fines surfaced soon after.

Assistant county prosecutor George Patricoff, head of the consumer fraud unit, said investigators could not tie the traffic ticket problems to Lowman. But an audit of the court's accounts revealed other discrepancies totaling $44,000 between receipts for money the counter clerks had reported and the deposits Lowman made at the bank after Jan. 1, 1995, Patricoff said.

Miamisburg Municipal Judge Robert E. Messham Jr. said insurance will cover any losses to the court and "the flaw in the system that we think she exploited has been closed." He said he hired an accountant to review the court's books back to when Lowman began working there in 1988.

Maria R. Lowman was hired by Messham's predecessor, Charles A. "Bud" Lowman. She is the judge's former sister-in-law.

I believed Maria Lowman was taking a fall for Judge Messham! It was preposterous. Lowman told me; in a recorded telephone conversation, *I just push the paper, Mr. Metz. You know that.*

It was time to go to work in earnest, on the psyche of Judge Gilvary. From a motion I filed:

... If parties within the DA's office seek the truth, as does the Defendant, it is a certainty that Miamisburg Municipal Court Judge Robert E. Messham, Jr. and Assistant Prosecutor Laurence A. Lasky face serious difficulties. On the other hand, serious breaches and violations of the State's responsibility places the Defendant in the position of a conviction, and a prison sentence.

...The Court is advised that business losses that involve the complainants were caused by the Defendant's resources in time, money, and attention to regrettable civil cases involving a member of the State.

In other words, the complainants seek justice by turning to the State; the very State whose member(s) caused the losses suffered by the complainants.

... This Defendant believes, and the evidence shall show, that poor Maria Lowman was merely the *hen* misused by two corrupt roosters named Judge Robert E. Messham, Jr. and Attorney/Prosecutor Laurence A. Lasky.

... In past filings, the Defendant has referred to television comedies entitled *Everybody Loves Raymond*[4] and Due Process. The Defendant draws attention to another new show that follows 60 Minutes entitled *Touched By An Angel*.[5]

In matters before the Court, the Defendant has the assistance of as many as 280 angels. And, the Defendant believes that *accidents* like the prosecutorial use of *Raymond* and the person who paid his fine getting a warrant are the workings of the Defendant's angels.

More about angels from the Old and New Testaments:

The Visionary Ass

Numbers 22:

21 And Balaam rose up in the morning, and saddled up his ass, and went with the princess of Moab.

22 And God's anger was kindled because he went: and the angel of the Lord stood in the way for an adversary against him. Now he was riding upon his ass, and his two servants *were* with him.

23 And the ass saw the angel of the Lord standing in the way, and his sword drawn in his hand: and the ass turned aside out of the way, and went into the field: and Balaam smote the ass, to turn her into the way.

24 But the angel of the Lord stood in a path of the vineyards, a wall *being* on this side, and a wall on that side.

25 And when the ass saw the angel of the Lord, she thrust herself unto the wall, and crushed Balaam's foot against the wall: and he smote her again.

---

[4] Aired on CBS for 211 episodes; 9-99 to 5-05.
[5] Aired on CBS for 9 years; 9-94 to 4-03.

26 And the angel of the Lord went further, and stood in a narrow place, where *was* no way to turn either to the right or to the left.

27 And when the ass saw the angel of the Lord, she fell down under Balaam: and Balaam's anger was kindled, and he smote the ass with a staff.

28 And the Lord opened the mouth of the ass, and she said unto Balaam, What have I done unto thee, that thou hast smitten me these three times?

29 And Balaam said unto the ass, Because thou hast mocked me: I would were a sword in mine hand, for now would I kill thee.

30 And the ass said unto Balaam, *Am* not I thine ass, upon which thou hast ridden ever since I *was* thine upon this day? Was I eve wont to do so unto thee? And he say, nay.

31 Then the Lord opened the eyes of Balaam, and he saw the angel of the Lord standing in the way, and his sword drawn in his hand: and he bowed down his head, and fell flat on his face.

32 And now the angel of the Lord said unto him, Wherefore hast thou smitten thine ass these three times? Behold, I went out to withstand thee, because *thy* way is perverse before me:

33 And the ass saw me, and turned from me these three times: unless she turned from me, surely now also I had slain thee, and saved her alive.

34 And Balaam said unto the angel of the Lord, I have sinned; for I knew not that thou stoodest in the way against me: now therefore, if it displeases thee, I will get me back again.

35 And the angel of the Lord said unto Balaam, Go with the men: but only the word that I speak unto thee, that thou shalt speak. So Balaam went with the princess of Balak.

The modern day saying, *talking out of his ass*, comes from the Book of Numbers in the Old Testament. The original meaning of the saying was one of inspiration and beauty and wisdom and truth. Balaam learned the error of his ways, and faithfully served the Lord.

But down through the ages something was lost.

The Dumb Ass

II Peter 2:

8 (For that righteous man dwelling among them, in seeing and hearing vexed his righteous soul from day to day with their unlawful deeds;)

9 The Lord knoweth how to deliver the godly out of temptations, and to reserve the unjust unto the day of judgment to be punished:

10 But chiefly them that walk after the flesh in the lust of uncleanness, and despise government. Presumptuous *are they*, selfwilled, they are not afraid to speak evil of dignities.

11 Whereas angels which are greater in power and might, bring not railing accusation amongst them before the Lord.

12 But these, as natural brute beasts, made to be taken and destroyed, speak evil of the things they understand not; and shall utterly perish in their own corruption;

13 And shall receive the reward of unrighteousness, as they that count it pleasure to riot in the day time. Spots *they are* and blemishes, sporting themselves with their own deceivings while they feast with you;

14 Having eyes full of adultery, and that cannot cease from sin, beguiling unstable souls: an heart they have exercised with covetous practices; cursed children:

15 Which have forsaken the right way, and are gone astray, following the way of Balaam *the son* of Boser, who loved the wages of unrighteousness;

16 But was rebuked for his iniquity: the dumb ass speaking with man's voice forbad the madness of the prophet.

17 These are wells without water, clouds that are carried with a tempest; to whom the midst of darkness is reserved for ever.

18 For when they speak great swelling *words* of vanity, they allure through the lusts of the flesh, *through much* wantonness, those that were clean escaped from them who live in error.

19 While they promise them liberty, they themselves are the servants of corruption: for of whom a man overcome, of the same is he brought in bondage.

In a direct parallel to Biblical times, the average citizen in our nation has been forsaken. The average citizen is viewed as the *dumb ass* to be held in contempt of. In large measure the Democrats steal via the government; the Republicans via the corporation.

… the new president of the American Bar Association, Roberta Cooper Ramo wrote an article for the August 5, 1996 issue of *The National Law Journal*. From notes:

> *Perceptions of corruption or incompetence on the part of the judicial system are stains upon democracy itself that demand the response of the legal profession….*
> *Lawyers must speak out in defense of the Constitution and its Bill of Rights.*
> *… American lawyers…must remember that they are by oath not just advocates for the interests of their clients, but are sworn to uphold the Constitution… Freedom, justice and liberty would be empty words in this country without strong, ethical independent judges and lawyers.*

The New Testament's "spots *they are* and blemishes" become Ramo's "stains upon democracy." Amen, ms. president!

This assault on the psyche of Judge Gilvary was intended to be part of his *continuing education.* Left unwritten, but most assuredly thrust deep within his soul was that the judge had become a judicial whore; one of Ramo's *stains upon democracy.* And he knew it.

CHAPTER SIX

Stand By With Me

I continued my assault on the psyche of Judge Gilvary the following day, November 14, 1996:

> Now comes the Defendant, pro se, before the Honorable Court in a motion calling for the removal of court appointed advisor, John P. Kolesar.
>
> The Defendant understands that a conviction on eight felony counts carries a potential sentence of twelve years. The words to the song go, *"Are ye able, said the Master, to be crucified with me? Yea, the sturdy dreamers answered, to the cross we'll follow Thee,"* and are easier to sing than they are to live by.
>
> The Defendant's faith in the system is shaken to the point that he cannot absolutely believe that Mr. Kolesar wasn't a *plant*.... Mr. Kolesar derives a part of his case work, i.e. his income from court-appointed cases like this one. Most are probably plea bargained. It is unjust to Mr. Kolesar and unjust to the Defendant to have him advise the defendant, in a case that has annoyed, or worse threatened reputations and/or careers of many within the legal fraternity in Dayton.
>
> Mr. Kolesar is two years[6] out of law school, and a newer member of the fraternity. The Defendant remembers well what he faced as a twenty-one to twenty-seven year old in the life insurance business.
>
> Therefore, the Defendant desires to *wing it* **alone**, he and a few hundred angels. The Court is reminded that he's not the dumb ass he's been treated by the system as, but the visionary ass who, at this late date in our decaying civilization, still

---

[6] On the date this motion was filed, Kolesar had been licensed to practice law for one year and one day.

believes in America, and the beauty of her constitutional guarantees.

He believes so deeply that he's willing to bet twelve years of his life in prison against rediscovering the simple beauty and power of a thing called *the truth, the whole truth, and nothing but the truth*. And, he believes his fate is in better hands with angels as assistants than with a member of the fraternity.

The stage was set for the final pretrial hearing in Gilvary's chambers. I had spent twelve hours in University of Dayton's law library, developing a strategy. My desire to *wing it alone* was an integral part of that strategy.

A final pretrial conference is the last meeting of parties prior to trial. It was scheduled for November 19, 1996 in Judge Gilvary's chambers.

The Second District Court of Appeals of Ohio, with five appellate judges ruling on cases in several counties, was on the fifth floor of the Montgomery County Courts Building. The Montgomery Court of Common Pleas, with eleven judges, was located on floors two to four; directly below them.

So Gilvary's courtroom was in close proximity to the appellate judges he assisted. I decided to create a minor quake, within the appellate court. There would be little time for a quake to reverberate down to Gilvary's chambers. But I was certain this one would.

Before leaving home on the morning of November 19th, I telephoned the appellate court.[7]

"Court of Appeals."
"Yes, is Angie in please?"
"This is she."
"Angie, what's your last name? This is Ray Metz in Cincinnati."

---

[7] Conversation is taken from a transcription of the recorded conversation with Angie House.

"Unhunh."

"What's your last name?"

"I'm sorry. This is who?"

"This is Ray Metz in Cincinnati, Ohio."

"Ray Metz?"

"Yeah."

"From?"

"Ah ... I've had some cases in the court of appeals that were dismissed."

"Okay."

"And I wanted to serve you with a subpoena to appear in court and I didn't know your last name."

"Why do you want me to appear in court?"

"Ah ... to be a witness."

After a pause, Ms. House asked, "Which cases are you talking about?"

Come on, Angie, I thought. *How many times have you been asked to send a court order dismissing a civil appeal, a day before it was filed; intended to lure me into the court house for an arrest?* I responded, "Well, this is a criminal case that I want you to appear as a witness in, but it was civil cases that were dismissed ah ... back ah ... when I was arrested in February."

House gave me her last name (that I already knew). I was certain; as soon as we hung up, she made a bee-line for Judge James A. Brogan or Judge Mike Fain.

It was 9:42 a.m. when we finished our conversation. The final pretrial conference was scheduled for 2:00 p.m. – just below the appellate court. The geniuses had four hours to react.

There are certain abilities that must be used with care and utmost discretion. For example, the master salesman can, in effect, reach in; take out another's mind; play with it for awhile, *coo-chi-coo-coo-coo;* put it back; and the targeted party would never even know it had been missing. A criminal mindset made ethically challenged attorneys extremely susceptible.

I decided it might be advantageous for chambers meetings to be recorded by a court reporter. Any request by me would have been declined. So I had made other provisions. The way I did this was to include in my November 13, 1996 motion for a change of venue:

> The Court is reminded that the Defendant voluntarily agreed to a trial date set *after* the elections, as *no one wanted this case to become political.*

I assumed Judge Gilvary would have asked Judge Langer if we had all *agreed* to anything of the sort; and Langer would have told him it was nonsense. It never happened.

I assumed Gilvary would not take any chances that wise-guy Metz could fabricate what happened in *his* chambers meetings. The way to avoid that would be to have a court reporter present, for posterity.

I believed: With the phone call to House, appellate judges had reason to become unnerved. Three of them had conspired in arranging for my arrest in the courts building. The judges would contend I was *crazy,* and only *imagined* they had been involved in my arrest.

Certainly, a staged competency examination would do the trick! Gilvary had reason to order one; I would rather be represented by angels of the Lord than by John-boy. *Angel* logistics supported probable appellate judges' assertions – I had imagined a lot of things.

And so, I went to Gilvary's chambers fifteen minutes early, prepared to face my enemies. Kolesar came in and sat down beside me, as we waited. Parties whom I assumed were involved in another case were in Gilvary's chambers.

"John, don't worry about my motion to dismiss you. There is a method to my madness that I'll explain to you later," I assured.

"That's alright, Mr. Metz." Kolesar said with his nervous little laugh.

Gilvary summoned us in. I did not recognize the
people in chambers. Gilvary made introductions to a
court reporter named Donna Jean Flock.

Vicky Whisman of the Montgomery County Prosecu-
tor's Office was present; and Robert K. Hendrix of the
Greene County Prosecutor's Office represented the
State of Ohio.

The parties were not in chambers for another case.
Judge Gilvary had met with ~~prosecutors~~ persecutors
without us. This violated due process.

Gilvary began with,[8] "Let the record show that we're
here in Case Number 95-CR-2317, State of Ohio versus Horace Raymond Metz. Is that the name you want
to be known as?"

"That's not my name, Your Honor," I pointed out.

Gilvary corrected himself, "Horace Ray Metz."

"Yes, sir."

Gilvary went on, "The case of Horace Ray Metz.
We're here on a final pretrial conference. Let the record further reflect that his court-appointed auxiliary
attorney, or whatever his role, is Mr. Kolesar."

"Legal advisor," Kolesar contributed.

Gilvary continued, "Also here, and is it Robert Hendrix?"

"Yes, Your Honor."

Gilvary said, "H-e-n-d-r-i-x is also here. And then
we've already noted that Vicky Wiseman is here. Let
the record further reflect that both the defendant, and
Mr. Schenck and Mr. Hendrix for the State of Ohio,
asked for a continuance of the trial set for November
25, 1996.

"Mr. Metz, I have read your motion on that score
and I'm not clear as to the basis for your wishing a
continuance, but I'm going to grant you one anyway."

How about, I'm not really in any hurry go to prison, I
thought. I said, "Thank you Your Honor."

---

[8] Conversation taken from the official transcript.

Gilvary let me off the hook with, "You won't have to explain it to me. And the state has set forth their reasons for a continuance so I'm going to grant that. While we're on the record, Mr. Hendrix, I want you and Mr. Schenck to file an entry of appearance."

"We will do so by the close of business tomorrow, Your Honor," Hendrix promised.

How in the hell did special prosecutors file motions in court prior to filing an appearance? I wondered to myself. *Ah, I almost forgot. This is Montgomery County – Dayton, Ohio, where anything goes.*

Gilvary pressed on, "One of the things – and there are some pending motions by Mr. Metz that has not been ruled on – one of the things; he says in a November 13th motion for a continuance is that he doesn't even know who the witnesses are for the State nor what the exhibits of evidence are to be. And I know that there has been a changing of the guards, and maybe in that changing he somehow didn't get the discovery packet that we usually give here in Montgomery County, Ohio, so I'm looking to the new counsel for the State to provide him with the discovery package which would contain a list of witnesses and what proposed exhibits you would use at trial, and likewise, Mr. Metz, I'm going to order you to do the same thing for the State."

"Yes, Your Honor," I acknowledged.

Gilvary addressed me, "But you will have to do so within two weeks of the time that you receive that discovery packet, I want you to furnish them with witnesses and an exhibit list."

"No problem, Your Honor," I assured. "Excuse me, Your Honor. I was provided initially a discovery package that was compiled by Mr. Lipowicz or whoever does that. Mr. Lipowicz provided that to me."

"Okay."

"But it was not complete."

"That may all that he has and so I'm going to let Rob Hendrix review the file and whatever they're going to use at trial they will disclose to you."

"Okay."

Gilvary changed subjects, "Let's talk about the new trial date and then there's one other thing I want to work on. February 17th is Washington-Lincoln Day; the court will be closed. I want to begin this trial on February 18th which is a Tuesday. Be advised – as you know, today, Tuesday afternoon, we don't have trials so we will have a jury in on the 18th and perhaps we can get a jury sworn in and do some of those things in the morning. We will not have the trial in the afternoon, but after that, it is all yours, and I will put out an order to that effect, and your address is still P.O. Box et cetera?"

"Yes, Your Honor," I acknowledged.

"One other thing, pursuant to Ohio Revised Code Section 2945.37.1, the Court on its own motion is of the opinion that there is a question as to the competence of Mr. Metz to stand trial, and I'm going to order you, Mr. Metz, to present yourself to the Forensic Psychiatric Center for Western Ohio on November 27th at 12:30 p.m. to be interviewed and examined to determine your competency to stand trial.

"I'm going to give you a copy of this memo from the prosecutor's office which simply sets forth that information. It is not a voluntary thing on your part. If you choose not to attend, I will issue a warrant for your arrest."

A warrant similar to the one you expected to issue until I surprised you, and showed up for a phony meeting in chambers, scheduled orally by you on the same day you were appointed to my case? I thought.

"Could I ask what caused this?" I wanted to know.

Gilvary looked at me and said evenly, "Reading the material that you have filed so far gives me cause to pause as to your competence to stand trial."

Goody-gum-drop! I thought. I said, "All right."

Gilvary started to hand me a paper, paused and addressed Whisman, "And is there any problem with him having the memo? It has the information in there that he needs."

Whisman nodded negatively, and Gilvary addressed Hendrix, "And do you need a copy of this?"

"I don't think so, Your Honor," Hendrix replied.

"Where will this be?" I asked.

"It is 12 Wenger Road, Englewood, Ohio, just north of town. And they will probably also contact you, but I don't know that and here is a copy."

I looked at the form Gilvary handed me, and mentally noted, *Copy, my ass. This is the original with Heck's seal in gold and black and 'Vicky' written in blue ink next to her typed name. It is the only copy in existence.*

The memorandum stated the files of the case had been in the Greene County Prosecutor's possession prior to today. It meant the decision to appoint Special Prosecutors had been decided prior to my ploy with Angie House. They had been appointed to free George Patricoff for the Lowman cover-up!

But Whisman's form, resplendent with *Vicky* in blue ink, was dated the 19th; and we were in chambers on the 19th. *This is the original of a hastily arranged competency exam – following my call to Angie House,* I analyzed mentally.

Everyone had been waiting for me to finish reading the short memorandum. Whisman finally said, "It is my understanding he will receive a letter of confirmation. Could we get a good address just to make sure?"

Gilvary checked his file and responded, "His home address – I will give you two addresses – his home address is... I wouldn't call it a business, but when he corresponds with the court, he usually uses Ray Metz, P.O. Box 0293, Cincinnati....His phone number where he can be reached is...."

"Thank you," Whisman said politely.

Gilvary continued on, "I'll put this ruling in writing. With reference to your legal assistant, I'm not going to let him out of the case, at least until after we have the hearing on competency."

"All right," I agreed.

"He's going to stand by with me," Gilvary admitted.

That's the reason I wanted him removed, dumb ass. I need someone who will stand by with me, I thought.

The timid young Kolesar contributed again, "That's fine with me."

Gilvary ended with, "I will get out some orders. The case is continued, and I will be back in touch. Thank you."

Dysfunctional - Montgomery County Style:

Judges	Prosecutors
Judge Robert E. Messham, Jr.	**Laurence A. Lasky**
Acting Judge Mark E. Landers	Richard A.F. Lipowicz
Judge William H. Wolff, Jr.	Diane Friday-Brown
Judge James A. Brogan	Susan Finch
Judge Mike Fain	Thomas G. Rauch
Judge Frederick N. Young	Robert Skinner
Judge Thomas J. Grady	George B. Patricoff
Judge Robert L. Moore	Mathias H. Heck, Jr.
Judge Larry W. Moore	Vicky E. Whisman
Judge Patrick J. Foley	David P. Mesaros
Judge John W. Kessler	Robert K. Hendrix
Judge Dennis J. Langer............*Dennis J. Langer*	
Judge Barbara P. Gorman	William F. Schenck
Judge James J. Gilvary	

Judge Gilvary wanted to ascertain my competence to stand trial. What possible standard could I be compared too, in Montgomery County, Ohio? A *nonexistent Raymond* faced a prison sentence of twelve years; for a *nonexistent crime.*

And for Raymond's dream team defense, he had the judge's *stand-by-with-me.* He would be sent to prison by a judge lacking jurisdiction; a *nonexistent judge.*

His only hope was to be sent to a *nonexistent prison.*

CHAPTER SEVEN

Angels

Judge Gilvary filed an Order scheduling a final pre-trial conference on February 11, 1997. The trial would begin a week later.

Gilvary ruled on my motion for change of venue:

> This motion was filed by the Defendant in the alternative on November 13, 1996. Nothing in the Defendant's memorandum would support such an order and the motion is **OVERRULED.**

Next he dealt with the motion to dismiss Kolesar.

> This motion will be taken under advisement pending a hearing on Defendant's competency to stand trial, which is now set for December 23, 1996 at 10:00 a.m.

Gilvary dealt with the use of my name.

> It is not clear to the Court what this motion is all about but from now on he shall be referred to as Horace Ray Metz.

Gilvary might agree to *refer* to me as Horace Ray. But the heading of his Order indicated he would still send me to prison in the fictitious name of *Raymond*.

Through the years, I had enjoyed reading hundreds of *true crime* books. The criminals were always caught; the detectives and prosecutors were always the good guys. In the process, I developed a layman's familiarity with the criminal case process.

During the competency exam; I assumed one of the tests I would be given would be the Minnesota Multiphasic Personality Inventory-2. I had taken the "1" version of the test in the late 1970s, when test results indicated I was normal (or whatever medical term applied). There is no way to consciously *cheat* the test.

Careful review of the parallel to what happened to me in the 1960s; and what was taking place in the 1990s, provided a way to use a competency exam to my advantage. And so, *I decided:* Gilvary would decide I needed one. He accommodated me.

Fate is a funny thing. Prior to leaving Colorado in 1983, the psyche endured enormous pain resulting from the cold blooded murders of Rod and Marilyn Carlson by their son, Ross. They lived in Littleton, as I did. I purchased a book about the murders in 1993.

Ross Carlson faked having a multiple personality disorder. The idea was planted in his mind by Dr. Ralph Fisch. This was the *same* quack I was referred too, after testing "normal" on the MMPI-1 test. I quit seeing Fisch, once he inferred I suffered from multiple personalities!

Dr. Michael Weissberg wrote about *soul murder* as a form of child abuse.[9]

> Soul murder is the most subtle – and malignant – form of child abuse. It is subtle because soul murder does not depend on physical harm or neglect. Souls are murdered by glances; souls are murdered by ideas and distorted feelings. On the surface, parents who murder their children's souls often appear normal and good.
>
> And soul murder is malignant because parents who murder their children's souls are unable to see their children as they are, only as they expect them to be. Soul murdered children, as they grow, come to believe that they are who their parents think they are. They do not have their own identities. As Erik Erikson wrote over forty years ago, it is this very deprivation

---

[9] *The First Sin of Ross Michael Carlson – A Psychiatrist's Personal Account of Murder, Multiple Personality Disorder, and Modern Justice* by Michael Weissberg, M.D.; © 1992. Weissberg was a professor at University of Colorado's School of Medicine in the Department of Psychiatry. Ross Carlson's *first sin* was being born out of wedlock. His parents treated him as if it were his fault.

of identity, not frustration, which leads to murder. Physical evidence of child abuse is often sparse because, when a soul is murdered, there is no dead body.

While not a child, but a nineteen-year-old teenager when officials at University of Cincinnati betrayed me, the soul had been murdered in much the same way. Over thirty-five years were spent in efforts to reclaim it; to date. Sometimes when I was in a drunken haze; fleeting thoughts of murdering Wandmacher came to me, as I obsessed on how he had screwed up my life.

The dynamics in 1961 involved a sexual attack and a cover-up. They were assaults on the psyche, and the cover-up is what caused permanent harm. I accepted responsibility for the criminal acts of others, and suffered the consequences.

The dynamics from 1994 and beyond; involved the abuses initially perpetrated by Lasky, and the subsequent cover-up. Both were assaults on the psyche.

And again, the cover-up caused the greater damage. For now I was being involuntarily forced to accept responsibility for the criminal acts of others, and suffer the consequences – by going to prison.

One of the things the MMPI-2 picks up is an attempt by the patient to appear normal. This is known as a *fake good* result. And so it was; I got the idea of *faking* a *fake good* result on a MMPI psychological test.

If I were able to achieve it, and if the forensic psychologist misinterpreted the results of a MMPI-2, I could introduce evidence at a competency hearing; of how and why it had been misinterpreted. In theory, I could prove my innocence in open court, prior to trial.

Audacious ideas can best be filtered via conceptualization. I began with Milton and *Paradise Lost*:

> The mind is its own place, and in itself can
> make a heaven of hell, or a hell of heaven.

I would attempt to *recreate* - in the subconscious - the mental hell endured as a student, by secretly accepting full responsibility for the misdeeds of others. It was an ambitious undertaking.

In preparation, I collected props. Mother had given me letters and personal effects she had saved from college days. I chose a letter written to them, and several checks she sent me for expenses.

Beginning of letter to Mom and Dad

The amounts of the checks reminded me of the supreme sacrifice my parents had made, in sending me to college. The checks reminded me of the love they freely gave; and the love of them I experienced.

I set up a tape recorder, and holding Mother's checks in one hand; holding the July 16, 1961 letter in the other, I made a tape recording, by reading excerpts from the letter; written long ago by an abuse victim.

Dear Mom and Dad,

I received your letter yesterday. Sorry I haven't written before this. I was sick Tuesday and Wednesday. I had a slight fever and bad head cold.

... I've tried to study this week without much success. I've been thinking a lot about my situation. I think the thing which bothers me most is what everyone thinks of me. I've made quite a bad reputation for myself. Although no one says anything, it bothers me more and more. I feel so inferior, it's not funny. I think that's the reason I can't study right. All I know is, I'm getting out of here at least for a year. I don't think I could make it as things are now.

... Even after a full year down here, it's hard to take thinking of myself as a failure. I know I've let you down. If I sincerely felt I could snap out of it down here, I'd stay. But I'm afraid I've dug a hole too deep to get out of. I guess I just don't have what it takes. I don't know.

... The fact that people may laugh or scorn me bothers me a little. But that's not really important. I think I'll recover my faith in myself and get on my feet. It's horrible not to have any self-confidence or self-respect. That hurt my grades more than anything else this past term.... I'll be home this weekend to discuss things.

Love,

Ray

I hid the sexual attack from my parents. I did not do so out of shame over the attack. The predator was a sick man. I did it because I loved them; and wanted to spare them the enormous amount of anguish, I knew they would feel. I accepted responsibility for failing five final exams in the week following the attack.

It was an emotionally draining experience, reading the letter while holding Mom's checks. My voice wavering in some places, and breaking in others, it did not take long to make the tape recording. It seemed like an eternity. There were no retakes.

Next, I prepared a court motion, to be filed and time-stamped just before the competency examination. The content and theme of the motion, filed just before the forensic examination, would stand in stark contrast to conclusions of the psychologist. From the motion:

> Now comes the Defendant, *pro se,* before the Honorable Court, in gratitude and filled with humility, and thereby offers his very best to officers of the court involved herein.... [T]he profoundly positive influence of an earthly angel inspired...a Thanksgiving prayer. The Defendant hopes you like it.
>
> Thank You, Lord
>
> Thank You for giving me eyes to see,
> Your wondrous works; life's beauty.
> Ears to hear life's joyful sound;
> And cries for help that do abound.
> A tongue to speak out loud and strong,
> For what's right, and against what's wrong.
> A heart that's filled with love for me,
> And for You, Lord, and all humanity.
> A mind to think of good works to do,
> And hands and feet to follow through.
> I thank You, Lord, for all of these,
> As I stand before You on my knees.
> Of all the ones that I might be,
> Thank You, Lord, for making me – me.
> And one more thing before I'm through,
> Since it's from Your image I grew,
> Thank You, Lord, for being You!

Finished with my motion, I copied the taped message, over and over onto anther tape. Then I listened to the tape recording the rest of the day. On the morning of Wednesday, November 27, 1996, I got up at five o'clock. I listened to the tape, drinking black coffee.

I listened to the tape continuously on the way to Dayton. I filed the motion in the clerk's office at 10:13 a.m., and then drove to Richmond, Indiana and back to Englewood, killing time until the 12:30 competency evaluation.

I ate nothing, just drank black coffee and listened to the tape; over and over. I arrive at Forensic Psychiatry Center prepared for the examination, in every respect.

I had been correct. The first task was to take the MMPI-2[10] on a computer. I was ready; mentally, physically, and spiritually. And I answered 557 true/false questions in 35 minutes.

It equated to 15.9 questions per minute. When told I was finished with the test, the forensic psychologist was overheard to exclaim, "That's impossible!"

Forensic Psychologist Bobbie G. Hopes, Ph.D. was very professional. She made notes on her lap top as we went along. During the examination, the topic of religion was brought up.

"You consider yourself to be a very religious person, don't you, Mr. Metz?"

"Not at all," I replied.

"You don't consider yourself to be deeply religious?" she challenged me.

"Not at all," I replied again.

---

[10] The Minnesota Multiphasic Personality Inventory (MMPI) was developed by psychologist Starke R. Hathaway and psychologist J.C. McKinley in the late 1930s. True or false answers are given to questions like: *I have a good appetite*, or *I am easily awakened by noise.* Normally the test takes between 60 and 90 minutes to complete. Validity Scales include The F Scale. This is used to detect an attempt at *faking good* or *faking bad.* In essence, an attempt is made to appear better or worse than the party being tested really is.

"Well, I've read some of your court filings, and they would seem to indicate that to me. How would you characterize your religious beliefs?"

"To me, a religious person is often similar to the person depicted on television at a sporting event; holding up a John 3:16 sign saying in effect, *God so loved the world that...I got this great seat to the game! Nah na nah na nah na.*"

"Then can you elaborate on what you do believe?"

"I have a personal relationship with God that He seems comfortable with. If it suits Him, it suits me."

"Do you believe you can predict events happening in the future?"

"Sometimes I just write things down, and, later they seem to happen."

"Do you believe you can control what other people do, by controlling them mentally?"

"If I could, I wouldn't be sitting here taking a competency examination ordered by a judge in a criminal trial," I responded. And I thought, *That's precisely why I'm here!*

Finally Dr. Hopes completed her examination and turned off her lap top. She looked at me and her features softened, from objective professional to compassionate human.

"What are you going to do; if you're not allowed to put on all those judges and court officials as witnesses?" she asked in a kindly manner.

"I'm going to prison."

Body language gave away her thoughts, as I continued, "Don't look at me as though it were *my* idea. It's very simple. If I'm not permitted to put on a defense, I'm going to prison."

Dr. Hopes snapped back into her professional state, and wished me well as we shook hands. I left satisfied I had accomplished what had I intended.

I wrote Hopes on November 30, 1996.

Dear Doctor Hopes:

The session of last Wednesday was mentally and emotionally draining, and I forgot to request a copy of the release form that you had me sign. An *attorney* slip-up! Ha ha. Please forward a copy of the same.

... Thank you for the professional manner in which the examination was conducted, and thank you in advance, for your assistance herein.

Very truly yours,

Ray Metz, *pro se*

cc: The Honorable James J. Gilvary

    Special Prosecutors Schenck/Hendrix

    Court-appointed Advisor John P. Kolesar

I used stamps depicting the *Midnight Angel* for the four mailings, making copies in color of the four envelopes, for my records. This was the only purpose in writing Hopes.

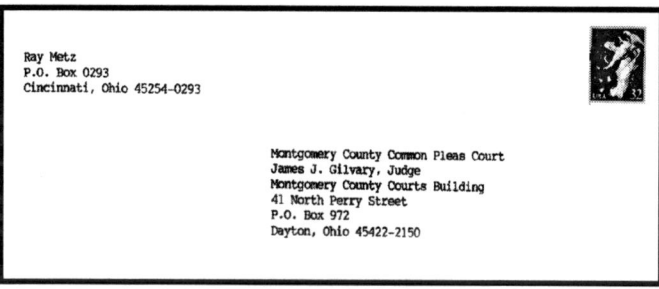

Midnight Angel
Heavenly herald.
Glorious guardian

The *Midnight Angel* First-Day Cover Envelope of October 19, 1995 read:

> "And the angel said unto them, Fear not: for behold, I bring you good tidings of great joy, which shall be to all people. For unto you is born this day, in the city of David, a Savior, which is Christ the Lord." In the Old and New Testaments, angels are messengers of God. Although genderless in the scriptures, angels are often portrayed with long flowing robes and "feminine" features. According to one classicist, Gilbert Highet, the image of the angel is a combination of Jewish mysticism and Greek imagery. The Jews thought that God was free of all human form and so he used messengers, angels, who were human in appearance to deliver His word. Greek artists and poets, on the other hand, did not think of the divine as formless, because it was artistically difficult to represent a nondescript being. Instead, God was the perfect man or woman in form and shape, and had superhuman powers. Because the angels of God traveled between heaven and earth, they therefore needed wings for a swift and graceful flight. Belief in angels is a matter of individual faith in many religions of the world. However the Roman Catholic Church states that angels were created in a realm above man but below God. The Biblical Christmas story depicts one of the most impressive roles of these heavenly beings. The angel Gabriel told Mary she was to bring forth a son and call him Jesus. After Christ's birth, an angel brought the good news to shepherds in nearby fields. More recently, angels have reappeared in movies such as *It's a Wonderful Life*.

I finally responded to Lasky's secular *World Peace through LAW* stamps, with the spiritual *Midnight Angel* stamp. Despite Judge Gilvary questioning my sanity, I put absolute faith in my *angels!*

Satisfied with the outcome of entire competency issue, I wondered in quiet reflection:

What kind of angel will Gilvary become,
after I put him through hell on earth?

CHAPTER EIGHT

Mind Control

The competency report was seven pages long, with "CONFIDENTIAL Client must consent to further disclosure of this information." It read in its entirety:

CONFIDENTIAL FORENSIC EVALUATION
NAME: Horace Ray Metz
EXAMINER: Bobbie G. Hopes, Ph.D.
FORENSIC NO: 9611-0578
DATE EVALUATED: 11-27-96
DATE OF BIRTH: 1-16-42   COURT CASE: 95-CR-2317
COUNTY: Montgomery   JUDGE: James J. Gilvary

COMPETENCY TO STAND TRIAL – O.R.C. 2945.371

Horace Ray Metz was referred to the Forensic Psychiatry Center for Western Ohio by the Honorable James J. Gilvary of the Montgomery County Court of Common Pleas to assist the Court in determining current Competency to Stand Trial in accord with Section 2945.371 of the Ohio Revised Code, an issue which was raised by the Court. He was charged with eight counts of Theft. He was informed of the purpose and nonconfidential nature of the evaluation, and he signed this agency's informed Participation Statement. He was clinically interviewed at the offices of the Forensic Psychiatry Center for Western Ohio on November 27, 1996 for approximately two hours and fifteen minutes. He was administered the Minnesota Multiphasic Personality Inventory-2 (MMPI-2) and the Georgia Court Competency Test – Mississippi State Hospital Version. Sources of collateral information included court documents and law enforcement investigative reports pertaining to this case.

SELF-REPORTED BACKGROUND INFORMATION

Family

Horace Ray Metz was raised in Beavercreek, Ohio. He is the oldest of four children. His father is age 85 and his mother, 79. There is no history of mental illness in his family, but his two brothers have been treated for substance abuse.

Education

Horace Ray Metz attended regular classes at Beavercreek High School in June 1960, then attended the University of Cincinnati for one year before dropping out. He told a rather long and complicated story about having been molested by a professor whom he reported to school officials but not to police. He said the school kept quiet about the incident, and he was so distressed by the events that he could not continue and eventually dropped out of school.

Employment

After completing an alcohol treatment program at Greene Hall in December 1983, he became a Fuller Brush salesman, then manager of an Olan Mills telephone solicitation studio. Following his divorce, he began working in the phone sales room for RainSoft, then at Enting Water Conditioning for approximately nine months. In April 1989, he began his own business until July 1, 1995. He then worked at the Cincinnati airport sorting mail as a laborer for one year, then he was trained and worked as a training instructor until the company for which he was employed lost their contract. He received unemployment payments for seven weeks then found employment at an Adidas warehouse through a temporary service. He has not been employed since November 10, 1996.

Marriage

He married his first wife in February 1966, and they divorced in May 1984. He married his second wife in May 1985. He has two sons and a daughter from his first marriage and stepchildren from the second.

Legal

He was arrested three or four times for Passing Bad Checks, after he quit his job at RainSoft and went to work for Enting. He said he eventually paid all the money he owed and was placed on probation.

Chemical Abuse

According to the defendant, he began drinking at age 30 and drank eight to ten beers every day and occasionally some gin. He received treatment at Green Hall and has had no alcohol since December 2, 1983. He has never used illegal drugs.

Mental Health Treatment

In 1961, after being assaulted by a professor while attending University of Cincinnati, he was sent to a school psychologist for a couple months. However, he has never been diagnosed or treated for a mental illness and has never been psychiatrically hospitalized.

PSYCHOLOGICAL TESTING RESULTS

Horace Ray Metz was administered the Minnesota Multiphasic Personality Inventory-2 (MMPI-2). This defendant produced an invalid MMPI-2 profile, which is often referred to as a "fake good" profile. This type of test response is indicative of defensiveness, attempts to appear mentally healthy by naively denying minor foibles, or deliberate attempts to hide one's faults or problems. Despite his defensive approach to the test, his test results show he is hypersensitive to criticism and broodingly resentful. Though typically these individuals have severe underlying guilt, they tend to project their problems onto others, rather than accept blame for their own problems or wrongdoing. They are broodingly resentful toward others and hold long-term grudges when they perceive they have been wronged by others. They typically have a history of very disrupted interpersonal relationships which they found quite dissatisfying (usually due to their misinterpretation). They typically are suspicious of the motives of others and are guarded and defensive in their approach to others. These individuals tend to read malevolent meaning into neutral situations, and they jump to unwarranted conclusions (e.g., that others intend to do them harm) on the basis of little or no data.

MENTAL STATUS EXAMINATION

Appearance

Horace Ray Metz is a 54-year-old (d.o.b. 1-16-42) White man with fraying brown hair, balding on top. He wore metal-framed glasses and was dressed in clean, casual clothes and his hygiene and grooming were good. No scars or tattoos were observed or reported. He has a knot on the top of his head.

Behavior

The defendant was cooperative with the evaluation, and he maintained adequate eye contact. His movements were not unusually slow or rapid, and he showed no signs of lethargy, excessive distractibility, uneasiness, or hyperactivity. His behavior was not highly unusual or bizarre.

Orientation and Memory

Horace Ray Metz was aware of the time, place, and general circumstances for the present evaluation. His short-term and long-term memory abilities were not impaired, as evidenced by his IQ test results, his ability to track current conversation, and his ability to provide meaningful background information during this interview.

Speech and Verbal Ability

The defendant read this agency's Informed Participation Statement aloud without error, and he demonstrated adequate comprehension of the statement by restating it in his own words and by answering questions about it. His speech was clear, coherent, and spontaneous, and he was responsive to questions. He spoke in a normal tone of voice and at a normal pace. His vocabulary, sentence structure, grammar, and use of abstract verbal concepts were above average.

Affect (Observable signs of Emotions)

The defendant smiled, laughed, and cried during the evaluation. His affect was considered appropriate to the current circumstances and to the topics under discussion. Overall, he was experiencing high levels of emotional distress.

Perception (Hallucinations)

Horace Ray Metz said he has never experienced hallucinations, and he did not appear to be responding to hallucinations during this evaluation.

Thought Content and Processes

Horace Ray Metz reported no current thoughts, plan, or intent of suicide. He denied holding bizarre beliefs such as mind control or thought insertion. His judgment and reasoning abilities were fair. However, he was overly suspicious, had excessive expectations of harm or mistreatment by others, and tended to read malevolent motives into situations which may have been more neutral.

Mental Status Opinion

Based upon the results of this evaluation, it is my opinion that Horace Ray Metz has a paranoid and distrustful orientation toward potentially conflictional situations and he is experiencing high levels of emotional distress. However, he is not mentally ill, as defined in Section 5122.01(A) of the Ohio Revised Code. Based upon his academic background and verbal skills demonstrated during this evaluation, he is above average intellectually.

UNDERSTANDING OF COURT OBJECTIVES AND PROCEDURES

Understanding of His Charge

Mr. Metz was aware of the charges against him and he understood the nature and meaning of the charges. He knew that if found guilty, he could face serious penalties including incarceration, and he was aware of alternatives to incarceration, including probation or treatment. He also understood that by defending himself, he was exposing himself to the possibility of a lengthy sentence. He is appropriately motivated to defend himself, but he is also aware of the possible consequences of a guilty finding, and he is willing to accept the consequences of what he believes will be a fair trial.

Understanding of Pleas

He was aware of the pleas he could make and understood the meaning of each plea. He also understood the meaning and potential of plea bargaining.

Understanding of Roles of Court Participants

When provided with a picture of a courtroom, he pointed to where each of the court participants (judge, jury, defense attorney, prosecutor, witnesses) would sit, and he provided adequate definitions of the roles of each of the major participants in the trial process. He said the judge "monitors the proceedings and acts as the legal referee without any vested interest in the outcome." A jury "decided the facts that they're allowed to hear, the evidence, based on the instructions of the judge as to what the law is." A defense attorney "tries to protect the rights of the person accused to make sure that he has a just trial... (Goal?) In practice it's to get him off." The prosecutor "presents the evidence for the crime the person's accused of. (Goal?) In general his goal is to seek justice and truth...His goal should not be to convict if it is not justified, but that's the way the game's played in many cases." Witnesses "are oath-bound to tell the truth as to the questions that's put to them." He understood the behavior expected of him during a trial, and he was able to conform his behavior to those expectations.

He said that although he is acting as his own attorney, he has a court-appointed advisor, John P. Kolesar, who was appointed by Judge Langer. He explained that he is representing himself because he believes he cannot afford a good attorney and he is not eligible for a public defender. He also explained that there is a special prosecutor handing this case, because of a potential conflict of interest being that Larry Lasky, who is on the staff of the Montgomery County Prosecutor's Office, is involved in this case.

He said that although he has no formal legal training, he does have some practical experience in representing himself. He said he represented himself in a trial with the IRS. He explained that he earned only $5,000 in the year after he was discharged from Greene Hall, but he had a $13,000 debt written off through an insurance company, and the IRS tried to charge taxes and fines for the total amount of his earnings and the bad debt, but he won the case. He said he also represented himself in a civil case in Judge Foley's court and won. Actually, he explained he lost and had to pay $900 but he bargained with the plaintiff afterward and threatened to sue them, so they "forgave" the debt.

ABILITY TO ASSIST IN HIS DEFENSE

Mr. Metz said his strategy for his defense will be to call several prosecutors and Court of Appeals judges as witnesses, and if that fails, to ask for a change of venue. Although he acknowledged that strategy may not be permitted, his overall strategy is simply to try to prove that he had no intent to commit a crime and that his actions lacked mens rea. He stated, "Intent has something to do with it. I went out of business and I owe these people...no intent to defraud, but I was put out of business" by other matters in civil court. He stated, "The civil matters caused the criminal matters."

Although he expressed overly suspicious beliefs and tends to real malevolence into potentially neutral situations, he did not include all court participants in his suspicions. He acknowledged that this seems to be a very complicated case, but he expressed strong faith in his attorney advisor. He also indicated he believes the Greene County prosecutor who was assigned as special prosecutor for this case is an honest man who will treat him fairly. He stated, "I really think the special prosecutor has no ulterior motives, has no stake in railroading me...I believe the judge is doing things precisely the way things are supposed to be done... He has no ulterior motives... I had very positive experience with Judge Foley...with a federal judge in tax court, and I believe in the system."

Ability To Discuss Pertinent Facts About Alleged Crimes

Horace Ray Metz provided an adequately detailed, sequential account of the events that may have led to his arrest for the alleged offenses.

Georgia Court Competency Test - Mississippi State Hospital

A person who earns a score of 70 or more out of 100 on the Georgia Court Competency Test - Mississippi State Hospital Version is generally considered competent to Stand Trial. Horace Ray Metz earned a score of 98.

SUMMARY AND OPINION

Horace Ray Metz was referred to the Forensic Psychiatry Center for Western Ohio by the Honorable James J. Gilvary of the Montgomery County Court of Common Pleas to assist the Court in determining the defendant's current Competency to Stand Trial in accord with Section 2945.371 of the Ohio Revised Code. He was charged with eight counts of Theft. It is my opinion that Horace Ray Metz has a paranoid and distrustful orientation toward potentially conflictual situations and he is experiencing high levels of emotional distress. However, he is not mentally ill and not currently mentally retarded, each as defined by Ohio Revised Code. It is my opinion that he is capable of understanding the nature and objectives of the proceedings against him and of presently assisting in his defense, as well as working with his court-appointed advisor to defend himself. Therefore, it is my opinion that Horace Ray Metz is currently Competent to Stand Trial.

Respectfully Submitted,
Bobbie G. Hopes, Ph.D.
Forensic Psychologist

Hopes made an egregious miscalculation, in her analysis of the MMPI-2 test results. In her defense, the manner in which I prepared for her evaluation was unprecedented.

She overlooked exclaiming *"that's impossible,"* when told I had finished the MMPI-2 test in 35 minutes. Answering 557 true/false questions at the rate of 15.9 per minute (one every 3.77 seconds) would transcend being a pretty good human feat; to a supernatural act, *if* I had been able to *consciously* select answers in an attempt to control results.

In 1961, I accepted blame for the misconduct of others. I took responsibility for the sexual assault and responsibility for the predicament it left me in. In 1996, I had recreated the mindset of a nineteen year old covering up – not *his* misdeeds, but the misdeeds of others. I had been able to condition the subconscious mind to *fake* "a fake good" profile on the MMPI-2 test!

It had worked! Here, the State and the judiciary were forcing me to accept responsibility for the misdeeds of...*themselves!* It was an unadulterated rape of the psyche; cold, calculated, and unmerciful.

It was a rape so incomprehensible Hopes was unable to imagine it! I was paranoid. And it indelibly demonstrated the pain machinations of Lasky, Messham et al. created within my psyche. It actually *was* déjà vu!

These individuals tend to read malevolent meaning into neutral situations, and they jump to unwarranted conclusions (e.g., that others tend to do them harm) on the basis of little or no data.... He was overly suspicious, had excessive expectations of harm or mistreatment by others, and tended to read malevolent motives into situations which may have been more neutral.... It is my opinion that Horace Ray Metz has a paranoid and distrustful orientation toward potentially conflictual situations and he is experiencing high levels of emotional distress. However, he is not mentally ill and not currently mentally retarded...

It was a perfect report for me, *if* I were able to challenge Dr. Hopes' misguided conclusions. On the other hand, it was a perfect report for the State, *if* I were prevented from challenging those conclusions.

Taken at face value, I was competent to stand trial, but my claims were unbelievable; because of my paranoia, etc. The showdown was scheduled for December 23, 1996, at the competency hearing. It was time to work on some more *mind control* – or *thought insertion!*

CHAPTER NINE

Well Taken

Judge Gilvary had a criminal mindset that was sinister, and predictable; defying his public persona. His perceived lack of character would be put to the test.

I telephoned John Kolesar on November 29, 1996.[11]
"John, this is Ray Metz."
"Hello, Mr. Metz."
"How was your Thanksgiving?"
"Fine. How was yours?"
"Likewise. John, the reason I called you was to explain something. I have decided that I want you to remain on the case."
"Okay."
"But whatever you do, don't let on to Gilvary."
"I won't. But why do you say that?"
"I have a right to have witnesses testify at the competency hearing; don't I?"
"Well - yes. But normally these things are routine formalities. I think Judge Gilvary was just being cautious, making sure he covered himself."
"Oh, he covered himself, alright. Routine hunh? Not this time, John! This is going to be a humdinger. And *you* are going to be the star!"
"I don't know if I like the sound of that," Kolesar said with his nervous little laugh. "What'd you have in mind?"
"I don't have it all worked out yet, but we're going to piss Gilvary off, big-time, right in open court. And *you* are going to be the star player!"
"I'll have to see what you have in mind."

---

[11] Taken from a transcription of the recorded conversation.

"Don't worry. You're gonna love it. You'll be the talk of the legal fraternity, after we're done! Who do you want to play your part in the movie they'll make?"

"Ah - I'm not sure."

How about Pee-wee Herman? I thought as I talked to the meek little twerp. "Whatever you do, John, don't let on to Gilvary. Boy, is he ever gonna be pissed! I can't wait to see his fucking face."

"You'll have to give me more than that."

"I will, John, when the time is right, and I've got it all figured out."

"I don't know what you have in mind, but I am only to act in an advisory capacity for you."

"Hell, John! You'll probably *advise* me *not* to do it. But I'm going too anyway. We'll get together before court. Don't worry; you won't be asked to do anything illegal. But just remember, you're supposed to be on my side. Remember; not a word to Gilvary! Take care, my friend."

"Goodbye, Mr. Metz."

I counted on the little snitch running straight to Gilvary. That accomplished, I filed a motion that same November 29th entitled Defendant's Motion For A Change Of Venue. Since Gilvary had just denied the same motion, I expected a resounding response to this one. *Annoyance* would be turning to *anger.*

> Now comes the Defendant, *pro se,* before the Honorable Court, demanding that a change of venue be granted the Defendant, and that said change of venue be granted before any ruling as to the Defendant's competency to stand trial, pursuant to CrimR 18.
>
> ... The Defendant has been denied access to witness lists, exhibits of evidence and information that would exonerate him, by the State.
>
> The reason for this, in the Defendant's mind, is that officers of the court, up to and including judges on the Second District Court of Appeals, have a vested interest in convicting

the Defendant. The case has bounced from Judge Langer to Judge Gorman to Judge Gilvary.

It has bounced from Assistant Prosecutor Lipowicz to Assistant Prosecutor Rauch to Assistant Prosecutor Patricoff, and finally, the appointment of Special Prosecutors Schenck and Hendrix.

None of these reassignments were made in the interests of justice. None of these reassignments were made in the interests of the Defendant. None of these reassignments were requested by the Defendant.

... As Attorney/Prosecutor Laurence A. Lasky once told judges on the Court of Appeals, "*Nobody in Miamisburg Municipal likes Mr. Metz.*" (The Defendant had an inkling.) Nobody within the system has to *like* the Defendant.

However, the Defendant demands, if not respect for him, respect for the system and respect for the Constitution. With all of the changes, the one constant throughout has been the Defendant.

From a personal note, from one whose formal education ended with one year of college, it saddens that so many with bright minds, availed to the finest of educations squander their genius. It's a national disgrace.

... The question that the Defendant places before the Court is this: *If* the Defendant was perfectly competent to stand trial on November 25, 1996, without proper discovery having been proffered by the State, *what* would cause the Court to question his abilities for a trial at a later date, when he is amply prepared?

... The *appearance* is that the 9:35 a.m. call from the Defendant to Angie House provoked a call from the Second District Court of Appeals, that in turn provoked the Court to contact the prosecutor, that in turn provoked a call to the Forensic Psychiatry Center, that in turn provoked Vicky E. Whisman to detail the results of her efforts in memorandum form, which in turn provoked – due to time constraints – her showing up in chambers without having made any copies, which in turn provoked Judge Gilvary to simply hand the Defendant the original.

It's beautiful, with its nice seal at the top embossed on the paper. Reminds me of the original *Lowman* version of the bogus court order in my possession.

... Doctor Hopes was asked for a synopsis of her findings of the Defendant. Terms like *marginally competent* and *paranoia* were offered. A look at the history of matters before the court(s) render the good doctor's finding absurd.

There's been a lot of incompetence; a lot of paranoia; it hasn't come from the Defendant.

It is suggested to the good doctor that she broaden her horizons with the works of Emerson; the works of Thomas Moore, etc. In particular, Thomas Moore's marvelous book entitled *Care of the Soul* is recommended, for all parties enjoined herein.

WHEREFORE, the Defendant having fully discoursed, it is respectfully demanded that a change of venue be granted the Defendant, outside the dominion of the Second District Court of Appeals, and that the Court refrain from any ruling on Defendant's competency until after said change is in place.

The Defendant requests that the case be moved to Cincinnati, Ohio, as that is closest to his home.

Judge Gilvary would have received his copy of Dr. Hopes' evaluation. Hopes found:

A person who earns a score of 70 or more out of 100 on the Georgia Court Competency Test – Mississippi State Hospital Version is generally considered Competent to Stand Trial. Horace Ray Metz earned a score of 98.

What with Kolesar's blubbering in his ear; with my recent court filings; and with the competency test score, Judge Gilvary may have suffered a massive seizure within his mind, rendering him temporarily incapacitated. *Incompetent* described his condition best.

The demented judge lost his mind. I *knew* it was so, *because I had it*. Gilvary committed a major blunder.

He *knew* that removal of a defense counsel had to be done in open court, and then only when great caution was exercised. The right of counsel is fundamental. He *knew* he lacked jurisdiction to preside in my case. Yet he filed an Order reading:

> This matter came on to be heard on Defendant's Motion for Dismissal of Court Appointed Advisor filed November 14, 1996. Defendant accuses Attorney John P. Kolesar, his Court Appointed Advisor, of being a "plant". It is not clear from Defendant's memorandum if Mr. Kolesar is a prosecutorial "plant" or a judicial "plant". In any event, the motion is **SUSTAINED** and Defendant will be permitted and now required to "wing it" alone (as he puts it).
>
> This matter is also before the Court on Defendant's Motion for a Change of Venue filed on November 29, 1996. The Defendant seeks to remove the case from the jurisdiction of the Second District Court of Appeals. He alleges wrongdoing by the Judges of that Court as a basis for his motion. The Court finds the motion not well taken and the same is **OVERRULED**.
>
> SO ORDERED:
>
> JAMES J. GILVARY, JUDGE

I had written in my motion, *they were trapped. And there's no way out.* I vowed that *the Defendant shall serve a prison sentence long enough to repay the complainants.* And I had cautioned Judge Gilvary, quoting II Peter 2:19:

> For of whom a man overcome, of the
> same is he brought in bondage.

Mock my angels, would he? I would be *required* - by him - to "wing it" alone, would I?

The Honorable James J. Gilvary would soon be condemned to a prison of the psyche, *where I would become his warden.* Gilvary would serve his time in isolation; in solitary confinement, until his death. And in the end, the demented judge would be...*well taken.*

CHAPTER TEN

Fair Shake

Larry Lasky's associate, Attorney Steven C. Holloman had been indicted August 20, 1996, by a Montgomery County grand jury for forging Dayton Municipal Court Judge James Cannon's signature on court documents. Holloman surrendered his license to practice law.

Lasky and Judge Messham's *rubber stamp queen*, Deputy Clerk Maria Lowman had been fired August 6, 1996 for theft in Miamisburg Municipal Court. She had been indicted on November 5th by a Montgomery County grand jury.

Lowman's case had been assigned to Judge Barbara P. Gorman, after she recused from my case. George B. Patricoff became the prosecutor for Lowman's case, after he abandoned my case and special prosecutors were assigned.

Lasky prosecuted cases for the Fraud Division Patricoff now headed, that had charged me. The "fix" was on in Lowman's case! I wondered how they intended to keep her from blowing everyone's cover.

Lowman pled guilty to one count of theft in office. While she awaited sentencing; I decided to rattle a few cages. I telephoned Patricoff at the prosecutor's office. [12]

"George Patricoff."

"Hello, George. This is Ray Metz. How are you doing?"

"I'm doing fine. What can I do for you?"

"Ah the reason I called ah I understand Maria Lowman took a plea the other day to a count. Does your office have jurisdiction over any actions she might

---

[12] Taken from a transcription of the recorded conversation.

have done so far as forging a judge's signature on a court order – things like that?"

"Sure."

"Alright. I'd like to file a complaint."

"Well ah I think you need ah what did she forge? Ah what judge's signature?"

"Well, first of all she signed an order as judge. She signed Lowman as judge and notarized it on the bottom and then she or - she either did it or had someone do it ah forged Acting Judge Mark E. Landers signature on a -"

"Acting judge who?

"Acting Judge Mark Landers, who visits down in Miamisburg. He's a lieutenant colonel in the Air Force. And I know that he didn't sign it. I talked to him at home after it happened."

"Alright, well what you need to do – my complainant will be the two people whose names have been forged. So you need to have them call me and make a complaint."

"Okay, well what if they won't do that?" I mean you know they're not going to do it. First of all, they did it for Lasky."

"Well ah you know - I don't want to get into that."

I laughed as Patricoff said, "I don't know anything about it."

The hell you say! You do know; and that's why you don't want to get into it, were brief thoughts. But I responded agreeably, "I understand that."

"You know - I can't - you know," the prosecutor botched. *He sounds exactly like Maria Lowman, when cornered,* I thought in satisfaction.

... "Now, it could be that that guy - it could be the judge said Marie ah I'm on my way to lunch - can you sign it which she - she should - she should not sign *her* name - but you know."

The weasel sounds exactly like Maria Lowman! I thought again. "Well, she signed her name – ah - she signed her name on one copy and when I caught her-"

... "I've read your pleadings and to me they don't make any sense. But -"

I laughed. "Part of that's deliberate."

"Well I know that, but on the other hand, you're not making any legal points with anybody. And you need to make some legal points to get what you want done and you're not gonna do it."

The legal point is that I am involved with a den of thieves, George, and you are in the den, I thought. I agreed, "Unum, okay."

... "That's why we have trials."

"That's right. And ah - all I'm asking for is a fair shake, and if I get a fair shake it will all be resolved, but ah - to this point -"

"If you can't get a fair shake in this county, you're never gonna get a fair shake."

America is in deep shit then. Maria Lowman's not going to get a fair shake, I thought. "Well -"

"Ah well, there again we have a difference of opinion."

"Well -"

"You're making it harder on yourself."

"Not really, because I was in Judge Foley's court for - in a civil case and I represented myself against an insurance company and I was very satisfied with the outcome. Ah I prevailed after a two-day jury trial."

"Well I mean you can't -"

"I had to back into it but I did prevail. And I was very satisfied."

"Don't think you're Clarence Darrow because you won one, now."

"Hunh?"

"Don't think you're Clarence Darrow because you won one."

"Ah well, I won another one too, but no - not at all. Ah I won one against the IRS too."

... "Alright, good luck to you."

"Thank you. Bye."

I wonder how much he knows about Clarence Darrow,[13] I thought while hanging up. I laughed at the irony. Patricoff attempted to portray a comedian! *Good luck* was not in the equation.

If I had *good luck,* some of Patricoff's accomplices faced disbarment; and others prison. What I needed to spare Judge Gilvary a death sentence, and a long prison stretch for me, was - *a fair shake.*

---

[13] Clarence Darrow (1857-1938) was born in Kinsman, Ohio. In the 1920s the Agnostic was considered America's most famous lawyer.

His most controversial case was to defend John T. Scopes in **Dayton, Tennessee** in a trial known as The Monkey Trial. Scopes was accused of teaching the theory of evolution, in violation of a new law. The prosecution team included William Jennings Bryan, who believed in a literal interpretation of the Bible. Darrow made a fool of Bryan on the stand.

Unlike Darrow, I believed in God. And I believed the existence of God could be proven. Like Darrow, I saw the beliefs of fundamentalists like Bryan to be unfounded. And I *believed* Judge Gilvary would experience the fate of William Jennings Bryan - in the other Dayton in 1925. For he died five days after the Monkey Trial ended with a conviction (overturned on appeal). The day began by his attending church with his wife, and offering the prayer. After dinner, he laid down to take a nap. He never woke up. His personal physician concluded, "Bryan died of diabetes melitis, the immediate cause being the fatigue incident to the heat and his extraordinary exertions due to the Scopes trial."

CHAPTER ELEVEN

Gonna have a Party

A gambler's weakness is the *tell*. I had invaded the psyche of Judge Gilvary in a powerful and compelling way. He told me this by mimicking me with *wing it alone* - while dismissing Kolesar, in violation of Ohio Revised Code. High–stakes poker was getting too him.

It was time to introduce Gilvary to what life with his future warden would be like. George Patricoff told me that I needed an attorney, during our telephone conversation on Friday, December 13, 1996.

I filed a Motion on December 16th. I did not want to disclose George Patricoff's identity, so I referred to him as *a little birdie*. It read in part:

> Now comes the Defendant, via the authority granted in the Sixth Amendment of the Constitution of the United States of America, demanding that the Court appoint a new Legal Advisor for him.
>
> ... The Defendant imagines that the Court may view this as an example of his supposedly diagnosed *paranoia*. The Defendant would simply respond to that hypothetical by saying, while "winging it" **a little birdie** told him he'd better get an advisor that the Court and the State respected.
>
> ... Therefore, it seems logical that a *level playing field* can be attained by the Court's appointment of Neil Freund as the Defendant's Legal Advisor.

I filed for subpoena of eleven witnesses for the competency hearing of December 23, 1996; served on:

1. Miamisburg Municipal Clerk of Courts Janice Lowman
2. Common Pleas Clerk of Court Craig Zimmers
3. Appellate Judge James A. Brogan

4. Appellate Judge Mike Fain
5. Appellate Judge Thomas J. Grady
6. Dayton Mayor Michael R. Turner
7. County Prosecutor Mathias H. Heck, Jr.
8. Bar Counsel Jonathan Hollingsworth
9. Greene County Prosecutor William F. Schenck
10. Bobbie G. Hopes, Ph.D.
11. Attorney John P. Kolesar

I visited the *Dayton Daily News;* the *Xenia Gazette;* as well as television stations WDTN, Channel 2; WHIO TV, Channel 7; and WKEF, Channel 22; provided them documentation of what was transpiring, and invited them to attend the competency hearing.

My foes wanted to play in obscurity. And I wanted to play in the open; in the *court of public opinion.*

If all went as planned, as the song goes, we were *Gonna Have a Party!*[14]

---

[14] "Gonna Have a Party" was released in 1993 by Alabama.

CHAPTER TWELVE

Trembling Hands

Judge Gilvary was in a box. He dismissed Kolesar without doing so in open court and on the record. I filed for new counsel. A competency hearing was mandated. I had the right to counsel at the hearing. According to Ohio Revised Code, a hearing could not be conducted until I had counsel.

Gilvary could see why he was the *fourteenth judge* to deal with me. I was certain it was not a happy revelation for him.

On December 19, 1996, I received a **docket schedule** for Monday, December 23rd, at 10:00 A.M. My case was set for a Competency Report. This was my first notice that a competency hearing was not going to be conducted.

On December 20th, Mathias H. Heck, Jr. filed a Motion To Quash his subpoena. It read:

> Now comes Mathias H. Heck, Jr., in his capacity as the Prosecuting Attorney for Montgomery County, Ohio, by and through his counsel, and, for the reasons stated in the accompanying memorandum, respectfully moves this Court for an order quashing a subpoena recently delivered to his office commanding that he appear on December 23, 1996 at 10:00 a.m. in the above-captioned matter.
>
> Respectfully submitted,
> MAHIAS H. HECK, JR.
> PROSECUTING ATTORNEY
> By: CHRIS R. VAN SCHAIK
> Assistant Prosecuting Attorney

MEMORANDUM

On or about December 16, 1996, the Defendant in the above-captioned matter caused to be filed with the Clerk of Common Pleas Court of Montgomery County, Ohio a subpoena directed to Mathias H. Heck, Jr. (hereinafter "Movant"), commanding that he appear on December 23, 1996 at 10:00 a.m. ostensibly to be a witness and to offer testimony in the above-captioned matter. O.R.C. §309.08 clearly states that a prosecuting attorney is to inquire into the commission of crimes within his or her county and that such prosecuting attorney shall prosecute all complaints wherein the State of Ohio is a party. The Movant therefore stands in the capacity as the statutory counsel for the State of Ohio in the above-captioned matter and that, as such, he does not qualify as a witness who should testify on behalf of the Defendant. The Defendant cannot attempt to taint the criminal proceedings pending before him by calling the Prosecuting Attorney as a witness.

Based on the foregoing, this Movant respectfully requests that this Court issue an order quashing the subpoena issued by the Defendant in this matter.

> Respectfully submitted,
> MATHIAS H. HECK, JR.
> PROSECUTING ATTORNEY
> By: CHRIS R. VAN SCHAIK

Heck's hypocrisy is very unbecoming. If he adhered to O.R.C. §309.08 – as it "clearly states," he would be investigating "taint" in his office, I thought while reading.

I arrived early for the court session, and went to the basement coffee shop. I sat in quiet reflection, mentally preparing myself for what lay ahead.

Finishing, I made my way to the elevator for the ride to the floor where Gilvary's courtroom was located. The elevator was crowded after stopping at the lobby, and I overheard two parties in front of me.

"Something big is going on in Gilvary's courtroom. There are special prosecutors and the press is there."

"What's happening? I haven't heard about anything."

"I don't know, but it must be big."

The courtroom was packed, with standing room only. I saw a smiling Second District Court of Appeals Judge Mike Fain standing in the rear. A reporter from the *Dayton Daily News* was present.

Judge Fain appeared to be enjoying himself a little too much. But appearances can be deceiving. He had to have the criminal's normal anxieties; and fears of being exposed – no matter how slight the chances.

Janice Lowman, the clerk of Miamisburg Municipal Court approached me. "I don't know why I was subpoenaed, but I was told to let you know I am here."

Though I had subpoenaed him, Kolesar was not in court. There was no one present in the courtroom; that Gilvary could later claim represented me.

I finally persuaded two people to squeeze together, making room for me. I sat down next to an isle. Someone thrust a paper in my hands, and disappeared.

It was an Order from Gilvary denying me counsel. The heading used my *real name:* HORACE RAY METZ, aka RAY METZ. The order was time-stamped 96 DEC 23 AM 9:52. *Eight* minutes before court convened, Gilvary denied me counsel.

Gilvary-the-gambler was under immense pressure, as another *tell* indicated. A slip of Gilvary's pen told me so. The Order was filed on December 16, 1996. But the order read:

The trial date of **February 18, 1996** is firm.

How *firm* could a trial date be, that was ten months in the past? Gilvary, the gambler was sweating bullets at the enormity of what was transpiring.

```
                          FILED
                  COURT OF COMMON PLEAS

                  95 DEC 23 AM 9: 52

                     CRAIG ZIMMERS
                    CLERK OF COURTS
                  MONTGOMERY CO.. OHIO

         IN THE COMMON PLEAS COURT OF MONTGOMERY COUNTY, OHIO

                         CRIMINAL DIVISION

     THE STATE OF OHIO,        :    CASE NO. 95-CR-2317

                Plaintiff,     :    (Judge James J. Gilvary)

        -vs-                   :    DECISION, ENTRY AND ORDER

     HORACE RAY METZ, aka      :
     RAY METZ,
                               :
                Defendant.
                               :

                  : : : : : : : : : : : :

         This matter came on to be heard on Defendant's Motion For

     Appointment Of A Legal Advisor.  This motion was filed on

     December 16, 1996, some four days after the Court sustained the

     Defendant's motion to dismiss his previously appointed advisor.

     Defendant seeks the appointment of Neil Freund as his legal

     advisor.  If Defendant wishes to retain Mr. Freund at his expense

     for whatever purpose, the Court has no objection, but the trial

     date of February 18, 1996 is firm.  Although this Court did not

     appoint Mr. Kolesar originally, it has no reason to doubt his

     ability to serve as Defendant's legal advisor.  The motion of

     December 16, 1996 is OVERRULED.
```

A criminal using the pen often makes critical errors. They are not typos! It is akin to a bank robber in suburban Cincinnati, who wrote his stick-up note on the back of a printed deposit ticket, resplendent with his name and home address affixed. A comedian[15] joked:

> An accident is just premeditated carelessness.

It was one thing for appellate judges, Mike Fain, Jim Brogan, and Bill Wolff, Jr. to conspire with Common Pleas Court Judges Dennis Langer and John Kessler;

---

[15] Brother Dave Gardner 1926-1983) recorded "Rejoice, Dear Hearts" in 1959. He was a funny, funny man in my high school days of innocence.

along with Prosecuting Attorney Matt Heck, Jr. – in the secrecy of their den of iniquity, in creating *The Perfect Crime.*

Eventually, Gilvary had willingly agreed to rescue his friends. But now, it was quite another thing to have some of the conspirators subpoenaed to appear in court; when the press had received a personal invitation from the object of their affection. And it made Gilvary nervous; to say the least.

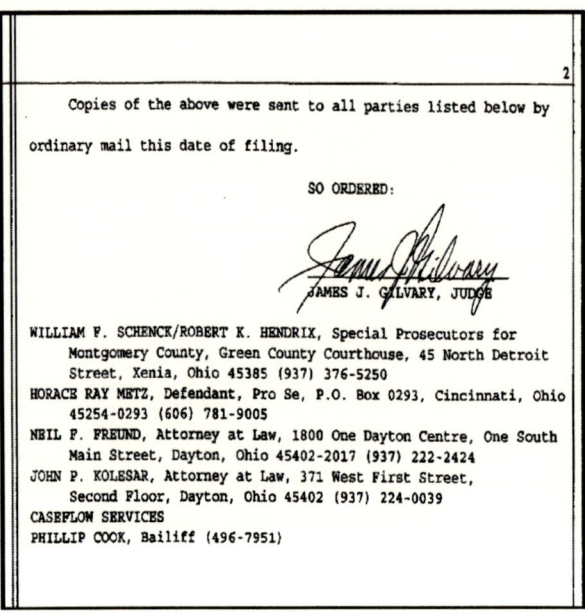

...this Court...has no reason to doubt his ability to serve...
(Except for one factor - Gilvary dismissed him.)

After our "all rise" and initial formalities, the bailiff called the first case. Following the conclusion of that matter, the bailiff said, "Next case ..."[16]

Judge Gilvary interrupted, "Why don't you call the Metz case next."

"Yes, sir. Top of page three, Horace Raymond Metz, 95-CR-2317.

---

[16] Conversation taken from the official transcript.

I rose and went to stand in front of the bench.

Gilvary began with, "Good morning, Mr. Metz."

"Good morning, Your Honor."

Gilvary's eyes turned to the prosecutor, who stood beside me, saying, "Good morning, Mr. Hendrix."

"Good morning, Your Honor."

Gilvary began, "Let the record show that Mr. Hendrix is appearing as special prosecutor in this case and that the matter is before the court on a report of competency to stand trial which the court ordered, with which Mr. Metz complied, and we now have a report dated December the 5th from the Forensic Psychiatry Center for Western Ohio signed by Bobbie Hopes expressing an opinion that Mr. Metz is currently competent to stand trial.

"Does the prosecution wish to waive anything further on that issue?"

"Yes, Your Honor," Hendrix agreed.

Gilvary addressed me, "Mr. Metz, I take it you don't have any argument with the conclusion reached by the psychologist. Do you?"

Very clever wording, you slimy shyster, I thought. I said, "No, Your Honor, except some of the conclusions that she made in her report I'm concerned about."

Gilvary held the report in his hands, and without making eye contact said, "All right. Well, the only conclusion that's of importance to the court, and I think to you at this time, is that she finds that you are competent to stand trial, and unless you have some quarrel with that, that's going to be the finding of the court."

You're one clever son-of-a-bitch, I thought; as I said, "Well, Your Honor, if I may?"

The pressure of playing high-stakes poker overcame the gambler. Gilvary became completely unnerved; his hands began trembling so badly that the papers he held rattled. His microphone picked up the sound.

Symbolically, the rattling papers echoed as though an unwelcomed extension of Gilvary's rattled psyche. He quickly laid the papers down, to quiet the noise.

The rattling noise ended in the secular world; while the psyche continued to rattle uncontrollably, in the spiritual world. I stood calmly with hands clasped behind my back, seeking eye contact to no avail; savoring the moment as I thought, *Gilvary's afraid of me; he's afraid of what might come next. I stand before him, facing twelve years in prison, and he's afraid of me! What a pathetic foolish, squalid little man!*

All I had to say was one of three things, to conclude matters:

(1) *Your Honor, you denied me counsel eight minutes before court began. I would respectfully ask that this matter be continued until such time as I am represented.*

(2) *Your Honor, I demand that this matter be set for a hearing as mandated by Ohio Revised Code.*

(3) *Your Honor, pursuant to Local Rules of Court, you have no jurisdiction; and therefore, you are compelled to dismiss this case.*

Prudence became the better part of valor. It was not up to me to assure that the lawless Gilvary, operating without jurisdiction, obeyed his oath. It was solely up to him to properly execute his judicial duties!

So I said, "I believe I'm perfectly competent to stand trial. However, some of her findings would indicate that I may suffer from paranoia which would tend to discount some of the things that I have written - reported in the past, and I really believe that those conclusions were made by analyzing the part of me that's the pro se attorney and not the defendant. And I'd like to challenge the veracity of those findings if the court would use that as a basis to limit my defense."

Gilvary responded, "I'm not going to use it for any purpose at all. The only conclusion that I'm going to use was the last line that says you're competent to stand trial.

"And Pat, on the docket sheet it doesn't indicate that there is a trial date and there is, February 18th."

"Thank you, Your Honor," Pat parroted.

Gilvary finished with, "That concludes the matter this morning. Thank you."

"Thank you, Your Honor," I acknowledged.

"Thank you, Your Honor," Hendrix parroted.

Though I would not learn of it until much later, line 0550 on the docket would be deleted. It was the line for the Order by Judge Gilvary, denying me counsel eight minutes before court began. It amounted to reversible error.

```
                                                        (PAGE:    3)
0520 12/16/96 <MD> DEFENDANT'S MOTION PLEADING THAT THE STATE NOT BE
                   SANCTIONED FOR NONCOMPLIANCE OF THE COURT'S ORDER FILED
                   SIGNED BY: DEFT HORACE RAY METZ  DUE DATE - 12/16/96
0530 12/16/96 <MD> MOTION FOR APPOINTMENT OF LEGAL ADVISOR FOR THE DEFENDANT
                   FILED  SIGNED BY: DEFT HORACE RAY METZ  DUE DATE -
                   12/16/96
0540 12/23/96 <CM> DEFT IS COMPETENT (IN DOCKET CALL)  SIGNED BY: 7001
0560 12/20/96 <MP> MOTION TO QUASH FILED  SIGNED BY: ASST PROS ATTY C VAN
                   SCHAIK
0570 12/24/96 <MP> MOTION TO QUASH SUBPOENAS FILED  SIGNED BY: SPECIAL PROS
                   ROBERT HENDRIX
0580 12/26/96 <OE> ENTRY AND ORDER THAT DEFT IS PRESENTLY COMPETENT TO STAND
                   TRIAL FILED  SIGNED BY: JAMES J GILVARY  SIGNER'S NBR:
                   0010
```

Docket Statement with line 0550 removed
0560 and 0570: motions to quash by Van Schaik and Hendrix
0530 is my motion for counsel; 0580 Entry and Order by Gilvary

```
0520 12/16/96 <MD>

0530 12/16/96 <MD>

0540 12/23/96 <CM>
0560 12/20/96 <MP>

0570 12/24/96 <MP>

0580 12/26/96 <OE>
```

0550 was deleted -
denying me counsel

I went to the clerk's office to review the file of the case, and was turned away. I did not make an issue of it as I *knew*, without seeing the files; Gilvary's order denying me counsel had to have been removed from the record. I obtained the docket statement.

Hendrix filed a motion to squash Schenck's subpoena on December 24th – *one day after* the "hearing" was held. I thought of Janice Lowman finding me while in the courtroom, and her words: *"I was told to let you know I am here." They were setting me up!* I thought incredulously.

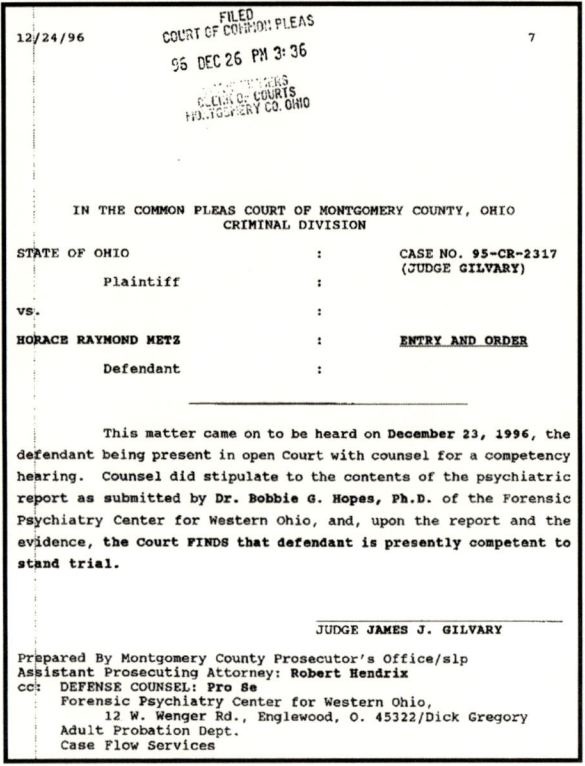

The order prepared by "slp" of the prosecutor's office

I will never forget standing calmly before a dishonorable Judge Gilvary - in the packed courtroom - hands clasped behind my back; alone and vulnerable, and watching him. One who held himself out as being all-powerful in his arena; behaved like a cornered punk.

I shall never forget those *trembling hands.*

CHAPTER THIRTEEN

Paradise Lost

Mahoning County patterned its *Local Rules of Court* after Montgomery County's. Youngstown and Dayton were sister cities; of sorts.

The day after Judge Gilvary's *trembling hands* debacle in Dayton, the criminal element struck with a vengeance in Youngstown. It was the Christmas Eve of 1996.

A mob hit man, Mark A. Batcho crept into the home of the newly elected Mahoning County Prosecutor Paul Gains. He heard Gains in the kitchen, talking on the telephone. He waited for the phone call to end.

Batcho fired the first time, hitting Gains in the midsection. He fired again as Gains fell to the floor. Gains was bleeding from the side and an arm.

Fate is a funny thing. As Batcho aimed at Gains' heart, the prosecutor-elect put up his hands; as if to ward him off. When the hit man pulled the trigger, the gun jammed. Panicking, Batcho ran from the house, leaving Gains to die in his blood.

But Paul Gains miraculously survived the assassination attempt. He recovered, took office, and began the enormous task he had been elected to do. Gains had campaigned on a vow to clean up corruption in Mahoning County.

And, just when it appeared his attempted murder would go unsolved, the county prosecutor received a phone call at home, on a spring night.

"Are you Paul Gains?"

"Yes. Who is this?"

"I know who shot you."

The phone call came from an ex-girlfriend of a mob hit man. Gains informed the police, who brought in the FBI. For the first time, a mob hit was solved.

Once the FBI was brought in; Gains joined forces with Special Agent Robert Kroner, a consummate professional. Kroner joined the FBI in 1971, and transferred to Youngstown in 1976. He dedicated himself to cleaning up corruption found in Mahoning County.

Everything fell in place for the two dedicated American heroes; Paul Gains and Robert Kroner. A cursory review of records of over seventy convictions included:

> Lenine Strollo – mob boss
> Bernard Altshuler – top mob associate
> Lawrence P. Garono – top mob associate
> Jeffrey Riddle – mob enforcer
> Lavance Turnage – mob enforcer
> Mark Batcho – mob hit man
> James Traficant, Jr. – US Congressman
> Charles O'Nesti – congressional district office
> Raymond A. Sinclair – congressional staffer
> Frank A. Lodi – county commissioner
> William Fergus – county engineer
> Andrew Rauzan – police officer
> Gerard Keish - police officer
> Phillip A. Chance – county sheriff
> John Chicase – county deputy sheriff
> Russell J. Saadey, Jr. – prosecutor's investigator
> Michael Paul Rich – city prosecuting attorney
> James A. Philomena – county prosecuting attorney
> James R. Wise – attorney
> Jack V. Campbell - attorney
> Peter J. Bozanich – attorney
> Edward A. Flask – attorney
> Richard D. Goldberg – attorney
> Walter David Hartsock - attorney
> Laurence Joseph Seidita - attorney
> Stuart James Banks - attorney
> Joseph A. Dubyak- attorney

Stewart I. Mandel – attorney
Paul Francis Gambrel - attorney
Andrew Polovischak, Jr. – judge
Patrick V. Kerrigan- judge
Fred H. Bailey – judge
Martin W. Emrich - judge
Edward A. Cox – appellate judge

A federal wiretap of mob leader Lenine Strollo and others had been in effect since August 23, 1996. Special Agent Robert G. Kroner, Jr., Special Agent John Stoll, and Special Agent Gordon Klau worked fourteen-hour days; for thirteen months. It was a seven-day-a-week ordeal.

The FBI had enough evidence to send Strollo to prison for life. Once they put the squeeze on him, he cooperated with prosecutors. Evidence gleaned from the mob boss was used to convict a multitude of others. He was sentenced to twelve years, eight months in prison.

Attorneys Jack Campbell, Stuart Banks, and Laurence Seidita were granted immunity from state prosecution in return for their cooperation. They sang like parakeets for the reduced federal sentences offered.

Mobsters Bernie Altshuler, Jeffrey Riddle, and Lavance Turnage were each sentenced to life-without-parole. Mark Batcho, the hit man who left Paul Gains to die, received twenty-eight years, with a mandatory twenty years in prison.

U.S. Congressman James Traficant, Jr. served over seven years in prison. Charles O'Nesti, the Director of Traficant's District Office died prior to sentencing. Attorney Raymond A. Sinclair was an attorney on Traficant's staff. He was paid $5,000 a month, and kicked-back half of it to Traficant in cash. His testimony helped convict the congressman.

Frank Lodi, a Mahoning County commissioner was sentenced to eighteen months. Michael P. Rich, City of

Campbell prosecuting attorney was sentenced to ten months.

Mahoning County Sheriff Phil Chance served about 62 months in prison. His approach to law enforcement was novel. The sheriff was in Strollo's pocket, accepting bribes from him.

Chance raided illegal gambling establishments competing against Strollo, while ignoring the mob's illegal operations. To create the public perception of being tough on crime, Chance would invite the press when he conducted a drug raid.

He would hold up clear plastic bags of powder cocaine for television cameras. But the bags contained flour, instead of cocaine. He pulled this ruse over and over.

James A. Philomena, the Mahoning County prosecuting attorney Paul Gains replaced, served six years in federal and state prison. He filed a motion for early release. An attorney described his client as a "broken, ruined man" while in prison.

His motion was denied. Two years after his release from prison, Philomena died in 2007, at age 60.

Youngstown Municipal Court Judge Andrew Polovischak, Jr., was sentenced to thirty months, as was his associate, Judge Patrick V. Kerrigan. Kerrigan was released after thirteen months. Judge Fred H. Bailey of the Mahoning County Court was sentenced to seventeen months, and two years of supervised control.

Stuart James Banks, Laurence Joseph Seidita, and Jack V. Campbell cooperated with the FBI. And they received reduced sentences from the feds. Banks and Seidita spent eight months in a halfway house and eight months on house arrest. Campbell spent sixteen months on monitored house arrest.

Seidita represented a drug dealer, Glen Martin. He told the FBI he paid Mahoning County Prosecutor James A. Philomena $20,000 to *fix* a drug case, giving Martin less time in prison. When Martin was arrested again, Seidita paid Philomena another $5-6,000. This payoff was made as they walked around the court-house.

Prior to this, Seidita paid Youngstown Municipal Court Judge Andrew Polovischak, Jr. $500 and Martin received a suspended sentence on a motor vehicle charge. He paid Polovischak $200, and Antoinette Anderson received a suspended sentence on an assault charge. Polovischak took six bribes from Seidita.

Seidita represented a jewel thief, Frank Susany. He paid Prosecuting Attorney Philomena $12,500 (who found no probable cause) to *fix* a case against Susany. Seidita paid a $2,500 bribe to County Judge Fred H. Bailey, who found no probable cause to bind Susany's charge of assault on a police officer over to a grand jury. Seidita paid Prosecuting Attorney Philomena $8,000 and drug dealer Daniel Boerio received probation; in a case that had mandatory prison time.

Seidita was approached by Walter Hartsock, who was a claims adjuster for Nationwide Insurance Company. From 1990 through 1999, Hartsock traded insider information in exchange for kickbacks.

Seidita was told he could make money, helping settle a case; if someone would contact Joseph Dubyak, who represented the plaintiff. Seidita contacted Stuart Banks. Banks contacted Dubyak. With insider information, Dubyak settled the case and paid a $15,000 kickback to Banks, who split it with Seidita and Hartsock.

In 1999, Dubyak was contacted by Banks, who offered insider information on a case in which Dubyak represented the plaintiff. Dubyak again agreed to pay a kickback. But this time, Banks was wearing a wiretap; in cooperation with law enforcement agencies.

Between these two cases, Hartsock contacted Seidita and told him he could provide insider information regarding a client of Paul Gambrel, if he would pay a kickback. Gambrel paid $2,500 to Hartsock.

Not to be outdone by Seidita, Attorney Stuart Banks informed the FBI that Judge Polovischak told him after election, "We are going to make some money."

Banks estimated Polovischak received bribes from him totaling between $10-15,000. He paid Polovischak $2,500 to vacate a DUI conviction against John Dunn. Polovischak transferred the case to Judge Patrick V. Kerrigan and Banks paid the second judge $2,500. Kerrigan found Dunn *not guilty.*

Banks paid Seventh District Court of Appeals Judge Edward Cox *bribes* of $600-700 for referring cases to him. He paid Mahoning County Judge Fred H. Bailey $1,000 to *fix* a case.

Banks estimated he paid Prosecuting Attorney Philomena $20-25,000 to *fix* cases. In one *fix,* Philomena allegedly split about $5,000 with James A. Vitullo, an Austintown assistant prosecutor.

According to court records, Seventh District Court of Appeals Judge Edward A. Cox had a gambling problem. He *borrowed* $20,000 from Attorney Richard Goldberg; and then $5,000 and $2,500 more. Judge Cox received *loans* from other attorneys. The *loans* were never intended to be repaid. They were *bribes.*

According to court records, Judge Patrick Kerrigan routinely shook down corrupt attorneys. Normally he demanded $1,000. He was shameless, aggressive, and unapologetic in his criminal endeavors.

Kickbacks and bribes went on ad nausea. In an unrelated case, a defense attorney insisted that a transaction was not a *bribe,* but rather, an *"unlawful gratuity."* The newspaper article did not say whether the attorney was laughed out of the courtroom.

As a result of these and similar activities, the United States charged Hartsock, Seidita, Banks, Dubyak, and Gambrel with using the United States mail in conspiring to defraud Nationwide.

There was a distinct difference in outcomes, for Lasky and Seidita. In Dayton, I threatened to go to the FBI the day I was arrested in the Montgomery County Courts Building. I did telephone the Dayton FBI office after the *trembling hands* debacle in court, but was practically ridiculed while expressing fear of physical harm. The nameless Special Agent I spoke too refused to look into allegations of criminal activity.

In Youngstown, Seidita had to actually deal with the FBI. He had to cooperate with agents, in order to be spared prison time for mail fraud conspiracy; in order to help convict a crooked county prosecutor and several crooked judges.

I was uncertain whether Dayton and Montgomery County had been inundated with organized crime, or simply disorganized slime; or perhaps a combination of both. In Dayton, I was forced to deal with a crooked county prosecutor and crooked judges.

There would be no FBI RICO probe. And I would go to prison, while Lasky et al. went to lunch. But what happened in Youngstown provides an indelible backdrop for what was endured in Dayton; in *Paradise Lost*.

CHAPTER FOURTEEN

Ten of Spades

On the morning of December 27, 1996, I sat Ann down for a discussion. It was time to let her know the seriousness of what lay ahead.

"Here is the way things are," I began deliberately. "If I plead guilty, I will be granted diversion and will not spend a minute in jail. I will pay the $7,040 and my record will be expunged. And they will have everything that they seek. I will be discredited; as a confessed convicted felon."

"And if you don't do that?" Ann wanted to know.

"If I don't do that, they are going to cheat, find me guilty, and send me to prison."

"How long could they send you for?"

"A long time; up to twelve years, if Gilvary wants too."

"How long would you have to serve?"

"Eight years."

"Well, we're going to have to hope he doesn't do that, because I know you, and I know you won't plead guilty."

"Are you with me in this?"

"You have *no right* to ask me a question like that!" Ann retorted with fire in her eyes.

Of course I didn't, I soothed, as I took Ann into my arms, and held her as she sobbed against my chest. Of course I didn't.

I reminded Ann I believed in what I was doing. We must believe in the teachings of Christian Scripture; we must *walk by faith, and not by sight.*

It was time to pay another visit to the psyche of my soon-to-be prisoner; time to really take off the gloves against the soon-to-be kidnapper. So I went to Dayton and filed three motions, along with a patriotic tape recording.

From the first motion:

> Now comes the Defendant, *pro se,* before the Honorable Court, in gratitude and filled with humility, and thereby offers his very best to officers of the court involved herein.
>
> ... At the Competency To Stand Trial Hearing on Monday, December 23, 1996, the Defendant stood before the bench, hands clasped behind his back, and calmly observed how *bothered* the good judge appeared to be.
>
> It seemed to the Defendant that His Honor suffered from, in the words of Bobbie G. Hopes, Ph.D., *"high levels of emotional distress"* and a *"paranoid and distrustful orientation."* It seemed that His Honor struggled to maintain a semblance of composure, with hands shaking uncontrollably.
>
> This Defendant witnessed, in awe, the might of...*the truth, the whole truth, and nothing but the truth...*as the Defendant sought out eye contact with the judge.
>
> This Defendant, stripped of any legal assistance, standing alone before the power of the State and the tyranny of the Court, and facing a possible twelve year prison sentence, observed the judge become unnerved, as the pious decorum of the court room crumbled.
>
> It was a memorable occasion!
>
> The Defendant hereby waives rights to confidentiality, and includes Doctor Hopes' entire Forensic Evaluation as a part of this filing.
>
> The Defendant viewed his being sent to the Forensic Psychiatry Center For Western Ohio as he would a visit to a massage parlor of ill-repute. Doctor Hopes received the same consideration that any *working girl* deserves from a *john*. The pimps are the State and the Court.
>
> ... If "prosecuted," the Defendant is willing to serve a sentence in prison however long; until the State finds that the claimants are whole, without ever having been repaid.
>
> ... This Defendant doesn't want your millions. This Defendant wants your inhumanity. He wants Aldridge and Wilcox to

be freed from the tyranny of the system. He wants a frightened little Centerville girl, unjustly tried as an adult, to be freed.[17] **In the name of heaven, what are you people about?**

… Made a part of this filing, and simultaneous filings…is a tape recording entitled Ohio v. Metz – Xmas 1996…

I began a tape recording with Gene Autry telling the story of One Solitary Life, based on an essay originally written by James Allen Francis (1864-1928).

There was a man born of Jewish parents in an obscure village, the child of a pheasant woman. He grew up in another obscure village. He worked in a carpenter shop until He was thirty and then for three years was an itinerant preacher. He never wrote a book. He never held an office. He never owned a home, or had a family. He never went to college. He never put his foot inside a big city. He never traveled two hundred miles from the place where He was born.

He did none of the things that one usually associates with greatness. He had no credentials but Himself. While still a young man the tide of popular opinion turned against him. His friends ran away. He was turned over to His enemies and went through the mockery of a trial.

He was nailed to a cross between two thieves. His executioners gambled for His coat while He was dying, the only piece of property He had. When He was dead He was taken down and laid in a borrowed grave through the pity of a friend.

Nineteen wide centuries have come and gone, and today He is the center piece of much of the human race. All the armies that ever marched, all the navies that ever sailed, all the parliaments that have ever sat, all the kings that ever reigned, put together, have not affected the life of man on this earth as much as has one solitary life.

---

[17] Parties referred too are Robert Dale Aldridge and M. Jenny Wilcox; and Rebecca Lynn Hopfer.

```
                          M - 835

                       Ohio v, Metz
                      Xmas 1996 Tape
                       (Revised)

       This tape recording is being made a part of the Defendant's
       filings in 95-CR-2317 of December 27, 1996: said filings
       entitled Defendant's Motion For An Inspirational Holiday
       Season For All Parties Herein Enjoined, Motion Celebrating
       "Virgin" Birth Of Appeals Case 15023, and Defendant's Motion
       Of Commendation For The Special Prosecutors.

       Side A:

              *    The Solitary Man by Gene Autry
          10-18-94  Attorney/assistant prosecutor Laurence A. Lasky
              *    (Town Without Pity by Gene Pitney)
          10-18-94  Miamisburg Municipal Deputy Clerk Maria R. Lowman
              *    Maria from West Side Story
          10-20-94  Visiting Judge Mark E. Landers
              *    Who Am I by Elvis Presley
          02-05-96  Eviction Police by WHIO-TV
              *    Town Without Pity by Gene Pitney
          10-25-94  Trial - Miamisburg Municipal Court - Judge Robert E. Messham, Jr.
              *    Happy Trails To You by Roy Rogers and Dale Evans
          12-22-94  Miamisburg Civic Center
              *    Oh Come All Ye Faithful by Al Martino
          12-27-94  Miamisburg Municipal Deputy Clerk Maria R. Lowman
              *    It Wasn't God Who Made Honky Tonk Angels by Kitty Wells
          01-18-95  Miamisburg Municipal Clerk of Courts Janice Lowman
              *    Back Home Again by John Denver
          05-19-95  City Manager of Milford, Ohio David Maynard
              *    Ragged Old Flag by Johnny Cash

       Side B:

          05-25-95  Miamisburg Municipal Deputy Clerk Maria R. Lowman
              *    It Is No Secret by Elvis Presley
          06-15-96  Montgomery County Assistant Prosecutor Dick Lipowicz
              *    God Bless America Again by Conway Twitty and Loretta Lynn
          07-27-96  Former customer and Delta pilot Greg Hurley
              *    I Believe by Elvis Presley
          08-06-96  (NOTE: MARIA LOWMAN FIRED)
          08-08-96  Court Appointed Advisor, attorney John P. Kolesar
              *    Walkin' In The Sun by Glen Campbell
          11-19-96  Second District Court of Appeals clerk Angie House
              *    Waterloo by Stonewall Jackson
          11-? -96  Second District Court of Appeals clerk Angie House
              *    Who's Sorry Now by Connie Francis
          05-19-95  Dan Rather's News - Fully Informed Jury Association (FIJA)
              *    God Bless The USA by Lee Greenwood
          10-18-94  Replay of Laurence A. Lasky/Maria R. Lowman
              *    In The Jailhouse Now by Sonny James
              *    Proverbs 24:10
       Prepared by Horace Ray Metz, pro se, P.O. Box 0293, Cincinnati, Ohio
       45254-0293 (606) 781-9005, on December 27, 1996.
```

Contents of tape recording filed in court

The tape recording ended in my words:

If thou faint in the day of adversity, thy strength is small. So reads Proverbs 24:10. A young man spent the night alone on a park bench, under a street light. In the early morning hours he opened his Bible, as he sought direction in his hour of

despair. And he found Proverbs 24:10. The setting was Burnet Woods next to the University of Cincinnati. It was the
Saturday morning of the week prior to Good Friday, in 1961.

On Saturday evening, December 28, 1996, Ann and I
went to younger brother Tom and sister-in-law Diane's
home in Kettering, Ohio, for a family Christmas party.
As is done at Metz family gatherings, Euchre was
played. We set up three tables, and rotated partners
and opponents.

I was being ribbed about my *paranoia* Doctor Hopes
said I suffered from. Everyone was laughing at the absurdity of it. But I was aware I faced a conviction by
hook-or-crook, and prison awaited me.

As I looked around, seeing my aging parents, enjoying the family closeness we all shared, I wondered how
many such gatherings I would miss. Too many!

Prison was a scary prospect, even though my faith
was strong. I felt detached from the others, in a sense.

It happened that my sister Karen's daughter was my
partner at the time. Michelle Lowry was a pretty senior
at Xenia High School that year. She was dealing.

I sought solace from the only Source I knew. I bowed
my head and closed my eyes, placing my fingertips on
the card table, and began saying in a voice that could
be heard: "I need a loan...I need a loan...I need a loan.
Turn up the...*ten of spades!*"

My niece turned up the ten of spades. All four players passed and it was turned down. The player on my
right passed; I named trumps and made my loan.

A marvelous peace settled over me. God was with me
in my hour of need, and I with Him. As I sat amongst
family members I loved and who loved me, assurance
was provided with an affirmation I could comprehend;
the *ten of spades.*

CHAPTER FIFTEEN

Who Am I?

Ann and I stayed at Mom and Dad's that Saturday night, after celebrating the Christmas season at Tom and Diane's house. On Sunday evening, December 29, 1996, we drove home to northern Kentucky.

As we rode in silence, I thought of the ten of spades; thought of Lasky's comment back when this all began: "*It's what we say in Vegas. You gotta pay to play.*"

I took a trip down memory lane; revisiting a gambler's troubled past. A 1980 trip to Las Vegas describes the world I lived in.

I stayed at the Frontier. On the final day, I entered the hotel casino and observed the blackjack tables, looking for a place to kill the hour before I caught a cab for the airport. I spotted a table with four attractive women playing against a four-deck shoe. The women appeared to be between thirty and thirty-five.

I approached the table and slid onto a middle stool between two of the women. "Good afternoon, ladies. How ya all doing?"

"Not so good," one exclaimed. "He's cleaning our clock!"

"Well now, we're going to change that!" I assured cheerfully.

Almost immediately the tides of fortune turned, and the women began winning. After a few hands one of them asked me jokingly, "Where have you been all my life?"

I smiled and replied, "In Denver. My wife sent me here and told me not to come home until I won *ten thousand dollars.*"

The women laughed and another remarked, "She must never want to see you again."

"I don't know. I'm doing pretty good so far, this trip."

"You are?" a third asked skeptically.

"Yeah; been here four days; only got eleven thousand to go!"

Everyone laughed, including the dealer and pit boss. It was an enjoyable time, as I played the women's emotions like a violin. The hour went by too quickly.

As the time neared for me to leave, I had a six of diamonds showing and a jack of spades in the hole, against the dealer's ten. I cleared my throat and ever so politely asked the dealer, "Can I double down?"[18]

The dealer looked at me with bemusement and asked, "Why would you want to do that?"

"Because you've got twenty and I've got sixteen," I calmly replied, without knowing the dealer's hole card.

"It's the worst bet in blackjack, but if you want to double down, you can," the dealer shrugged with the pit boss nodding approval.

"It may be the worst bet – or the best." I slid a five dollar chip beside my bet and paused for dramatics before removing my hand, saying, "Give me the...*five of clubs!*"

My finger left the chip on the felt dramatically, as though from inadvertently contacting a hot stove. The dealer slid a card from the shoe and cupped it, with hands on the felt, peeking before he turned it up.

His face gave him away before he flipped me the five of clubs. His hole card was another ten.

I had doubled down on sixteen against the twenty I predicted– and won while calling the exact card! The women gasped in unison as I stood and calmly gathered up my chips.

It was a momentous farewell. I paused before leaving the damsels, to protestations of *you can't leave now,* and addressed my fellow combatants.

"It's sure been nice playing with you ladies," I ended with a smile. "Where have you been all my life?"

---

[18] Double the bet on the table, and receive only one card. It should only be done when advantageous.

I left them in wonderment, cashed in my chips and headed for the casino exit, suitcase in hand. Baffled, I wondered, *What the hell just happened?*

Seduction takes on many forms, I observed as I got into a cab. And I chuckled as my thought process continued with; *I wonder how many of the babes had an orgasm, when they saw the five of clubs.*

If only momentary circumstance could sustain long-term reality. Though I won on this trip, it made little difference. For this gambler, losses would come tomorrow, the next day, or perhaps the week after that.

But one thing was a certainty; losses might be postponed, but could not be avoided. As certain as building a castle of sand, and then waiting for high tide, losses would come, sweeping away winnings.

On the plane back to Denver I sat alone, nursing a beer. I was always alone in those days; lost in life's wilderness. I wrote words to "Starwood in Aspen":[19]

> It's a long way from Vegas to Denver;
> It's a long time to hang in the sky.
> It's a long time to sit
> On a plane all alone,
> And ask myself, *why oh why?*
> And I wonder, *who am I?*
>
> And I'll have to tell her I've been there;
> And face the hurt in her eye.
> Though the tears soon be gone,
> Memories linger on.
> I can't help it, how hard I try.
> And I wonder, *who am I?*

Yes, I had an intimate understanding of Judge Gilvary and the high-stakes poker we were engaged in.

---

[19] "Starwood in Aspen" was written and released by John Denver in July, 1971. I used to joke: *When I got off the noon stage, I thought John really lived in Denver. So I moved a little south, and became Horace Littleton.*

In one sense, it was the dumbest game imaginable. Two intelligent men were playing in a game where one would go to prison; and the other would die.

However in another sense, it was the opportunity of a lifetime, for me. I was on the brink of escaping a life sentence in a prison of the psyche.

There was no upside for Judge Gilvary. Desecrating the oath, as he did repeatedly, was perilous.

Samuel Butler (1612-1680) wrote about oaths in Hudibrass, Pt. 1 [1663] Canto 1, and l.1:

> 22 Oaths are but words, and words but wind.
> 23 For truth is precious and divine –
>   Too rich a pearl for carnal swine.
> 24 He that imposes an oath makes it,
>   Not he that for convenience takes it;
>   Then how can any man be said
>   To break an oath he never made?
> 25   As the ancients
>   Say wisely, have a case o' th' main chance,
>   And look before you eve you leap,
>   For as you sow, ye are like to reap.

I had repeatedly danced around the fact he was the *third* judge assigned my case, without revealing my knowledge he was forbidden to preside - by his own courts' local rules. It was Gilvary's *sole* responsibility not to do so.

Perpetrating *The Perfect Crime* mandated that it be carried out within the jurisdiction of the Second District Court of Appeals. To force matters elsewhere, by forcing Gilvary to step aside, was unthinkable. I was concerned I would be murdered.

In 1980, on a plane from Las Vegas to Denver I wondered, *Who am I?* While composing the tape filed in court on December 27, 1996, I included excerpts from a conversation with Acting Judge Mark E. Landers, back in the beginning on October 20, 1994. The song selected to follow that conversation was Elvis Presley singing "Who Am I?"[20]

The higher purpose for my life had not involved exploring the outer reaches of the universe, as I had wanted to do so long ago. Instead, I explored the inner workings of the mind, the intimacy of the heart, and the sanctity of the depths of the soul.

I thought of how I forgave those at University of Cincinnati who betrayed me those decades before. I had considered that perhaps God had a different purpose for my life, and university officials were merely pawns on the chessboard of life, carrying out His plan for the grand scheme of things.

It was déjà vu. The same scenario was being played out in 1996; as when I was a teenager in 1961. With this perspective, Lasky, Messham, Langer, Gorman, Gilvary, Heck, Brogan, Fain, Wolff and Schenck et al. were merely pawns of the chessboard of life. They served my purpose. And so, I had forgiven them.

What mysterious powers lay within the seclusion of the mind and the intimacy of the heart? What forces exist within the depths of the soul? If God is within each of us, can we harness His powers, from within the depths of the soul? Can we create, or influence creation of events or miracles? Truth be told; no man really is an island?

I believed God was *Universal Supreme Court Justice* presiding over *The Universal Supreme Court,* governed by *Universal Laws of Life.* In this court, all were equal.

Inferior pro se status, as found in secular court, was nonexistent. I believed it is possible for anyone to petition this Court; possible to petition God in accordance to laws governing the universe. And I believed, with all my heart and soul, time would tell if I were correct.

---

[20] "Who Am I?" was written by Charles "Rusty" Goodman; © 1965 and recorded by Elvis Presley in 1969.

Life would become my laboratory. And Judge Gilvary would become my experimental laboratory rat. The objective would be to make certain he never abused another; as he did me.

I would take my rat, the kidnapper and extortionist, and would attempt to neutralize him; stripping him of secular power. In essence, I would attempt to kill him with my pen.

Looking back, it was an audacious undertaking. But at the time, caught up in the moment; it seemed perfectly logical. So in that regard, prison held an indescribable intellectual allure.

I intuitively understood this could mean the end of a decades-long obsession; a journey in which I had become lost in life's wilderness. The peace I yearned for, within the psyche would manifest itself; and so would answers to: *Who am I?*

CHAPTER SIXTEEN

On the Sands of Time

I began the New Year with a January 3, 1997 letter to Montgomery County Prosecuting Attorney Mathias H. Heck, Jr., sending a copy to reporter Wes Hills, at the *Dayton Daily News.*

> I am writing you as a response to your attorney's December 20, 1996 Motion To Quash (a subpoena).
>
> I am further writing you for your lack of any acknowledgment of my letter to you of August 8, 1996 (copy enclosed).
>
> I remind you that the August 8th letter followed by two days the termination of Maria Lowman on August 6th.
>
> I remind you of what was known of Mr. Lasky, Ms. Lowman, and myself by your office, at the time.
>
> I'll remind you that Maria Lowman's fate was made public the day <u>after</u> elections, on November 6, 1996.[21] I'll remind you that the raw odds of my having been assigned Judges Langer, Gorman, and then Gilvary, *and* Ms. Lowman being assigned Gorman are 10,000 to 1 (11 x 10 x 9 x 11). From the Motion To Quash:
>
> > *The Defendant cannot attempt to taint the criminal proceedings pending before him by calling the Prosecuting Attorney as a witness.*
>
> You shall be called as a material witness, should I put on a defense at trial. *Taint* will be explored, under oath. It is probable that you shall appear as the Montgomery County **Prostituting** Attorney.
>
> Perhaps a more satisfactory resolution of matters at hand, for all parties involved, is invited?

---

[21] I missed an 8-29-96 *Dayton Daily News* article about this.

That same January 3, 1997, I wrote the first of many letters to reporter Wes Hills of the *Dayton Daily News.*

> Dear Mr. Hills:
>
> In June 1995, I met you in the clerk's office of the Federal Courts. I promised you a great story at that time. Little did I know then.
>
> ... Much of my informal education can be attributed to the voracious reading of newspapers. *Your* role, and the power of a free press, does more for guaranteeing the future freedoms of Americans than any other force.
>
> I thank you for all that you provide for the community; for all you've given me over the years; for your continuing interest in matters herein.

On January 6, 1997, I approached the clerk's counter where criminal filings were made; and handed over my latest offering. The clerk glanced at it as she time-stamped the top copy, and exclaimed to a coworker, "Here's another one from Metz!"

She looked at me and said, "We just love reading what this guy writes. Sometimes we laugh until we cry while reading his motions."

"Well don't laugh too hard. Your boss doesn't find me very humorous; neither does Judy Johnson, sitting over there."

"Are *you* Ray Metz?"

"Yes I am. If you enjoy my offerings, you'll probably like this one. Just remember, there are a lot of people around the courthouse who don't like me. You don't want to let on that you're in my fan club."

From the filing in response to the prosecutors' phony filing of December 26, 1995:

> Now comes the Defendant, *pro se,* before the Court in response to the aforementioned filing, as prepared by "slp" of the Montgomery County Prosecutor's Office.
>
> Could "slp" mean *slow learning people?*

... The Defendant, having none of the advantages of a fancy education, will close by asking those involved as described herein and elsewhere, from the Montgomery County Prosecutor's Office, the Second District Court of Appeals, and the Common Pleas Court of Montgomery County, as this new year begins; one sobering question:

Have you people completely lost your minds?

Respectfully submitted,
Horace Ray Metz, pro se

Debra B. Armanini wrote to the Special Prosecutors:

Gentlemen:

Enclosed please find a copy of a letter from Ray Metz, the Defendant in the case of State of Ohio v. Horace Metz, case number 95-CR-2317, which you are handling as Special Prosecutors for our county. You should be advised that Mr. Heck was subpoenaed by Mr. Metz for December 23, 1996 and we filed the enclosed Motion to Quash. You may already know more about this than I, but I was told there was no hearing set for 12/23/96, but that the case was on the Court's docket for a status concerning Metz's competency evaluation. No witnesses would have been called. Also enclosed are other miscellaneous documents that Metz enclosed in his letter to me.

Thank you very much for your assistance in this matter.

Very truly yours,
MATHIAS H. HECK, JR.
PROSECUTING ATTORNEY
By: DEBRA B. ARMANINI
First Assistant Prosecutor

Debra B. Armanini had replaced Dennis J. Langer as First Assistant Prosecutor. Langer had been the ultimate double-agent, the legal predator that performed as First Assistant Prosecutor when the criminal case against me was *created;* and then the judge once the case was *persecuted.* It was contemptible!

In order to induce a sense of reality in Ms. Armanini, I wrote her on January 11, 1997. The letter read:

> I am in receipt of a copy of the letter you wrote to Special Prosecutors Schenck and Hendrix.
>
> It seems disingenuous. I never wrote *you*; I wrote to Mr. Heck — twice.
>
> It appears that Mr. Heck attempts to hide behind the skirts of another ignorant woman, ala Mr. Lasky, Judge Messham, and Judge Fain's hiding behind the skirts of Maria R. Lowman.
>
> In any case, you've become a potential witness. Who *told* you that no competency hearing had been scheduled? Who changed the scheduled competency hearing to a competency report? Who is calling the shots in Judge Gilvary's courtroom?
>
> If you people were honest and if you sought the truth, there would be no need of a shameless attempt at a cover-up. And nothing to fear.
> Very truly yours,
> Ray Metz, pro se
> cc: William F. Schenck
>   Mayor Michael R. Turner
>   *Dayton Daily News*

I wrote to Schenck and Hendrix when I sent them a copy of the letter to Armanini on January 8th.

> This is a response to Debra B. Armanini's letter to you of January 8, 1997, in which she wrote:
>
> *But I was told there was no hearing set for 12/23/96, but that the case was set on the Court's docket for a status concerning Metz's competency evaluation. No witnesses would have been called.*
>
> Quoting from Judge Gilvary's Decision, Entry and Order of November 22, 1996:

This motion will be taken under advisement pending a
hearing on Defendant's competency to stand trial which is
now scheduled for December 23, 1996 at 10:00 a.m.
   ... from now on he shall be referred to as Horace Ray
Metz.
   ... Ah America, ala Montgomery County, Ohio. The Court
graciously decreed that I could be *referred to* in my given
name. But I'm to be prosecuted, railroaded, and imprisoned
in the false name of Horace *Raymond* Metz to accommodate.
   I suffer from an overactive *imagination* and from *paranoia?*
Somehow that offends my sensibilities. It is hoped, sirs, that
soon, very, very soon, it offends yours as well.
Very truly yours,
Ray Metz, pro se
cc: *Dayton Daily News*
   Mathias H. Heck, Jr.
   Mayor Michael R. Turner

On January 9, 1997, Judge Gilvary filed an Order:

This matter came on to be heard on Defendant's Motion
For Two Separate Continuances filed herein on December 30,
1996. In the motion, Defendant seeks an extension of his discovery disclosure to the State set for December 31, 1996. The
basis for this motion is not clear, but indeference [sic] once
again to the Defendant's pro se status, the motion is **SUS-
TAINED**. Defendant's witness list and exhibit list will be fur-
nished to the State on or before January 28, 1997.
   The motion to continue the trial date on February 18, 1997
is **OVERRULED**.
   Copies of the above were sent to all parties listed below by
ordinary mail this date of filing.
              SO ORDERED:
              JAMES J. GILVARY, JUDGE

Gilvary sent a copy of the service to John P. Kolesar;
as if he could divine Kolesar back on the case *after* he
had been removed. The demented judge annoyed me
yet again; with his arrogance!

I seized on a typo in Judge Gilvary's order, reading *indeference* in lieu of *in deference*, taking an opportunity to savage my future prisoner's psyche yet again. *No more mister nice guy!* I thought, as I responded:

> Now comes the Defendant, *pro se,* before the Court, responding to the Court's aforementioned filing.
>
> On January 9, 1997, the Court wrote: *but indeference once again to the Defendant's pro se status...*
>
> This could not be a *typo.* For the dictionary defines:
>
>> Deference N. Courteous respect for or submission to another's opinion, wishes, judgment.
>
> The Court, by and through His Honor, has shown repeated contempt for the Defendant, *pro se;* contempt for due process; and contempt for the Constitution of the United States of America and the Ohio Revised Code.
>
> In *this* case, the Court has become compromised, which is a polite way of saying *corrupted,* which carries the implication that His Honor is dishonest, which is a polite way of saying a *crook.*
>
> The *creation* of the illusion that the State and the Court are fulfilling their sworn obligations is born of an arrogance found in absolute power, and gives credence to the saying,
>
>> Absolute power corrupts.
>
> ... When Mental-Pygmies plot against the master salesman, they *always* screw it up. His Honor has made Mr. Lasky's first team; Debra B. Armanini and others are second stringers.
>
> Things like *indeference* result.
>
> ... Shame on the Montgomery County Prosecutor; shame on Judge Gilvary.
>
> Trample me if you must; don't patronize me in the process.

I wrote a letter to Dayton Mayor Michael R. Turner on January 16, 1997; my fifty-fifth birthday:

Mayor Michael R. Turner
City Hall
101 West Third Street
Dayton, Ohio 45402

Dear Mr. Mayor:

In October 1994, Attorney/Assistant Prosecutor Laurence A. Lasky sent me a copy of a bogus court order with Maria Lowman as judge, in an envelope with postage stamps that read:

World Peace through Law

Subsequently, the eye of the world was focused on my birthplace, Dayton, Ohio, USA.

To my knowledge, Dayton has not seceded from the State of Ohio; has not seceded from the United States of America. However, *local custom* has achieved the same within the courts, locally.

As a citizen about to be imprisoned for *crimes* committed pursuant to *local custom* that involve his being denied the protections of both the Ohio Code and the Constitution of the United States and its Bill of Rights, I am formally approaching you with a simple and explicit command, as you are both a local attorney and the Mayor of Dayton:

fix it.

My understanding is that, as an officer of the court, should you discover that a client has deceived the court in a way that is fraudulent, you are *oath bound* to see that the fraud is disclosed.

Your friend and client, Mr. Mel Entingh, has provided your firm with a fictitious name for me of Horace *Raymond* Metz. He cannot provide any time or occasion where I used that name.

Your firm filed for a restraining order and injunction in the Common Pleas Court on behalf of Mr. Entingh, against me in the name of Horace *Raymond* Metz. This was filed *after* Mr. Entingh had knowledge that I had closed my business.

... The jury cannot get into my mind and my heart. I should be found *innocent*. However, I fully expect to be found guilty and to be imprisoned - unless you perform your *oath bound* duties, as charged by me.

Mr. Mayor, in that regard, I'd like to invite you into my home, at this time. You see, I live in a very rich and exclusive neighborhood. And I'd like to invite you there, to a little corner of my world.

Now, it's not the physical world to which I refer. It's not the one-bedroom apartment that my wife and I presently share, nor is it the pink 1985 Buick Regal with 147,000 miles on it that's parked outside.

No, it's another kind of home, in another kind of neighborhood. It's a spiritual and a mental one. For Milton wrote, long ago, that,

> *The mind is its own place, and in itself can*
> *make a heaven of hell, and a hell of heaven.*

This influenced a song I wrote in 1977 entitled "Heaven in My Mind."

You see, in my rich and exclusive neighborhood, I live in a condo building on January 16th. Others in my building include baseball great Dizzy Dean and William Joseph Kennedy.

My neighbor directly on my left, at January 15th, is Dr. Martin Luther King, Jr. My neighbor directly on my right, January 17th, is Mohammed Ali.

Others in the neighborhood include Andy Rooney (14th), Horatio Alger (13th), John Hancock (12th), Benjamin Franklin (17th), Daniel Webster (18th), Edgar Poe (19th), and George Burns (20th).

Oh, it's a wonderful neighborhood, where I live. It's America! My neighbors are my friends. We have our own *neighborhood watch* program. We help each other out, and we stand/stood for something that surpasses ourselves. And, while I reside in the most modest home on the street, my neighbors never let on that they're aware of it.[22] They are most unpretentious.

... My name is Horace Ray Metz. I was named Horace after my father; Ray after my maternal grandfather. I came from somewhere and I'm going somewhere.

While here, I'm reminded, daily, that I'm one of the most fortunate to have ever walked the earth. I'm an American citizen, with an unsurpassed heritage.

And so are you.

I enclosed a copy of the notification of my birth, and a copy of a photo of my baby footprint with my letter to Mayor Turner. I anticipated Gilvary would see it all.

*... on the **sands of time***

---

[22] Fate is a funny thing. Though my "home" was modest, Tony Patrick Hall and I shared it; were both born in Dayton, on January 16, 1942. Hall would serve twelve terms in Congress; and I would serve four years in prison. Mayor Turner was destined to replace Hall in Congress.

CHAPTER SEVENTEEN

Close to High Noon

When facing a prison sentence of an unknown duration, each day spent in freedom seems to pass by rapidly. I had less than three weeks left. And so it was that the end of January approached.

A January 28, 1997 motion read in part:

> Now comes the Defendant, *pro se,* before the Honorable Court in a motion of remembrance of the January 29, 1995, illegal eviction perpetrated by members of the State.
>
> ... The *majority* of the Court's and the State's filings have been willfully, intentionally, and wantonly misleading and/or dishonest. Period. It's all a matter of record.
>
> The publisher of Webster's II New Riverside University Dictionary wrote in the preface:
>
> > It is clear that the final lexicon
> > exists only in the mind of God.
>
> ... It is this Defendant's belief that, just as the tavern owner is liable when he serves a partaker, so are those who abuse their God given abilities, their advantage of a fine education, and their divinely inspired duties, as sworn officers of the court, liable when those victimized react badly.
>
> The people with whom I've skirmished since June 1994 are, from this Defendant pro se's viewpoint, without redeeming social value. The lot of you is guilty of unconscionable behavior that borders on treason.

I received a letter from Judge Gilvary dated January 30, 1997. I could not believe Gilvary's gall!

He acknowledged a waiver of counsel had to be done "on the record," even though he had removed Kolesar without being in open court. Gilvary admitted he was wrong. Now he asked *me* to take him off the hook.

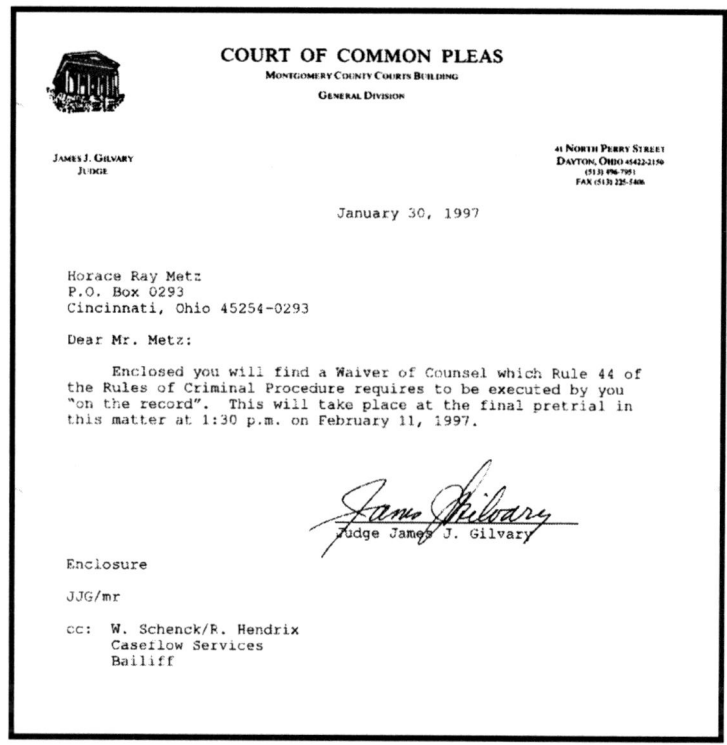

COURT OF COMMON PLEAS
MONTGOMERY COUNTY COURTS BUILDING
GENERAL DIVISION

JAMES J. GILVARY
JUDGE

41 NORTH PERRY STREET
DAYTON, OHIO 45422-2150
(513) 496-7951
FAX (513) 225-5406

January 30, 1997

Horace Ray Metz
P.O. Box 0293
Cincinnati, Ohio 45254-0293

Dear Mr. Metz:

    Enclosed you will find a Waiver of Counsel which Rule 44 of the Rules of Criminal Procedure requires to be executed by you "on the record". This will take place at the final pretrial in this matter at 1:30 p.m. on February 11, 1997.

Judge James J. Gilvary

Enclosure

JJG/mr

cc: W. Schenck/R. Hendrix
     Caseflow Services
     Bailiff

Letter from Judge James J. Gilvary

Gilvary's Waiver of Counsel was written *for me, by the judge!* Gilvary's latest inspiration provided renewed contempt for the demented judge.

Now comes the Defendant, Horace Ray Metz, and acknowledges that he has been charged with a serious offense; that he is financially unable to obtain counsel; that the Court previously assigned attorney John Kolesar to represent him in this matter; that he moved the Court to dismiss Mr. Kolesar, which the Court sustained; that he asked the Court to appoint Attorney Neil Freund at the State's expense, which the Court refused; that he knowingly, intelligently and voluntarily waives his right to counsel other than Neil Freund and desires to proceed Pro Se at the trial by jury on February 18, 1997. All of this pursuant to Rule 44 of the Rules of Criminal Procedure.

Signed: _____ Date: _____

       Horace Ray Metz

Gilvary simply could not comprehend that he was about to become *my* prisoner of the psyche. As his future warden, I did not look approvingly on an uppity inmate's demands.

It was time for another reality check. It was time to pay another visit to the psyche of my soon-to-be ward.

A February 4, 1997 motion read in part:

> Now comes the Defendant, *pro se,* before the Court in a motion of continuance until such time as the Defendant has the assistance of a Legal Advisor.
>
> The Defendant is in possession of the Court's own written Waiver of Counsel that His Honor has ordered the Defendant to comply with on February 11, 1997.
>
> Now, the Court may well be able to dictate the wording of a Competency Report to its liking, but the Court cannot ORDER the Defendant to waive his legal protections.
>
> ... The Defendant does not look forward to any further fiascos like his Competency Hearing turned Competency Report, and admonishes the Court and the State to modify and correct deviant behavior.
>
> To be clear: this Defendant demands that he have a Legal Advisor that has the interests of the Defendant foremost in mind, and that he be accorded the protections of any Defendant charged with serious criminal matters.
>
> The Defendant shall NEVER waive his right to counsel, and expects that the Court shall proffer an official apology, on the record, for demanding that he do so.
>
> WHEREFORE, the Defendant hereby demands competent counsel be appointed him in the form of a Legal Advisor, and that all proceedings be halted and continued until such time as said counsel can review matters and advise the Defendant

properly (how to get the case removed from the domain of the Second District Court of Appeals and the goons who "practice" therein).

In corrupt judicial systems; *pretense of ignorance is bliss.* I took away that pretentiousness, via my political statements mislabeled "motions"; but made part of the record. A February 5, 1997 motion read in part:

> Now comes the Defendant, *pro se,* before the Court, in a motion of acknowledgement of the six month jail sentence for Maria Lowman and the shameless cover-up that has been enforced.
>
> Included herewith are two time-stamped documents from the Miamisburg Municipal Court.
>
> ... Who would be involved? Maria Lowman acted as Judge Messham's moll; his *rubber stamp queen.* She did the banking. Who else? Who knows? How much? Who knows?
>
> ... The "criminal" case should not be in court. If it is to be in court, it shouldn't be tried within the dominion of the Second District Court of Appeals.
>
> In the meantime, let it be acknowledged that Maria Lowman received perhaps the correct sentence, for all the wrong reasons. Eventually, it will not set well with the public.

On February 7, 1997, Judge Gilvary issued a Decision, Entry and Order. It read:

> This matter came on to be heard on the motion of the Defendant for a continuance of the final pretrial conference in this case set for February 11, 1997 at 1:30 p.m. The motion is **OVERRULED**.
>
> SO ORDERED:
> JAMES J. GILVARY, JUDGE

The final pretrial hearing was held in Gilvary's chambers. I was introduced to Craig King, who was replacing Special Prosecutor William F. Schenck. King was instructed to file a motion of *appearance,* in the case. (He never filed any appearance.)

Gilvary put me in a straight jacket by limiting opening and closing remarks to thirty minutes for each side. I was further instructed, with emphasis; under no circumstances, was I to inform the jury of what I thought the law required. That was Gilvary's job.

I was told that it was *my choice* concerning a legal advisor. The choices: it was Kolesar or no one. I agreed to take Kolesar back as Legal Advisor.

Forcing me to appear at the final pretrial hearing without counsel, and then reappointing Kolesar as counsel the following day was yet another flagrant violation of due process. It was a reversible error, *if* there had been anyone I could appeal too.

February 12, 1997, the day following the final pretrial conference, Judge Gilvary filed the following:

> With the advice and consent of the Defendant, John P. Kolesar, Attorney at Law, is reinstated as Defendant's legal advisor in this case until further order of the Court.
>   SO ORDERED:
>   JAMES J. GILVARY, JUDGE

On February 14, 1929 Al "Scarface" Capone, leader of Chicago's South Side Italian gang, had seven mobsters in George "Bugs" Moran's Irish/German North Side Gang slaughtered in an attempt to eliminate Moran. Moran escaped death because he was not there, during the infamous St. Valentine's Day Massacre.

Two of Capone's men, dressed as policemen, pretended to be making a routine sting, and tricked Moran's men into lining up facing a brick wall within the S-M-C Cartage Company. They were slaughtered with a Thompson machine gun. In that era, mobsters assassinated each other; but their women were "off-limits."

However in Dayton, with its phony sophistication mislabeled *political correctness,* a defenseless woman was made a sacrificial lamb for the criminal element within the judicial system. It offended the sensibilities.

Maria Lowman was sitting in county jail while the real criminals went free. I decided it would be nice to arrange for a *card shower,* acknowledging her on Valentine's Day.

I filed a motion encouraging the Valentine's Day remembrance of Maria Lowman.

> Now comes the Defendant, *pro se,* before the Court in a motion that encourages all to remember Maria Lowman this Valentine's Day, as she sits alone in a jail cell, with "justice" incomplete.
>
> Maria's address is:
>
> > Maria Lowman
> > Inmate Number 97-2478
> > Montgomery County Jail
> > 330 West Second Street
> > Dayton, Ohio 45422
>
> Congratulations are also in order for "retired" Judge Richard Knepper, of Lucas County, who presided over her "case." His address is:
>
> > Visiting Judge Richard Knepper
> > % Judge Barbara Gorman
>
> I had a mental image of who the candidate for Maria Lowman's cover-up would be. I created a mental profile of a *judicial-transvestite.* The culprit would be Republican; would have seemingly impeccable credentials; would be "down on his luck."
>
> And so, on Wednesday afternoon, February 12, 1997, I drove to Toledo to check out the deviant who ruled over Maria Lowman's fate. The accompanying articles from the *Toledo Blade* are prima fascia: Tough on crime; against plea bargains; against cover-ups. Ha ha.

Whatever are the good folks up Toledo way going to think? Here's a man who almost became Lucas County District Attorney by attacking another for the very thing he was secretly doing...while he attacked her! A newly appointed judge to the Sixth District Court of Appeals; the *retired* Richard Knepper,

> Caught in *drag* in Dayton, consorting with the likes of Democratic Montgomery County **Prostituting** Attorney, Mathias H. Heck, Jr.

Little wonder that Special Prosecutor for Montgomery County, Greene County Prosecuting Attorney William F. Schenck bailed out of my case on February 11, 1997. Whoredom has scaled new heights.

All that's needed to perfect the cover-up is to place me in a cell next to Maria. I'm probably on my way.

... Considering Miami University President James C. Garland's column in the January 31, 1997, *Dayton Daily News*, I envision the day when Ohio's university presidents hire the likes of Sally Struthers to do commercials.

With teared eye she'll say, "Won't you please help, governor? Let Ray Metz out of jail so that one of our poor downtrodden creatures can be *educated*."

And, I'll reply, "Not so fast, little lady. A bunch of *educateds* is why I'm here."

And as the message fades from the screen, a serious and grave voice will match new words on the screen, ala the thought provoking United Negro College Fund,

> The mind would be a wonderful thing to have!

It was getting very *close to high noon.*

CHAPTER EIGHTEEN

The Day of Adversity

It was time to say goodbye to both sets of parents. Saturday, February 15, 1997, we visited Ann's folks, Harvey and Thelma Grushon. Harvey and I sat and talked in one room, as the women did in another.

"I'm still not sure what this trial is all about, Ray. Is this about money?" Harvey asked me.

"They say it's about money; but it's really not. It's about a bunch of crooks masquerading as lawyers and judges. And I caught them."

"You better watch yourself, Ray."

"I will, Harvey. But sometimes a man has to do, what a man has to do."

"I'm not too sure but what Bill Schenck isn't a crook," Harvey offered.

"We'll soon find out," I ended the discussion of the topic.

It was the harshest comment I ever heard the ninety-four-year-old gentleman make about another person. It was the last time I saw Harvey alive.

We spent Saturday night and Sunday at Mom and Dad's. On Sunday we played Euchre. I made oblique references to the fact that I *may* go to prison.

"Don't talk like that!" Mother admonished.

"That's what Ray wants to happen," Dad interjected.

"Oh, Buss, *it is not!*" Mother insisted. (Dad's nickname; in lieu of Horace Arthur.)

It was a strange thing. Though Dad's health was failing, he seemed to intuitively understand something escaping others. By this point, I simply wanted it to all end. I was weary of the endless mind-games played against the dumb asses who opposed me. In a sense; I *wanted* to go to prison; even fanaticized about it.

I experienced a sad melancholy state, as though I understood the inevitable. It was the last time I saw my father alive.

Monday, February 17, 1997 was President's Day. It was the day before the trial began. It was time to make my final spiritual preparations for the rape of the psyche about to occur.

I drove to the University of Cincinnati campus and quietly walked through the adjacent Burnet Woods, where I had gone the night of the sexual attack in 1961, when I was a college freshman. On the partially sunny winter afternoon with the temperature in the high thirties, I ended up on a park bench, just as I had that long-ago night.

I had taken along the Bible given me in 1951, when I was nine years old. It was the same Bible I carried into Burnet Woods as a nineteen year old, in the middle of the night in the spring of 1961. I opened it and read the words; the words etched into the psyche those long years before, in my hour of need.

If thou faint in the day of adversity, thy strength *is* small.

I also had a copy of Patrick Henry's inspirational speech with me, with his often quoted "Give me liberty or give me death" summation. While that was his most memorable quote, Henry is known for refusing to attend the Constitutional Convention in 1787, saying:

I smell a rat!

Henry insisted a written Bill of Rights be included, that the government could not take away from American citizens, before he could support ratification of the U.S. Constitution. As a result, the first ten amendments to the Constitution were ratified December 15, 1791, and called the Bill of Rights. I sat with Henry's speech in hand, mentally and spiritually preparing to be cast into prison. Etched in the memory were words written in a court filing, when *I smelled a rat* in October, 1994, concerning Attorney Larry Lasky:

> It seemed my smell of a rat had been accurate, and that "when the judge is away, the rats will play." I decided that unusual measures called for the same; I decided I needed a rat trap. Caught me one....
>
> If we ran against each other for **HOODLUM OF THE WEEK**, I wonder who would get the most votes.

The patriot's *give me liberty* speech was delivered to the Second Virginia Convention March 23, 1775. Henry was among the 120 delegates meeting in St. John's Episcopal Church; to debate the need to raise a militia to resist civil rights violations by the British Government, ruled by King George III. In attendance were George Washington and Thomas Jefferson.

Afterwards, Henry was credited with single-handedly convincing the Virginia House of Burgesses to pass a resolution in favor of providing troops for the Revolutionary War. I read his immortal speech once again:

> No man thinks more highly than I do of the patriotism, as well as abilities, of the very worthy gentlemen who have just addressed the house. But different men often see the same subject in different lights; and, therefore, I hope it will not be thought disrespectful to those gentlemen if, entertaining as I do opinions of a character very opposite to theirs, I shall speak forth my sentiments freely and without reserve. This is no time for ceremony. The question before the house is one of awful moment to this country.
>
> For my part, I consider it as nothing less than a question of freedom or slavery; and in proportion to the magnitude of the subject ought to be the freedom of the debate. It is only in this way that we can hope to arrive at the truth, and fulfill the great responsibility which we hold to God and our country.

Should I keep back my opinions at such a time, through fear of giving offense, I should consider myself as guilty of treason towards my country, and of an act of disloyalty toward the Majesty of Heaven, which I revere above all earthly kings.

Mr. President, it is natural to man to indulge in the illusions of hope. We are apt to shut our eyes against a painful truth, and listen to the song of that siren till she transforms us into beasts. Is this the part of wise men, engaged in a great and arduous struggle for liberty?

Are we disposed to be of the numbers of those who, having eyes, see not, and having ears, hear not, the things which so nearly concern their temporal salvation? For my part, whatever anguish of spirit it may cost, I am willing to know the whole truth, to know the worst, and to provide for it. I have but one lamp by which my feet are guided, and that is the lamp of experience. I know of no way of judging of the future but by the past. And judging by the past, I wish to know what there has been in the conduct of the British ministry for the last ten years to justify those hopes with which gentlemen have been pleased to solace themselves and the House.

Is it that insidious smile with which our petition has been lately received? Trust it not, sir, it will prove a snare to your feet. Suffer not yourselves to be betrayed with a kiss. Ask yourselves how this gracious reception of our petition comports with those warlike preparations which cover our waters and darken our land. Are fleets and armies necessary to a work of love and reconciliation?

Have we shown ourselves so unwilling to be reconciled that force must be called in to win back our love? Let us not deceive ourselves, sir. These are the implements of war and subjugation; the last arguments to which kings resort.

I ask gentlemen, sir, what means this martial array, if its purpose be not to force us to submission? Can gentlemen assign any other possible motive for it? Has Great Britain any enemy, in this quarter of the world, to call for all this accumulation of navies and armies? No, sir, she has none. They are meant for us; they can be meant for no other.

They are sent over to bind and rivet upon us those chains which the British ministry have been so long forging. And what have we to oppose them? Shall we try argument? Sir, we have been trying that for the last ten years. Have we anything new to offer upon the subject? Nothing.

We have held the subject up in every light of which it is capable; but it has been all in vain. Shall we resort to entreaty and humble supplication? What terms shall we find which have not been already exhausted? Let us not, I beseech you, sir, deceive ourselves.

Sir, we have done everything that could be done to avert the storm which is now coming on. We have petitioned; we have remonstrated; we have supplicated; we have prostrated ourselves before the throne, and have implored its interposition to arrest the tyrannical hands of the ministry and Parliament.

Our petitions have been slighted; our remonstrances have produced additional violence and insult; our supplications have been disregarded; and we have been spurned, with contempt, from the foot of the throne! In vain, after these things, may we indulge the fond hope of peace and reconciliation.

There is no longer any room for hope. If we wish to be free – if we mean to preserve inviolate those inestimable privileges for which we have been so long contending - if we mean not basely to abandon the noble struggle in which we have been so long engaged, and which we have pledged ourselves never to abandon until the glorious object of our contest shall be obtained – we must fight!

I repeat, sir, we must fight! An appeal to arms and to the God of hosts is all that is left to us! They tell us, sir, that we are weak; unable to cope with so formidable an adversary. But when shall we be stronger? Will it be the next week, or the next year? Will it be when we are totally disarmed, and when a British guard shall be stationed in every house?

Shall we gather strength by irresolution and inaction? Shall we acquire the means of effectual resistance by lying supinely on our backs and hugging the delusive phantom of hope, until our enemies shall have bound us hand and foot? Sir, we are not weak if we make a proper use of those means the God of nature hath placed in our power.

The millions of people, armed in the holy cause of liberty, and in such a country as that which we possess, are invincible by any force which our enemy can send against us. Besides, sir, we shall not fight our battles alone.

There is a just God who presides over the destinies of nations, and who will raise up friends to fight our battles for us. The battle, sir, is not to the strong alone; it is to the vigilant, the active, the brave.

Besides, sir, we have no election. If we were base enough to desire it, it is now too late to retire from the contest. There is no retreat but in submission and slavery!

Our chains are forged! Their clanking may be heard on the plains of Boston! The war is inevitable – and let it come! I repeat, sir, let it come.

It is in vain, sir, to extenuate the matter. Gentlemen may cry, Peace, Peace – but there is no peace. The war is actually begun!

The next gale that sweeps from the north will bring to our ears the clash of resounding arms! Our brethren are already in the field! Why stand we here idle?

What is it that gentlemen wish? What would they have? Is life so dear, or peace so sweet, as to be purchased at the price of chains and slavery?

Forbid it, Almighty God! I know not what course others may take; but as for me, give me liberty or give me death!

After a time of quiet reflection, savoring the sense of duty and unwavering commitment found in Patrick Henry's eloquence of long ago, I marveled at the sacred American heritage I was privileged to share. In a less significant way, I would do my part to protect it; and hopefully, to enhance it.

Next I read the letter from Associate Dean Cornelius Wandmacher; who wrote Mother May 3, 1961. He was the one person at University of Cincinnati, whose unconscionable rape of the psyche did permanent damage to me. And he got away with it.

Judge James J. Gilvary had been juxtaposed into Dean Wandmacher's role. Gilvary was about to rape my psyche in an even more unconscionable manner than Wandmacher had.

The healing of my psyche would come through the determination to hold Gilvary accountable. Intuitively I understood; I could be freed from the decades-long prison of the psyche – by standing against Gilvary and the band of oppressors, guilty of egregious spurious crimes Patrick Henry would have described as *treason.*

Next I opened my Bible again, and read the wise words of Proverbs over and over and over; repetitiously just as I had done those many years ago.

I sat in Burnet Woods for over two hours, savoring the atmosphere and the significance of being there. It was a very meaningful time, as I sat in the quiet of the park; in the presence of God.

When I left the University of Cincinnati campus area, I was mentally and spiritually prepared for the heinous rape I was about to endure. I would not faint in *the day of adversity.*

CHAPTER NINETEEN

Star Chamber

Tuesday, February 18, was the day after President's Day. I sat in Judge James J. Gilvary's chambers with Legal Advisor John Kolesar, while we were waiting for prosecutors to arrive, prior to jury voir dire.

"Welcome back to the case, John," I began.

"Thank you."

Though we had talked on the telephone following the final pretrial conference; this was our first meeting.

"I'm glad you're here, because I sure need some advice, pronto!"

"What is it, Mr. Metz?" a wary young Kolesar wanted to know.

"On the way up here, a question came to mind, that is very troubling to me, John. If I testify, I will have to take an oath; right?"

"Of course; everyone does," the ever-clueless legal eagle confirmed.

"The oath still goes like this, John? *I swear to tell the truth, the whole truth, and nothing but the truth, so help me God.*"

"It hasn't changed," Kolesar said with a discernible air of smugness, intended to belie his naivety.

"Just how the hell can I take that?" I asked with feigned indignity.

"What's the problem, Mr. Metz?"

"The problem is self-evident," I began patiently. "You were just reappointed to the case.

"Since you were dismissed, the judicial wizard you affectionately refer to as His Honor held a competency hearing-turned-report in open court, *after* denying me counsel; and held a final pretrial hearing in chambers, again *after* denying me counsel. What are the specific ramifications of his doing so?"

"That could be reversible error," Kolesar quickly asserted.

"Close, John; but no cigar. That *is* reversible error! But that will never happen."

"We don't know that," Kolesar answered meekly.

"Well, I know this. For me to vow to jurors; to God and country, to *tell the truth, the whole truth, and nothing but the truth* would be an audacious exhibition of blasphemy!

"Because we and everyone else involved in this dog-and-pony show knows; my telling the jury the truth will never be permitted. Everyone, including *Dayton Daily News* reporters, knows it; everyone except dupes who will sit in the jury box as shills."

Kolesar remained mute, shifting uncomfortably in his chair. I enjoyed these little intellectual excursions I took him on. I quickly continued on.

"John, when I am administered the oath; what if, instead of answering '*I do,*' I respond with '*no.*'"

"You must know you can't do that, Mr. Metz!" Kolesar blurted in alarm.

"And why not?" I asked devilishly. "Suppose I said, '*I would like too, but the judge and prosecutors are not about to let that happen.*'"

"You know you can't do that, Mr. Metz," John-boy restated. "Judge Gilvary is already extremely pissed off at you. Please don't make matters worse for yourself."

"I'm about to be railroaded into prison. Just how the hell much worse could it get?"

"I don't think that will happen," Kolesar answered meekly. "But I have to say, you don't do yourself any favors by angering Judge Gilvary."

"John, have you ever heard of John Lilburne?"

Judge Gilvary called us into his inner chamber before Kolesar could answer. The following is a brief synopsis:

> John Lilburne (1615-1657) spent much of his life in English prisons, for political dissent. When he

printed unauthorized Puritan books in Holland and distributed them in London, he was arrested in December 1637. When brought before England's Court of Star Chamber, he refused to take the oath requiring him to testify against himself. He claimed his prosecution was illegal.

His sentence was to be publicly whipped; then imprisoned until he admitted his guilt. The sentence was carried out April 18, 1638, with Lilburne receiving 500 lashes on his back. He loudly proclaimed he had committed no crime.

Though whipped unmercifully, he refused to admit to any crime, and continued to speak out. His head was clamped in a pillory. Though very weak from his ordeal, he still spoke out, describing the injustice he endured, and why he refused to take the oath.

He was then gagged, with his mouth bloodied in the process. And even then, he pulled pamphlets from pockets and distributed them among the crowd who approached. After two hours he was taken to prison, where he spent the next two and a half years.

Lilburne became a part of our American heritage. This case was cited in 1966, in *Miranda v. Arizona.* It is often credited with being the foundation for the Fifth Amendment of the U.S. Constitution; that reads:

> No person shall be held to answer for a capital, or otherwise infamous crime, unless on presentment or indictment of a Grand Jury, or in the Militia, when in actual service in time of War or public danger; nor shall any person be subject for the same offense to be twice put in jeopardy of life or limb; nor shall be compelled in any criminal case to be a witness against himself, nor be deprived of life, liberty, or property, without due process of law; nor shall private property be taken for public use, without just compensation.

The Court of Star Chamber was created by King Henry VII in 1487. It used the inquisitorial system of justice developed by the Catholic Church in the medieval period. There were no juries and no appeals.

The defendant was forced to take an oath, forced into promising to answer any question honestly. Torture was routinely used to extort a confession. The court would ignore its own rules of procedure and law; judges did whatever they wanted, with no accountability.

The Court of Star Chamber was utilized to persecute Puritans, many of whom fled to America. It was finally abolished in 1641.

Webster's New Universal Unabridged Dictionary defines:

Star Chamber. 1. a former court of inquisitorial and criminal jurisdiction in England that sat without a jury and that became noted for its arbitrary methods and severe punishments, abolished 1641. **2.** any tribunal, committee, or the like, which proceeds by arbitrary or unfair methods. [1350-1400; ME]

Judge Gilvary began:[23]

"Gentlemen, this is Lisa Rae Wirkner, the court reporter. Let the record show, we are in chambers at 9:00 a.m. on the trial date.

"State of Ohio is represented by Robert Hendrix and Craig King, representing the State. Mr. Metz is present, along with John P. Kolesar, his legal advisor.

"A question, Mr. Metz."

Repeating "state" is a tell. The crooked son-of-a-bitch isn't used to being pinned down, and is very, very uneasy, I thought as I answered, "Yes, sir."

---

[23] Conversation is taken from the original transcript.

"When we parted after the final pretrial, you were gonna let us know what role Mr. Kolesar is going to play. Have you arrived at that conclusion?"

"Well, we have a problem that I'd like you to address. I would like Mr. Kolesar to be my legal advisor during the trial; however, I want to call him as a witness for one specific narrow area, and I wondered if the court would have a problem with that."

"What area?"

"After Mr. Lasky confronted Mr. Kolesar and in Judge Foley's chambers and accused me of harassing him, of threatening him and went so far as to say that I had threatened his life. Now, I had lived –"

Gilvary cut me off with, "Was Mr. Kolesar a witness to all of –"

I interrupted Gilvary, "He was the one Mr. Lasky addressed."

Gilvary feigned surprise, "He said that?"

"Yes, he did. And I wrote to Mr. Heck immediately that day and told him that I had no contact whatsoever with Mr. Lasky and - -"

Gilvary did not want to get into that area, on the record. He interrupted again with, "Okay, enlighten me what that has anything to do with the eight separate thefts."

"Well, I think that the involvement that I had with Mr. Lasky and Maria Lowman and Judge Messham in Miamisburg during that time, has impacted my life very negatively to the point that it influenced what happened."

Gilvary pretended ignorance. "You'll have to give me more than that. I don't understand."

The devious Gilvary *knew* all that, in minutia, thanks to my voluminous court filings. The shallow facade, *pretense of ignorance is bliss,* was belittling; insulting to both of us and our intelligence.

Still, I understood we were on the record, and my court filings were not. Judge Gilvary wanted to create a record of being blissfully ignorant as to *why* we were in court. It was simply another of the pitfalls of taking on the state and the court, in concert.

I refused to put on my defense in chambers, prior to trial. I continued with, "Well, I really believe –"

Gilvary impatiently interrupted, "It might have negatively impacted your life, but what does that have to do with whether or not the State alleges you stole money by deception?"

"Mr. Lasky is a *member* of the State, Your Honor. I didn't know that until after my arrest, which Mr. Lasky arranged here in the court's building."

Gilvary made his first blunder on the record, with an acknowledgment, "I understand all that. Once again, what difference does that make?"

If you understand all that, what are we doing here? Of course, we both know the answer, I thought about Gilvary's confessional. *I called you a "crook" and your court "corrupt," and you are affirming it.*

I continued, "I think all of that will come out during the trial as I present my case."

Gilvary was under extreme pressure. It was akin to a bank robber knowing every act was being recorded.

But it was worse for Gilvary. The judge *knew* he lacked authority to conduct the trial; he *knew* he was committing a robbery much more egregious than one involving money. He was robbing me of my freedom, with every act duly noted for posterity.

He continued with, "Well, there is a motion pending that I want to deal with at this time that has to do with a motion in limine to prevent you from calling witnesses who don't know anything about whether or not you did or did not steal by deception. And have you received a copy of that motion?"

"Yes. I went to the Post Office yesterday."

"And I want to deal with that motion at this time. And let's start with Mathias Heck, Jr. What does he know about this case that's of any substance, other than the fact that it's in his office?"

I continued in an attempt at reasoning. "Your Honor, this places me in a position that I don't want to be in. I can understand the State's reluctance for asking the truth be revealed in this matter, but the State brought me here. I didn't come here willingly or – well, I came here believing that this matter shouldn't even be put to trial."

"I'll take this motion under advisement at this time but unless, between now and the time these people take the witness stand, if they show up, unless you point out to the court what relevant testimony you believe they have, I'll stay the motion in limine."

The problem I had was a tactical one. I had to subpoena some parties whose testimony could only be used as a rebuttal to the prosecution's case. To get them into court, they had to be served as witnesses.

Proving the crime of *theft by deception* is, by its definition, difficult to prove. It was intentionally designed to prevent what was happening to me. The *truth* would make Heck's prosecutors appear to be blundering, opportunistic, and deceitful criminals. And they were!

Judge Gilvary's charge to the jury would include:

> It must be established in this case that at the times in question there was present in the minds of this defendant, a specific intention to permanently deprive another of his or her or its property.

A time-line existed showing the cause-and-effect between civil cases involving Lasky, and the criminal counts. In none of the instances, did I anticipate the criminal actions of others impacting my civil cases; when I made the sales.

At no time, did I collect money with a specific intention of permanently depriving another. In the course of my business, extending over a six year period, over 700 parties, most of whom had built new homes in Montgomery, Greene or Warren counties, had done business with me. Each customer had their installation completed in a timely manner; without exception.

To deny any connection between what happened in civil cases and the criminal case was preposterous! But I was going to be denied any opportunity to show the jury what was in my mind and heart during these times.

On the other hand, the jury would be *misled,* via out-of-context testimony and circumstantial evidence, about what was in my mind at the time of sale. For me, it was the most chilling rape of the psyche imaginable.

The psychic pain I endured was unlike anything ever experienced. There was nothing to do, except permit them to have their way with me. It was not fun.

Gilvary continued, "This morning on voir dire I take it that you all picked up a copy of the questionnaires. We have a pretty good turn out in there today from all different zip codes, et cetera; and to repeat myself from the other day, I don't want either side to go over the same stuff that's in the questionnaires, unless there's something in there that piques your curiosity that you want to explore further.

"I am putting a time limit on voir dire of thirty minutes and putting a time limit on opening statements to thirty minutes a side. If, you don't want to use thirty minutes, fine. Don't take any more than that. Other than that, is there anything else? Who is gonna do voir dire for the defense?"

"Well, since I know the most about the case, I suppose I should," I decided.

"It's up to you."

I was pissed. *I'll be damned if I sit here silently, and submit to this asshole without a fight,* I thought angrily.

Remembering Gilvary's low threshold for stress, as shown by his trembling hands in open court, I went on a fishing expedition, in an effort to create a more favorable record - for posterity.

"Back to the motion, if I can't present a defense in, there's no use to have a trial, if the truth can't come out of it."

By his body language, I knew Gilvary was surprised by my assertiveness, but never let on by what he said. "Well, you have submitted a witness list that includes people other than the ones we've talked about today.

"Some of the same people the State has identified, you know, lots of witnesses, but I'm not going to permit this trial to be a platform for your views of the Mayor of the City of Dayton and the Prosecutor of Montgomery County, of Jonathan Hollingsworth from the Dayton Bar Association."

Thank you, thank you, you demented sanctimonious ass, I thought. I responded, "I wouldn't expect you to."

Thrown off track, Gilvary began again, "Unless they are on the witness list –"

They are, you damned fool. Keep talking! Gilvary attempted to recover from his judicial faux pas, **"You see, what's happened here since June of '94, is people have been dragged into something that should never have happened. If due process had been followed in civil matters, we wouldn't be sitting here, but they weren't."**[24]

Gilvary just confessed – on the record! Well done, dumb ass! And thank you very much, I thought with satisfaction. But I agreed verbally, "Yes, we wouldn't."

---

[24] Judge Gilvary immediate realized the magnitude of his misstatement. He admitted – on the record – that we were only there because *due process* had been thwarted in civil cases involving me. As a pro se defendant, it would have been impossible for me to have corrupted the system. Coupled with Gilvary's lack of jurisdiction, he was a confessed kidnapper! And the court reporter was an independent party, duly taking the confession down! Soon after my trial, Judge Gilvary equipped his courtroom with a video recording system; eliminating the "need" for a court reporter, and creating a means of editing, should it ever become necessary; because of another egregious slip of tongue.

The spoken word can never be retracted. Here, Gilvary confessed, on the record; I had been raped in civil matters – as he raped me in criminal matters!

High stakes poker was just not Gilvary's game! I could discern from body language, his immediate realization of the enormity of the blunder he made.

Gilvary continued to attempt to recover from his verbal diarrhea, "The defense in this case isn't that it's really a civil case, and I'll let you tell them that."

I'll bet you do, I thought. I leveraged my position, for the record.

"All these things that happened since '94, people weren't interested in correcting injustice. People are interested in saving reputations, and that's to my detriment. Now, I wouldn't insult the Court before the jury from here on, but the kind of motions that are filed aren't factual.

"I'm not faulting Mr. Hendrix or Mr. King. They have been given this case to prosecute. That's their job. But this motion is just not factual, in fact, and I would just ask that you reserve ruling."

Gilvary was back on track, stating, "I just told you I was reserving ruling."

"Thank you, Your Honor. That's fine."

"Anything else that we want to talk about?"

Craig King spoke up, "No."

My thoughts were uncharitable, as we ended the chambers meeting. *Marvelous, you ignoramus! We could talk about how you never filed an appearance as Special Prosecutor, in my case in Montgomery County.*

Your jurisdiction ended at County Line Road. Oops, silly me – the judge has no jurisdiction either.

Hendrix assured everyone, "We are ready."

Gilvary went on concerning prospective jurors, "We wanted to show them a film. I don't know if he got the VCR working. Let me check on that. And the jury has been here since 8:30; I might give them a short break."

Not so fast. I spoke up, "So are we clear? Is this open that Mr. Kolesar can represent me in court, but possibly be a witness for the one limited area?"

"I'm not saying that I think that's relevant at this time, but should you need him as a witness, I'll permit him to testify."

"Thank you, Your Honor," I humbly acknowledged.

"Okay, thank you and I'll see what the jury is doing."

After taking a break, we went into the courtroom to select the jury. Looking at approximately fifty of my fellow citizens, all of whom were there to perform an important civic duty; I experienced momentary depression. *These fine citizens, have been led to believe twelve of them are about to be chosen to have a role in the American justice system. The only role they'll play is to act as shills; as pawns of the state and the court.*

I shook it off as Gilvary addressed them. Hendrix spoke for the state. He observed that the state would rather see guilty parties go free, than convict even one innocent man. It was pure hypocrisy.

Craig King was funnier. He read the charges against me. He began by telling the prospective jurors how nervous he was, as this was his *first time.* It was: King had been admitted to the Ohio Bar on November 12, 1996; had been an officer of the court for ninety-eight days. A virgin!

I could sense we were all pulling for him; *Take a deep breath and relax. We're all with you, in this. You can do it!*

It was so effective, I wondered if King had found a great way to get jurors to identify with him. I wondered if he would use it *every time,* in the future.

One prospective juror asked Hendrix why they were there as special prosecutors. He responded adroitly, "Because we were asked."

Having selected the jury, we ended for the day. Tomorrow morning the trial would begin in the notorious court of *Star Chamber.*

CHAPTER TWENTY

The Trial

I knew the trial was not going to be much fun. But I had no inkling; just how much fun, it was not going to be!

The two-day trial began Wednesday, February 19, 1997. Kolesar and I met on the sidewalk, in front of the courts building.

"Mr. Metz, Hendrix is offering a final deal. You can plead *guilty* to some of the charges, and avoid a trial."

"Well, isn't that nice of him?"

"I told him I doubted you would, but I'd relay the offer. He said for me to tell you that, unless you did, he was going to provide evidence that you forged rescission form signatures on American General contracts."

"Hell, John, that's no secret. American General knew I signed the forms. They were for the file, in case of an audit. Each customer received my 90-day guarantee that replaced them. Tell the extortionist he can run his railroad, and I'll run mine. I would go to prison for the rest of my natural life, before I deal with the devil."

While going through the metal detectors in the lobby, I looked for Deputy Sheriff Bruce McGill, who arrested me in the courts building. It took awhile, but I finally located him.

"Officer McGill, do you remember me?"

"Of course, Mr. Metz. How are you?"

"I'm fine. Trial begins this morning. Were you served a subpoena to appear for the defense?"

"No. I wasn't."

"Don't worry about it. You probably wouldn't have been allowed to testify anyway."

"Good luck to you, Mr. Metz."

"Thank you."

I had filed eleven subpoenas with the clerk of courts, for the competency hearing, per their instructions. They were served. I had filed forty subpoenas for the trial in the same manner, per clerk of courts instructions. It conformed to what was done two months earlier. They were not served.

It was breathtakingly audacious! I would be permitted *no* defense. It was consistent with the manner in which my civil cases had been handled by appellate judges; consistent with the treatment so accurately summed up by Judge Gilvary in chambers:

> If due process had been followed in civil matters,
> we wouldn't be sitting here, but they weren't.

It was intriguing. Denial of *due process* in my civil cases, instigated by appellate judges via creation of a criminal case, provided Judge Gilvary with case precedent – my own - to deny *due process* again. It had worked once; and was bound to work again.

Miranda Rights of *you have the right to remain silent* had denigrated to:

> *You have the right to plead guilty. If you*
> *refuse to plead guilty, you can rest as-*
> *sured you will be found guilty, by what-*
> *ever means necessary.*

The State's opening statement was not made a part of the transcript. I cannot remember what was said.

In any event, knowing I would have no witnesses, I had no idea of what to tell the jury in an opening statement. So I decided to defer it until the prosecution rested. It was Show Time.[25]

"All rise. Court of Common Pleas in and for Montgomery County/State of Ohio is now in session. The Honorable James J. Gilvary presiding."

---

[25] Conversation is taken from the official transcript.

Honorable. If only he would live up to his billing, I thought as Gilvary entered.

Gilvary began, "Please be seated. Good morning, ladies and gentlemen. Is the state ready to proceed?"

Robert Hendrix responded, Yes, Your Honor."

"You may proceed."

"Thank you."

Asshole didn't ask if I was ready, I thought, interjecting, "Your Honor, we move to separate the witnesses."

"That motion will be granted."

Craig King spoke up, "Your Honor, State will call William Wilson Green."

Investigator George Brown sat at the prosecutor's table. He would hear testimony from all the other witness.

Damn it! I swore under my breath. "Excuse me, Your Honor," I interjected again. "Mr. Brown is a witness."

Gilvary looked at me with a slight smile, as he ruled, "He's State's representative. He's exempt from that order."

So the witnesses aren't separated, you asshole, I thought. But out loud I simply said, "Thank you, Your Honor."

"You're welcome."

Special Prosecutor King examined Will Green, identified as the president of a one-man company. He testified I done him wrong. I took his $1,200 January 16, 1995 and never installed his equipment. I also had not refunded his money.

King had his witness read a letter into the record, he sent to me March 13, 1995.

Judge Gilvary asked, "Is that an exhibit?"

King replied, "No, sir."

Green ended reading the damning letter by stating copies had been sent to several outside parties.

What happened next was farcical. And it exposed the *reason* Green's letter was not made an exhibit, which would be available to jurors during deliberations.

I had been pissed off upon receiving Green's letter. My response pointed out egregious discrepancies. And I ripped him a new asshole, for misrepresentations. Furthermore, I wrote, he would receive no refund from me unless, and until he provided a retraction to everyone who received his misleading letter.

Craig King, who previously had informed the jury pool he was nervous since it was his first time (much the way a virgin might react), apparently confused the rape he was involved in committing; with the foreplay accompanying a more mundane seduction of jurors.

In any event, King forgot the script! This followed.

"And you sent copies of that letter to all those people?" King asked.

"Yes, I did."

"How often do you write letter like that?"

"That' probably my first," Mr. Green acknowledged.

"I'll be handing you now what's been marked as State's #9 for identification purposes only. I'd ask you to read it as well."

Judge Gilvary interjected; revealing a rehearsal with the prosecutors, prior to trial, "Let me intervene. Just give us the *highlights* of Exhibit #9, please. Do you have a copy with you, Mr. Green?"

"Yes, I do. I'll keep this marked one."

Judge Gilvary helped the rookie Special Prosecutor King out. "So that's a letter from whom?"

"A letter from Mr. Metz."

"Dated?" the ever helpful judge wanted to know.

"Dated March 24th 1995."

Satisfied they were back on the conspiratorial script, Gilvary addressed King, "Go ahead counselor."

A contrite Craig King responded, "Yes, Your Honor. *I apologize.*"

"That's okay," the judge charitably said with a smile; in forgiveness.

Fifteen people in the courtroom had no clue of what was happening; twelve jurors, one alternate juror, Legal Advisor John Kolesar, and a female reporter from the *Dayton Daily News;* identified later as Ellen Belcher, via a newspaper photograph.

Belcher sat in the courtroom in a casual nondescript flowered dress, with a note pad in hand. The future Editor of the newspaper's Editorial Page was married to Judge Dennis J. Langer.

Langer was the county's double-agent; was the First Assistant Prosecutor when my criminal case was created; and then was the first judge assigned to *fix* the case; once my case was persecuted.

Oh, yes, others were present. A nun had a group of grade school children in the courtroom, to observe the trial. I had some uncharitable thoughts about Gilvary, in the moment.

The demented judge is raping my psyche, in a contemptuous violation of his sacred oath to God, and he invites innocent school children to watch? What a perversion of his Catholic faith.

Special Prosecutor King continued, "Mr. Green, this is again a letter written you by Ray Metz?"

"Yes."

"The date was?"

"March 24th of '95."

"Read the first paragraph please, for the jury."

"This is a response to your letter of March 13th 1995."

"The second and third paragraphs," King instructed.

"Will Rogers once said, 'Stupidity got us into this mess. Stupidity ought to be able to get us out of it.' It applies here. Your letter, while fluently written is a vulgar and willful misrepresentation of reality. It would be one thing to send it to me, but it's quite another to send copies to those you indicated."

"The sixth paragraph beginning with 'as both.'"

A detail almost overlooked by King when forgetting the script; certain parts of the letter destroyed their case. Judge Gilvary quickly rescued the nervous rookie prosecutor; and preserved the persecution.

This was what I had written, between the third and sixth paragraphs Green read to the jury:

> In no manner would your letter indicate, explicitly or implicitly, that I have offered to install your equipment on different occasions, and that you have refused to allow me to do the same.... On Monday, January 30th an offer was made to install the equipment that week.... I spoke with you on Thursday, February 9, 1995, when I again offered to install your equipment on Saturday, February 11, 1995.... Write me with two separate dates and times for an installation, and we shall do so.

The State had to prove, pursuant to Gilvary's charge to the jury:

> It must be established in this case that at the times in question there was present in the minds of this defendant, a specific intention to permanently deprive another of his or her or its property.

I had maintained, in court filings, that the criminal case against me was fraudulent. Prior to indictment; the State possessed crucial evidence making a conviction for theft by deception impossible to attain; *unless* Judge James J. Gilvary, Special Prosecutor Craig King, and Special Prosecutor Robert Hendrix *duped* the jurors.

To dupe the jurors, a script had been carefully prepared. It included suborning perjury; forcing Mr. Green to give contrived, out-of-context testimony. In open court, they created irrefutable evidence of a *conspiracy* to persecute me!

If I had it in mind to permanently deprive Will Green of his $1,200 at the time of the sale, I must have *lost* my mind later. I had offered to install the equipment repeatedly, as was detailed in writing.

As Mark Twain observed, *truth is stranger than fiction.* No one could make this stuff up. What a show! The vaudeville actors performing this scene were:

- A judge with trembling hands, but no authority to preside;
- A prosecutor with a nervous demeanor that aroused sympathy, since it was his first time, but no jurisdiction to prosecute;
- And me, the object of their affection; with a name that did not exist, from a place that did not exist, persecuted for a crime that did not exist.

Nothing *ever* existed in this make-believe judicial Land of Oz, except one reality. And that reality was; I would serve a year in prison for Count One, involving Will Green. And my foes were hell-bent on making sure it happened.

Finally King finished with, "Nothing further, Your Honor.

Gilvary addressed me, "You may cross-examine."

"I have no questions at this time, Your Honor.

Gilvary continued, "Very well. You may step down. Leave the exhibits there. You may call your next witness.

"State would call Shannon Green."

King soon ended with, "Nothing further, Your Honor."

Gilvary asked me, "Any cross-examination?"

"Not at this time, Your Honor."

Gilvary continued, "Thank you. You may step down."

The same thing happened with witness after witness. Special prosecutors examined them; Gilvary asked if I had any cross-examination; and I declined.

It appeared I believed that, since I had subpoenaed them for the defense, I would examine them on direct, in my defense case. The truth was; there was nothing material to ask the victims. I had received the funds to install eight parties' water softeners and/or reverse osmosis units, and the work had not been performed.

They truly were victims. But were they victims of mine, or victims of the state and the courts? Gilvary had confessed the truth, in chambers. But the jury would never be permitted to consider the question.

Things were progressing nicely for the judge and the prosecutors. I had been very accommodating, with no cross-examination. With the first two counts put before the jury, uncontested; it was time for improvising, while continuing the script.

Judge Gilvary followed my refusal to cross-examine a witness with, "Thank you. You may step down. Why don't we take a fifteen minute break at this time. Ladies and gentlemen, don't talk about the case or let anyone else talk to you about it. And please be back in the jury room within fifteen minutes. Thank you."

Hendrix, King, Brown and I used the same restroom. They made friendly acknowledgments. Hendrix graduated from University of Cincinnati's School of Law. He asked me, "How was the trip up this morning? Have any problems with traffic, in the cut-in-the-hill?"

"No. I take I-671 from Cold Spring, so I avoid I-75 going into Cincinnati."

"That's a real good thing, being able to avoid that nightmare," Hendrix said, ending our small talk.

I understood Hendrix's unspoken message. *This is nothing personal.* But it was personal for me. I thought of professional wrestlers; imagining them faking a show for the public, and then going out together afterwards, to have a beer.

The only difference here; only one of us was faking. And Hendrix would be going home, while I would go to prison. But it was nothing personal with him.

I measured my foe. Rob Hendrix was probably in his early thirties; and had been around long enough to acquire some seasoning. After working in the cesspool of the criminal courtroom for a time, after seeing the human misery flowing through the system, day after day; he could measure me, in comparison to others. Still, he willingly participated in raping me.

Hendrix appeared to be a young, friendly, competent prosecutor. But looks can deceive. Underneath that facade was a skilled practitioner, with the tenacity of a barracuda. He had the ability to get down-and-dirty.

I do not like this sanctimonious piece of shit, I reflected upon leaving the restroom. *The son-of-a-bitch tells jurors he would rather see guilty suspects go free, than convict an innocent person. The hypocritical fool says it in my presence, during vior dire. Then he wants to engage in friendly banter with me; as if I were deaf and dumb? What an ass!*

We went back on the record with the bailiff proclaiming, "All rise. Court is again in session."

Gilvary addressed Hendrix, "Call your next witness."

And Hendrix, apparently feeling the mixed emotions just described, momentarily forgot the spontaneous change in the script. "Call George Brown or - -"

Catching himself, he continued, "I'd like to call Pamela Thrash, if I can."

Every gambler has a *tell.* Hendrix was betting reputation and/or career, by assisting in covering-up criminal activity in Montgomery County. Unlike King, Hendrix was no rookie. His stress showed, by asking Gilvary, *if I can.*

Thrash was the branch manager for American General Finance Company. She had only been a branch manager for four months, when events of June 13, 1994[26] wrecked havoc in my life. Her testimony was laced with perjury; and ended with this:

---

[26] The day the world learned of the brutal murders in Brentwood, California, of Nicole Brown Simpson and Ronald Goldman by O.J. Simpson.

"At some point did somebody decide to bring this as a criminal matter?" Hendrix queried.

"Yes."

"Who made that decision?"

"I did with my supervisor."

"Who did you contact?"

"I contacted George Brown."

"Of the Montgomery County prosecutor's office?"

"Yes."

"All right. Did you tell him everything that you just told me here today?"

"Yes, I did."

Hendrix addressed Judge Gilvary, "I have no further questions, Your Honor." This was a slight, ever so slight change, in the manner that Hendrix used with his other witnesses.

Gilvary addressed me, "You may examine." He made a slight, ever so slight change too.

The slight differences and their overt meaning would go undetected by anyone present, or anyone reviewing the transcript at a later date. I was the lone exception.

Picking up the subtle change, I responded, "I'll defer for a later time."

Gilvary placed his cards on the table with, "She may not be around for your case. If you are going to cross-examine her, let's do it now. It's up to you."

"I'm really not prepared to, Your Honor."

Gilvary was in the driver's seat. And he was enjoying every second of it. "You've had plenty of time to prepare, Mr. Metz. So you can cross-examine or you can waive."

I sat mute, refusing to acknowledge Gilvary. Finally, he silently mouthed *NOW*, in an angry commanding gesture. Dynamics were intriguing. What happened in this case typified the conduct, and the mindset of the notorious criminal element.

In conspiring together, each participant is intent upon covering his own ass, and while doing so, each is

less than candid with others involved. Here, Gilvary
had been placed in a box.

He had agreed to persecute me. It was an enormous
personal risk to take. And then those who solicited
him to commit the crime; exhibited a lack of faith in
his ability to pull it off.

I had not been the only one who witnessed Gilvary's
trembling hands, in open court during the competency
report. Furthermore, my foes had received copies of
court filings, wherein I blistered the demented judge in
detail; mocking him about those trembling hands!

Ironically, in yet another Shakespearean twist; fearing Gilvary might not be able to control defense witnesses to *their* liking, the crooked judge who was solicited to betray me, was betrayed himself - by his so-
licitors. I would be permitted no defense witnesses!

It looked like I had unknowingly walked into a con-
venient trap; not cross-examining anyone in Counts
One or Two. Now Gilvary exhibited judicial knowledge
on the record; there would be no defense witnesses.

My options narrowed. Refusing to cross-examine
Thrash could compromise the significance of any later
claim: when Counts One and Two were presented to
the jury; I had *believed* I would have the ability to call
the same prosecutorial witnesses, as defense witnesses. Now I knew better.

It would diminish my (accurate) allegation: the purpose of the break was to create the illusion Gilvary
first learned I would have no witnesses, *when* Hendrix
informed him – during the break. I acquiesced and
cross-examined Thrash.

At one point I asked Pamela Thrash, "Now, did you
receive a subpoena from me to testify as a witness in
this trial?"

She testified, "No, I didn't receive anything like that."

"I was afraid of that," I lamented for the record.

Secretly, I was relieved. It was mortifying to face my accusers in court. It was excruciating to face victims, whose trust in me had been defiled; even with extenuating circumstances.

I never intended to put any of the victims on the stand, as defense witnesses. It had simply been a strategic ploy to create a reversible error, if I were denied a defense.

But in open court, while being portrayed as a ruthless Manson-type predator before the jurors, the soul cried in anguish at the injustice. The anguish I experienced was exacerbated by the presence of innocent school children.

I do not care who you are, or how tough you are, or how strong your faith is; there are times when the torture to the psyche is so overwhelming, it seems impossible to endure. This is when a man's true character is measured.

As I sat in the courtroom, I experienced such a time. A stifled impulse to cry out came to me again; and then again: *"Please stop it! This is not the man I am. I beg of you, with all my heart, let the truth set me free."*

I had summed up my angst in a court filing to Judge Gilvary on December 27, 1996:

> This defendant doesn't want your millions.
> This defendant wants your inhumanity....
> In the name of heaven, what are you people about?

And as I sat there in the courtroom, suffering excruciating psychic pain, I *received* their inhumanity. And it was being duly recorded. In the process of enduring, I experienced a very real transformation.

I was being set *free* from my prison of the psyche, where for decades; I had served a life-without-parole sentence. *This time, the rapist would be held accountable!* As I experienced the miraculous recovery within the psyche, another transformation was taking place.

While brutalizing me in the presence of innocent little school children; while an indisputable record was made, of the transference of his inhumanity to me; Gilvary unknowingly entered his prison of the psyche.

Gilvary's greatest fear was public disclosure of the rape that was occurring. It would destroy his carefully crafted persona. The rapist was caught red-handed, on the record; and would pay the ultimate price!

So as I endured, I vowed the demented judge would never do to another, what was being done to me! And just as I gratefully exited the prison of the psyche; he fearfully entered therein. Yes, it was Shakespearean!

It had all been promised, in a court filing of November 29, 1996, as defined in II Peter 2:19:

> For of whom a man overcome, of
> the same is he brought in bondage.

Hendrix began calling those who had purchased from me, and financed the purchases through American General Finance. None of the parties had suffered a financial loss. In the middle of a Hendrix next examination, he was interrupted.

Judge Gilvary said for posterity: "Thank you for coming, students from Saint Helen's School. Come again. You have been very well behaved."

Innocent children witnessed the fictitious Raymond, about to be cast into prison. It was one of the many perils in Dayton, Ohio, for seeking justice via *the trial.*

CHAPTER TWENTY-ONE

Inspector Clouseau

Hendrix addressed Judge Gilvary, "Your Honor, our other witnesses – we have proceeded much more quickly than I anticipated. Our other witnesses are not here. I can proceed and go ahead and call Mr. Brown what I had intended to do but -"

Judge Gilvary affirmed, "Why don't you do that, please."

Q. Sir, would you please state your name and your occupation for the record?

A. George Brown and I'm an investigator for the Montgomery County prosecutor's office.

Q. How long have you held that position, sir?

A. I came to the prosecutor's office in October of 1992.

Q. That particular position that you hold as an investigator is that in any particular unit?

A. I'm one of three investigators in the consumer fraud economic crime division of the Montgomery County prosecutor's office.

Q. Where did you work prior to the Montgomery County prosecutor's office?

A. I was a criminal investigator for the U.S. Department of Defense for a period of about ten years prior to coming to the prosecutor's office.

Q. Prior to that did you also work in law enforcement?

A. Yes, sir. I have been in law enforcement since 1971. I served as the chief of police in Brookville, Ohio and I worked as an undercover narcotics agent for the state, and I was an investigator in the United States Army for three years.

Q. Now, through your position in the Montgomery County prosecutor's office, have you had an occasion to come in contact with or investigate a man by the name of Ray Metz?

A. Yes, sir.

Q. Again, is this Mr. Metz (Indicating)?

A. Yes.

Q. Can you tell me how it was that Mr. Metz first came to your attention as an investigator with the Montgomery County prosecutor's office?

A. We first became aware of Mr. Metz when we received a complaint from American General Finance, the branch located on Miamisburg Centerville Road. As most of our complaints come in, either via a telephone call or someone gives us highlights of their situation or in this case, they prepared a written complaint and outlined the allegations concerning Mr. Metz.

Q. And Mr. Metz in his questioning of Ms. Thrash indicated a date of September 1st of '94?

A. That's fairly accurate.

Q. Upon receiving a complaint with American General, what did you do?

A. We evaluate the complaint. The crimes that we investigate are most crimes involving a considerable paper trail. When I looked at the documents and talked to Ms. Thrash and then ultimately attempted to contact Mr. Metz.

Q. Tell me about your attempts to contact Mr. Metz?

A. What we do is to run a check on the individual's operator's license. We were told that attempts to reach Mr. Metz by American General had reached to the point where they were unsuccessful.

So then I utilized resources that I had available to me to try to find Mr. Metz to try to find a good phone number for him and to reach him and let him know that I had received a complaint, and I needed to discuss it with him.

Q. Did you find a good phone number for him?

A. Ultimately, I did.

Q. Can you give me a time frame when you obtained that phone number?

A. It was fairly soon after the complaint was received.

Inspector Clouseau showed his investigative prowess. The number Pam Thrash had given him had been 859-7021. It was the same number he *ultimately* obtained. It had been my phone number for nine years!

Q. Did you call that phone number?

A. Yes.

Q. Did you speak to Mr. Metz or did you speak to a recorder?

A. I spoke to a recorder.

Q. Did you leave a message on that recorder?

A. Yes.

Q. What did you say?

A. Something to the effect that I identified myself and I needed to discuss a complaint that I had received concerning him.

Q. You identified yourself as an investigator with the Montgomery County prosecutor's office?

A. At least on one occasion.

Was the bumbling inspector deliberately attempting to deceive the jurors? Brown knew I taped recorded conversations involving Larry Lasky. But he did not know I had not kept a record of messages from him, because at the time, I had no knowledge Lasky was an assistant prosecuting attorney. He called me *one* time; he left *one* message in which he identified himself. Look at what follows.

Q. Did Mr. Metz return your phone calls?

A. I recall having one telephone conversation with Mr. Metz after having left multiple messages.

He left *one* message in which he identified himself. I returned *one* phone call.

What the hell kind of messages did he leave all those other times? *If* he called any other time. Me thinks Inspector Clouseau exaggerated, just like he did in attempting to obtain my phone number.

If Hendrix suborns perjury over this seemingly innocuous matter, and Brown willingly commits it, what else would they do to persecute me? Stay tuned.

Q. Okay and tell me the gist of that particular conversation?

A. I told Mr. Metz that we received a complaint and it was important that I sit down with him and talk to him, which is the same way we would have done with anyone else in a similar position to try to get from him his side of the story and basically, what had taken place.

Q. All right. And what was Mr. Metz's response?

A. Well, I didn't want to do it over the telephone. I asked him to come to my office to sit down and meet with me. I may have even offered the opportunity to meet somewhere else. I just don't recall, but the gist of the conversation was to have him sit down with me and tell me what had taken place.

Q. Did he take you up on that offer?

A. No.

Q. Did he ever make any further contact with you?

A. The last even – I believe, in that conversation, he told me that I would hear from his attorney.

What took place is that I was eager to get together with George Brown. But after hearing some of what transpired, he lost interest. There was *no* mention of an attorney. It was blatant perjury, couched with an experienced witness's way of phrasing things, by conditioning testimony with *I believe.*

Q. As a law enforcement officer, once he says attorney, what does that mean that –

A. Basically, that eliminates that and we would then contact – or wait for the attorney to contact us or at least, wait a reasonable amount of time to be contacted by an attorney.

Q. Were you ever contacted by an attorney?

A. No.

Q. Were you ever contacted by Mr. Metz?

A. I don't recall having any subsequent conversations with him.

Brown almost said he would contact the attorney, and caught himself. For no attorney existed. Brown testified he backs off once the word *attorney* is heard; *at least, waits a reasonable time.* I knew he backed off once the letters FBI were heard.

Q. What turns did the investigation take after that?

A. We found additional complaints, additional people that allegedly had been victimized by Mr. Metz.

Q. We are talking about Will Green and the Caupp family?

A. That's correct.

Q. And did you talk to those folks?

A. Yes, I did.

Q. And after you talked to them, what did you do?

A. I contacted ultimately the Cold Spring Police Department. I advised them that we were interested in finding Mr. Metz and basically because there was no effort on his part or his attorney's part to sit down with me, then we secured a warrant for his arrest.

Again, Brown committed perjury to enhance his story. He had no reason to discuss an *attorney* with an out-of-state police force. At any time Brown had called me; I would have willingly sat down with him to discuss matters.

Q. Do you recall the date on which you secured that warrant for his arrest?

A. No, sir. I don't.

Q. Would approximately July of 1995 sound correct?

A. Probably late July, I would assume.

Q. And that complaint or that warrant was obtained from the Kettering Municipal Court?

A. Yes, sir. That's correct.

Q. How long did that warrant lay dormant?

A. Many, many months.

Q. And do you recall Mr. Metz being arrested?

A. Ultimately, yes.

Q. And where was he arrested?

A. He was arrested while entering or I believe that he had already entered the building in which we are currently in.

Q. In the Montgomery County Court of Common Pleas building?

A. That's correct.

Q. When he was arrested, did you talk to him that day?

A. Briefly, yes.

Q. What did he have to say on that day?

A. He was arrested by one of the uniformed security people as you enter the building and go through the metal detector. Ultimately, one of the representatives from that unit arrested him. They brought him upstairs to me.

I had a brief discussion with him about what had taken place, specifically, about the contracts that I'm trying to remember if, in fact, there was a rights waiver that exists in the folder. Our conversation was fairly brief.

Q. Did he make any statements to you about why he had failed to deliver on these contracts?

A. He said that he had run into some problems, and that's why he did not fulfill his part of the contract.

Q. How did you find out that Mr. Metz had been detained?

A. I was called by security and advised that he had been arrested on the warrant that I had issued.

Q. Did you have any idea that Mr. Metz was going to be in the building that day?

A. None whatsoever.

Q. What was your feeling when you were told that we have Ray Metz in custody?

A. I was quite surprised.

Q. What else, if anything, did you do in the investigation of this particular case?

A. There would – we would have then requested the original checks, other documents that were involved.

Q. Now, on the day Mr. Metz was arrested, was he placed into the Montgomery County jail?

A. No, sir.

Q. Why was that?

A. He was not placed in the Montgomery County jail.

Hendrix royally screwed up, asking, "Why was that?" The *only* reason I was not jailed was that I threatened to go to the FBI, *if* I were arrested. But Brown adroitly covered, ignoring Hendrix by repeating himself.

Q. Did he post bond that day?

A. No, sir. I actually took him. I called the Kettering Municipal Court and made arrangements to have him arraigned that day.

Q. As opposed to putting him in the jail and having him arraigned?

A. That's correct.

Q. You personally drove Mr. Metz over to Kettering Municipal Court?

A. Yes, sir.
Q. He was arraigned that day?
A. Yes, sir.
Q. Released on his own recognizance?
A. Yes, sir.
Q. Didn't have to post any money?
A. No, sir.

What a guy! I had been arrested in the courts building, on a warrant that had been outstanding for many months. And out of the goodness of his heart, he personally drove me to the municipal court, and saw that I was released on my own recognizance.

I was free to go back out of state, to the place where Brown testified he called the police department; in a failed effort to take me into custody.

A word about the jurors: To a person, they followed the testimony intently. Interest never wavered. It was a panel of decent citizens, motivated to perform their civic duty.

But they were inexperienced in legal matters. And just like I had been in the past, they wanted to *believe* in the integrity of the professionals who performed for them. They could not be expected to see through the outlandishly sinister debacle taking place.

Q. Ultimately, did you present the case to the grand jury?
A. Yes, sir.
Q. All right. And he was indicted and that's why we're here today.
A. That's correct.

"And I have no further questions then, Your Honor."
"You may examine," Gilvary addressed me.
"Your Honor, I have quite a bit to cover with Mr. Brown. Would you want to break for lunch before we begin?"
"Go ahead and use some time," Gilvary decided.
"All right."

Q. Good morning.

A. Good morning.

Q. Mr. Brown, we heard yesterday during Mr. Hendrix's voir dire that he said this was not an O.J. kind of trial; did we not?

A. Yes, sir.

Q. Do you recall that he said that reasonable doubt exists at the beginning at the time of indictment? Do you recall him saying that yesterday?

MR. HENDRIX: I'll object to any further questions in voir dire."

JUDGE GILVARY: Sustained.

Q. All right. Well, I guess, I will just dig into it this way. Mr. Brown, on the date that I was arrested, I believe it was February 29th of 1996. Would that date ring a bell to you?

A. Could have been, yes.

Q. And you were quite surprised that I was arrested in the court's building; is that correct?

A. I was surprised you were arrested in the court's building. Yes, sir.

Q. And was it a Sergeant S.L. Buck that telephoned you to inform you in your office that I was placed under arrest?

A. Yes, sir. That's correct.

Q. And as I recall at that time, you came down to a room that's off the lobby downstairs and visited with me briefly; did you not?

A. I identified myself to you and I think that I went back upstairs and then you ultimately were brought up by one of the uniformed people.

Q. Did you make notes of our conversation during this time?

A. No, sir.

Q. During that time that you were downstairs in the room off of the lobby, I don't know what else to call it, but it's right off the lobby, within the lobby. Did you – do you recall that I asked you what was going to happen and that you stated to me that I

was going to jail until an arraignment would be arranged?

A. Traditionally that is normally what –

Q. Would that be a normal response that you
would make?

A. It is one of many options.

Q. If I said that you made that statement to me,
would you dispute it?

A. What, that you were going to jail?

Q. Yes.

A. I could have said that, but I also, to qualify
would have said, if there is not an arraignment, if
the Judge is not in Kettering Municipal Court, that
that was one of my options to physically take you
to the county jail and book you in.

George Brown imitated Inspector Clouseau very well.
He testified an option was to physically take me to jail.
However the courts, the prosecutor's office and the jail
were contiguous. He slyly inferred there were two
similar choices; take me to jail – in the building – or to
municipal court in another city. Then Brown claimed
it was an *option* for me to be arraigned, unless *the
judge is not in Kettering Municipal Court*. Because
Brownie knew where I was headed with questioning;
and he knew the real reason for my not going to jail.

Brown could routinely commit perjury and get away
with it. He could get away with it time and again. But
once he reached a spiritual table limit, just one time,
in the casino called *life,* he stood to loose his reputation, profession, and possibly his freedom. Ordinarily,
it was a reckless gamble; except in this courtroom.

Q. Now, I believe February 29th was on a Thursday of that year. As I recall what you told me, was
if I wasn't arraigned that day, I may remain in jail
for up to a week before I'd be arraigned?

A. No, sir. I wouldn't have said that. We have requirements as to once a person is incarcerated,
when they have to be arraigned.

Q. All right. Now, after the time that – from the time you met with me briefly in that room and went upstairs to your office, didn't you receive another call from Sergeant Buck?

A. I may have conversed with her again.

Q. At that point it was arranged for me to be brought up to you?

A. That's correct.

Q. And then you and I engaged in some conversations at that time?

A. Well, if you remember, I told you that you were physically under arrest.

Q. Well, I came into your office in handcuffs.

A. Right. So it was obviously - to both of us - that you were under arrest, and at that point then, I did not ask you questions. You proceeded to respond to me voluntarily.

Oops! Caught again with, "If you remember." We both remember, and that s the cause of your anxiety. Brown never told me I was under arrest when I entered his office. In the lobby, he had explicitly told me I was going to jail; and instructed Deputy Combs to take me.

Q. Did I appear to be someone that had something to hide?

A. At that point, Mr. Metz, I wasn't sure. You had been arrested. All I knew was what I had gathered from that point from the people that had lodged complaints concerning you.

Q. Let's go back a little bit to some of your testimony on the direct. It's my understanding that you received a complaint from American General Finance on or about September 1st of 1994. Would that be correct?

A. Yes, sir.

Q. And you evaluated that complaint at that time?

A. Yes, sir.

Q. And you claimed that you tried to contact me, to reach me several times unsuccessfully. Is that your testimony?

A. That was my testimony.

Q. But you also said that you had made contact with me fairly soon?

A. That I had contacted you. I don't recall exactly when it was. I mean, I know that it wasn't within the next day or two or three.

Q. Would you disagree with the statement that I immediately called you as soon as you had left a message for me and talked with you in person over the phone?

A. I don't recall that having occurred.

Q. Did you make notes of your attempts to call me or attempts to reach me or any notes of any conversations we did have?

A. I made notes of the attempts to contact you. Yes, sir.

Q. Did you make notes of our conversation once we did talk?

A. Yes, I would have.

Q. Do you have those notes with you?

A. No, sir.

Q. Do you know what happened to those notes?

A. No, sir. I don't. I would assume they are part of the jacket, part of an investigative file.

Q. As a defendant, do I have the right to have access to any notes made by a law officer as a criminal?

MR. HENDRIX: Objection.

JUDGE GILVARY: Sustained.

Q. Are you clear on the fact that I said to you that you would be hearing from my attorney?

A. I believe that's what you told me, yes.

Q. Do you believe that your notes would establish that?

A. I'm testifying as to what I recall. And I recall you having said that.

Q. But you acknowledge that I'm here in court pro se?

A. Yes, sir.

Q. Now, you took this complaint you had from American General Finance Company in September of 1994 and you had six serious charges against me, according to us being in court here, but you did nothing with it until July of 1995. Was there a reason for that?

A. That's not true, sir.

Q. All right. What did you do?

A. You were one of probably two hundred complaints that we have in our office in white collar activity for economic-type crimes. I did attempt to locate you.

Q. Locating me was easy. I mean, I lived at 521C Shawnee Run. My phone number was 859-5021. I had lived there over four years. I was in this court's building probably forty times from the time you became aware of me until my apprehension, probably more than forty times.

JUDGE GILVARY: Is that a question?

MR. METZ: I'm sorry, Your Honor.

JUDGE GILVARY: Why don't you rephrase the question and ask -

Q. What did you do to try to find me?

A. I do know that I left messages. I left those messages as primarily what I did. I figured that you would contact me.

Brown *never* attempted contacted me after *one* message, I responded too. It was scandalous perjury.

Q. All right. Now, when we had this conversation, I believe that you told me on the phone that you had a slam-dunk case against me. That you had never seen a case so clear cut and easy to prosecute as the case you had against me. It was a nobrainer. Do you recall having made any statement like that?

Q. No, sir. I have never used the words, slam-dunk in my twenty-six years in this profession.

A. So you would dispute my recollection as to that particular term?

Q. What I am saying is that I requested you to come to my office so we could discuss the allegations against you.

Q. You did that initially early on in our conversation; would that be correct?

A. Could have been during the course of our conversations.

Q. Okay, but then after you heard some of what I had to tell you, you lost any interest in having me come in and talk to you any further, didn't you?

A. No, sir. That's not correct....

A. There are multiple reasons why these cases do not move as quickly as let's say a homicide or a burglary or a robbery. There is a considerable paper trail on each of these cases, and if my inventory of cases only consisted of your case, your argument would be valid.

Q. It's not an argument. It's a point of fact, isn't it?

A. No, it's not a point of fact.

Q. Did you take any criminal activity against me from September 1st of 1994 until July 26th of 1995?

A. Well, a warrant was issued for your arrest, and you were ultimately arrested.

Q. On July 26th of '95 from September 1st would be ten or eleven months later?

A. Yes, sir.

Q. All right. Now, isn't it true that after our visit in your office on the day of my arrest and after our conversation at that time, that you decided on the spot not to place me in a cell, but you called the Court in Kettering and told them to have my judge stand by and not to leave for lunch until we got out?

A. No, sir. That's not true. I'm an investigator. I'm not a judge, and I don't direct judges to do things like that.

Q. That wasn't your conversation with the Kettering Municipal Court?

A. No, sir. I asked if the judge would be available for arraignment.

Q. Well, I was under arrest and my recollection could be foggy in some areas, but the fact is that you did make a call to Kettering Municipal Court, and we did go out there and you did go into chambers, and in the courtroom in front of the judge and a court reporter, and I was arraigned and released on my personal recognizance.

Brown chose a different inventive avenue to venture onto. Perjured creativity on the spot, while on the witness stand; is perilous.

A. Specifically, you said that you didn't want to go to jail and that's the *only* reason why I did it.

Q. Do you do that to every person that doesn't want to go to jail?

A. I'm a pretty compassionate person.

Q. Are you compassionate enough to get a person's name right when you file it under a warrant?

MR. HENDRIX: Objection

JUDGE GILVARY: Overruled.

A. I'm not perfect, Mr. Metz.

Very, very few investigators would claim that the *only* reason he offered personal limousine service to and from a municipal court in a different city, for an arraignment, was because the accused *didn't want to go to jail.* It demeaned the stature of the profession of perjurer! Yet Brown did so while exhibiting no sense of shame. The criminal mindset is a work of art. It was intriguing to explore Inspector Clouseau's, while he was under oath.

Q. After that criminal indictment, which was February 29th of '96, what was the next contact that I had with you?

JUDGE GILVARY: Let's get the date right.

MR. METZ: I'm sorry. What did I say?

JUDGE GILVARY: You gave him the date of the indictment.

Q. Oh, after the arraignment of February 29th of 1996, what was the next contact we had with each other?

A. It would have been at a scheduled preliminary hearing, I believe, in Kettering Municipal Court.

Q. And as I recall, we got it continued for a week and I went back in a week, and they gave me a chance to get a lawyer. And I went back in that week and told them that I would represent myself pro se, and then we set the preliminary hearing.

So you weren't there in the interim, but you were there for a preliminary hearing, and from my records, that preliminary hearing was set for March 15th of '96. Would that sound reasonable?

A. It could have been. Yes, sir.

Q. And so you and I met in the Kettering Municipal Court, and I believe at that time we had a different judge than we did during the initial session; we met in the Kettering Court before the Honorable Robert L. Moore for this preliminary hearing.

A. It could have been. Yes, sir.

Q. Who did you call in for this preliminary hearing?

A. There were people subpoenaed. I don't recall exactly who was on that list. I believe the Caupps, Schmidts. There were four or five people there.

Q. As I remember, both Caupps were there and the Greens from Cincinnati were there, would that -

A. It could have been. Yes, sir.

Judge Gilvary interceded, "Why don't we take our break now. Ladies and gentlemen of the jury, we'll break until – why don't you be back in your jury room by 1:15. We may or may not get started on time, but let's recess until 1:15. Don't talk to anyone else about the case. Don't let anyone talk to you, and we'll see you hopefully at 1:15."

Leaving the restroom, I saw Brown, and shrugged my shoulders with a grin. It was nothing personal.

The Gold Coin Restaurant was a good place to get a quick lunch at a decent price. Located close to the *Dayton Daily News*, it was a popular downtown spot.

I had one of my favorites; a roast beef hotshot. I chose milk over coffee, hoping to avoid bladder problems later.

As I ate amongst the downtown business people, all with busy lives and personal agendas, I was very aware I would soon eat my meals in a different atmosphere. Few would claim that the Gold Coin had any special ambience. But for me, on that day, it did. And I lingered as long as possible, experiencing each precious last moment of freedom.

Back in the courtroom, the bailiff proclaimed, "All rise. Court is again in session." Judge Gilvary began, "Mr. Brown, you may resume the stand. Mr. Metz, you may resume cross-examination."

Q. Okay, as we broke for lunch, I believe we were at March 15th of 1996, in Kettering Municipal Court; is that your recollection?
A. I guess. I don't know.

I had to wonder if anyone critiqued Brown's morning performance for him. He seemed a little out-of-sorts, as we began.

Q. All right. And what did you tell me at that time?
A. I don't recall.

Q. Did you tell me that the case would be going before the grand jury? You would take it to the grand jury?

A. I probably said that ultimately the case would be presented to the grand jury, yes.

Q. Did I indicate to you that I'd like to testify at a grand jury?

A. Yes, you did.

Q. Did you indicate that you had any problem with that?

A. It's not my decision, but I did relay it to the person responsible to –

Q. Did you indicate to me that you didn't believe that would be any problem for me to appear?

A. I indicated to you that that was not my decision to make. It was out of the ordinary, but it certainly is not unheard of.

Q. Okay, would I have been left with the impression after our conversation that so far as you were concerned, I was probably gonna be able to appear before the grand jury?

A. I don't know how to answer that question.

MR. HENDRIX: Your Honor, I'm going to object to the entire line of questioning.

JUDGE GILVARY: Well, that question, the objection will be sustained. What impressions you may have had in your mind from what he said is not something he can testify too. Move onto the next question.

Q. I understand, Your Honor.

I would not get Brown to admit he explicitly informed me he saw no problem in my appearing before the grand jury. I could not go into plea bargain offers of diversion, because of the prejudicial impact they could have on the jury.

But Brown and Hendrix carefully created a scenario wherein I avoided Brown extensively. But as shown by the testimony, the State had repeatedly obfuscated.

Gilvary was wrong. Brown should have been made to testify as to his *impression* of what I was led to believe.

If, for example, I asked Brown to give me three quarters for a dollar bill, and he asked why; and I replied, "Your wife couldn't make change last night," I could testify that I thought; Brown would be under the impression I had just called his wife a two-bit whore.

Q. During the time that you drove me out to Kettering and brought me back to my car that was parked on the street here in Dayton, we had conversations, did we not?

A. I'm sure we did, yes.

Q. And as I recall, at one point you told me that you had a son that was going to the University of Toledo and how proud you were. Do you recall that?

A. I recall that, but I see no relevancy.

Q. You do recall it?

A. Yes, sir. And I am still very proud of him.

Q. Do you recall that I shared with you the experience that I had in my college years?

A. No, sir.

Q. Do you recall that I had been sexually molested by a college professor?

MR. HENDRIX: Objection.

JUDGE GILVARY: Sustained.

Q. During the time that we were traveling out to Kettering and back, did I share with you that I had the possibility of a lawsuit against a party coming to fruition and that there would probably be monies coming from that lawsuit?

A. You did say that, yes.

Q. Did I mention a particular name of Laurence A. Lasky, as a person who was a party as an attorney involved in this lawsuit?

MR. HENDRIX: Your Honor, I'm going to object to the line of questioning.

JUDGE GILVARY: Sustained! That's sustained!

Q. Are you aware of how my arrest took place in the court's building lobby that morning, other than the fact you got a phone call?

A. I was not there when you were arrested. The only thing I can testify to is what I was told by the Sergeant.

Q. All right. Did you tell me I was mistaken for another person and that my arrest was just a fluke?

MR. HENDRIX: Objection.

JUDGE GILVARY: Overruled.

A. I told you when I was contacted, and I had a conversation with Sergeant Buck, I related to you what she told me.

Q. Would that have been the impression I was left with?

MR. HENDRIX: Objection.

JUDGE GILVARY: Once again, you're going with your impressions.

MR. METZ: I apologize, Your Honor.

JUDGE GILVARY: That's all right.

Q. Was I informed by you that I was mistaken for someone that looked like me who had a beard and that you had seen a picture of?

A. No. That's not entirely true.

Q. Okay, what would be true?

A. I was told by Sergeant Buck that there was a picture that existed. Where that picture existed, I do not know, but that you were – it was actually a fluke that you were arrested. That's what Sergeant Buck told me.

Q. Now, this warrant that was issued on July 26th of 1995 for the Kettering Municipal Court was issued under the name of Horace Raymond Metz also known as Ray Metz. Do you have recollection of how you came into contact with the name of Raymond for me?

A. No, sir. I don't.

Q. All right. Can you testify that I never used that name, to your knowledge with any of the complainants?

A. I don't quite understand what you are asking.

Q. Well, when American General came to you in – no later than September 1st of 1995, did they use the name of Horace Raymond Metz for me in any way?

A. No, sir. They did not.

Q. But you filed a complaint against on behalf of Horace – American General, excuse me in the name of Horace Raymond Metz and my question to you is why would you do that?

A. Your question as to the name that was used?

Q. Yes. Mr. Hendrix provided me, this morning, with a copy of this complaint that was filed. May I approach, Your Honor?

JUDGE GILVARY: Yes.

A. And your question?

JUDGE GILVARY: He wants to know where you got the name Raymond.

A. I can't recall where the name Raymond derived or where I got the name Raymond. No, I can't...

The most memorable moment of the day was eliciting the obvious; "I'm not perfect, Mr. Metz," from the bungling *Inspector Clouseau.*

CHAPTER TWENTY-TWO

Judgment Day

In a sidebar, Special Prosecutor Hendrix said, "We are ready to rest."

I spoke up, "Your Honor, I have a problem. To my knowledge, my witnesses have not been subpoenaed."

"That is a problem," Judge Gilvary agreed.

"I don't want to given opening statements and mention peoples' names and I'd ask you if you have ever had this happen before."

"Yes."

"What do we do?"

"Well, I don't do anything," Judge Gilvary schooled me.

John Kolesar interjected, "You didn't file the subpoenas with the court and arrange for service. That's correct. He did bring the subpoenas to court and has the right to have them served."

"Right," I said with feigned defensiveness. "I got time-stamped subpoenas."

"They just have not been served," Kolesar added.

"How do you know?" Gilvary asked.

"I talked to three people. I filed them before Mr. Hendrix filed a motion to – whatever you call it."

"Well, just a second," Gilvary decided. "I don't think the jury has to wait."

Stipulations were explained to the jurors by Judge Gilvary. Then he said, "With the stipulation, the State of Ohio is gonna rest its case, and will move for the admission of its exhibits into the record as evidence. We will take care of that outside of your presence.

"There is a logistics problem that has arisen, which we'll dialogue about, once again, outside your presence.

"It's not really your problem, so we'll recess for your purposes now, and please be back in your jury room by 9:00 a.m. I have got a scheduling conference at 8:30. We'll be ready about 9:00 so have a good evening. Do not discuss the case among yourselves or with anyone else and we'll see you tomorrow."

The bailiff proclaimed, "All rise." The jurors departed.

Back on the record the State's exhibits were admitted into evidence, without objection from me. We then went through the State's motion in limine, objecting too many of my witnesses.

If my witnesses were present and available to testify, Judge Gilvary informed me who he would allow. But since subpoenas had not been served, ah...

Gilvary ended with, "Having said that, tomorrow morning, shortly after 9:00, are you going to give an opening statement?"

"Yes, I will."

"And then we are going to take your witnesses after you are finished with your opening statement?" Judge Gilvary asked.

"Yes."

"And when you are finished with your witnesses, supposedly we'll rest your case, so I should be ready to charge the jury tomorrow."

"Sounds right," I agreed.

"Okay, I'm working on the charge right now and I'll have it ready when the folks get here in the morning so you know what's going on. Anything else that we have to do today? If not, thank you very much and court's adjourned."

On the sidewalk Legal Advisor John Kolesar became very animated. "You didn't file the subpoenas properly, Mr. Metz."

"Why didn't I, John?" I asked the young legal eagle.

He explained what I had needed to do. It seems there had been a recent change in procedure.

"John, the clerk's office instructed me on what I had to do, prior to the competency hearing. In December, they accepted eleven subpoenas. They served those subpoenas. Hell, Heck filed a motion to quash his.

"This is less than two months later. I filed over forty subpoenas with the clerk's office, just as I had done in December. They accepted them, just as before. But this time, they simply did not serve them! Judy Johnson was sitting *ten feet* from where they were accepted. *Ten feet,* John! Others were right in this building. That cannot possibly be my responsibility!"

"It is, Mr. Metz."

"The hell, you say! Had I known that, I would have simply jumped the counter and stuck one in Judy Johnson's face. I'd have charged into Craig Zimmers' office and slapped one on him. Get real, John.

"They accepted the subpoenas, and didn't even find time to serve them on themselves? Johnson was sitting *ten feet* from where they were time-stamped.

"Once they accept them, they are bound by Ohio Revised Code to serve them. If they weren't gong too, after accepting them, I should have been notified."

"I don't know what to say. But I can get some of them served tonight. I know I can get Lasky in here to testify."

"Hell no! I forbid you to even make an attempt to drag anyone in, after the fiasco today."

"What do you mean?"

"Never mind. I'll have to go forward without a defense," I ended.

"But Mr. Metz –"

"Forget it, John. Tonight I'll pray for forgiveness; for committing blasphemy, as I take the oath tomorrow."

On the way home I thought, *If they could put me in the darkest hell-hole in Ohio, those I served time with could not be worse than the scumbags I just spent the day with. If you can go to hell for hypocrisy, Gilvary, Brown, Hendrix, and King are well on their way.*

The morning of February 20, 1997, I took Ann to her job at the Northern Kentucky - Greater Cincinnati Airport. As she had done, throughout, she would ride the bus home.

I got emotional as I kissed Ann goodbye. Because I knew I would not be coming home. It was my role, as her husband, to love and protect her; to comfort her and nourish her. And I felt like an abysmal failure.

I watched as she walked away. And I cried. I knew I would not be there for her, for a long time to come.

The bailiff proclaimed, "All rise."

Judge Gilvary began, "Have a seat. Let the record show we are here in open court outside the presence of the jury. The State having rested and it's my understanding, Mr. Kolesar, that you want to make a Rule 29 motion on the record."

"That is correct."

It was news to me! Hell would freeze before Judge Gilvary granted a motion to *acquit,* after all the trouble they had gone too just to get to this point. But I sat quietly.

"You may proceed."

"As the Court knows, the Rule 29 defense may move for acquittal after the close of the State's case or at any time after the close of either case.

"In this case, we are alleging that the State has failed to prove, that at the time these incidents occurred, that Mr. Metz had any knowledge that he was going to deprive – intent to deprive the owners of property, in this case being money...."

All of the principles present *knew that!* But that was not the point. It was the jurors who were being duped. It was the twelve civic minded citizens (and an alternate) who were callously being used as shills.

Hendrix made his argument, against the Rule 29 motion, which Kolesar did an admirable job in preparing. And then Gilvary spoke.

"The Rule 29 motion will be overruled. My bailiff indicated to me that Mr. Metz, you wanted to talk to me about subpoena problems."

"Yes, Your Honor. As you know, I have subpoenaed people into court, and I had gone down to the clerk's office and I had filled out one form that I wanted the sheriff to serve the subpoenas and I don't remember the clerk who waited on me, but she indicated to me that she would rather do it by process server.

"And so we changed the check marks to process server and she gave me one copy of the forms and I left and she had them served. And I know that Janice Lowman appeared here in court as a response to that subpoena."

Gilvary added, "So did Judge Fain."[27]

"I thought he was here, but I –"

"Yes, I saw his smiling face," Gilvary replied in a satisfied voice.

I had done the same thing this time! But they had not served the subpoenas, nor had they notified me that they did not intend to do so, I pretended to explain to the wise-assed judge. *Prior knowledge* diminished the spirit of *explanation.*

By now, Gilvary had learned all about "my learning" the subpoenas not being served. He *knew* I had forbidden Kolesar from dragging a few people into court.

---

[27] In a May 24, 1997 *Dayton Daily News* article, with a heading **County officials mistakenly gauged the boy's sanity,** a sentence read: "The appeals judges, Frederick N. Young, Mike Fake and Thomas J. Grady, said both Fujimure and the juvenile court magistrate missed the point of the hearing." A typo? F-A-I-N became F-A-K-E. I thought not, as I read the article in prison. In the May 24, 1997 article, Judge Fain acknowledged a *competency hearing* had taken place in Fujimure's case.

Fain had been present in open court on December 23, 1996 and had witnessed Judge Gilvary's trembling hands. So had a reporter! Perhaps someone did not agree with the hypocrisy, of the son of a former editor of the *Dayton Daily News.* And perhaps that someone slipped **MIKE FAKE** past editors – whose newspaper published nothing about my case.

And I *knew* Gilvary had to be very, very annoyed
that his co-conspirators had so little faith in his ability
to control his courtroom, that they never served the
subpoenas – on themselves or anyone else! It was insulting to the judge, and placed him in an untenable
position.

"Are you telling me you don't have any witnesses to
go with today?" Judge Gilvary asked.

"No, sir. The Delta Airlines pilot even called his su-
periors and the way he gets off flights, is to have a
subpoena. And I mean, these gentlemen with the
prosecution team knew I had subpoenaed their people
and they didn't object to me subpoenaing their people
as witnesses, but I assume they are not gonna be
available today."

"Well, if they haven't been served a subpoena, I assume they wouldn't be available."

"And I believe they knew they hadn't been served
when I asked them yesterday. I think they probably
knew ahead of time."

"Probably did."

"I'm not saying that's their responsibility."

"It's your responsibility to have your witnesses here
ready to go to trial," Gilvary lectured. "The case has
been set since when? How long ago did we set this
case for trial?"

How long did I go without legal counsel, dumb ass?
Oh, since six days before trial, right after a final pretrial
hearing, I thought. I replied aloud, "In November."

"Right. Why don't you take a seat. The jury is here.
It's 9:25. I've overruled the Rule 29 motion. What do
you propose to do? Mr. Metz, I'm addressing you or
Mr. Kolesar."

"So far as?" I asked.

"What are you gonna do? When I bring the jury back
in, are you going to testify? What are we gonna do?
This case is going forward."

"Your Honor, in my testimony can I inform the jury
why I don't have witnesses here?"

"Yes. You can tell them you didn't get them served with subpoenas, which is what happened."

"Can I explain the circumstances of it?"

"Yes."

"Thank you, Your Honor. We'll continue."

"Very well. Anything from the State on this issue?"

Hendrix said, "No, Your Honor. Thank you."

"Okay, bring in the jury."

In the American adversarial system of justice, the limits of propriety are often pushed. A rationale is that there is a higher court to review any errors in the trial court. That safeguard was not in play here. For the judge, prosecutors, and appellate court judges were acting in concert, while perpetrating *The Perfect Crime.*

A crime of the magnitude of kidnapping and extortion, committed by an officer of the court, would involve careful consideration of every possible contingency. To deny a criminal defendant constitutional protections afforded by the First, Fourth, Fifth, Sixth, Eighth, and Fourteenth Amendments would be ample grounds for overturning a conviction. Yet that is what was happening.

How did Gilvary intend to get away with it? I had spent hours in the law library at University of Dayton, exploring possible escape avenues available to the criminal. I finally determined there was only one possibility that was practical; abuse of *res judicata.*[28]

The problem for my foes was that I was always able to figure out what they were planning, before they executed their plan. The problem for me - even though I

---

[28] The legal principle of *res judicata* explicitly defines when issues have to be raised. For example, if appellate issues were not raised at the first opportunity, they were lost forever. All Judge Gilvary had to do was create a bogus appellate issue that could be raised by an attorney brought in on the *fix;* who ignored what really took place. The intentionally created issue would be appealed; to the exclusion of addressing violations of the 1st, 4th, 5th, 6th, 8th and 14th Amendments.

knew what was going to happen, I could not prevent it.

The bailiff announced, "The Court of Common Pleas is again in session and will now come to order.

"Good morning, ladies and gentlemen," Judge Gilvary welcomed the jury. "The State has rested. Is defense ready to proceed?"

"Yes, Your Honor, I'll begin with my opening statement. Good morning, ladies and gentlemen of the jury. I stand before you as the defendant in this case, as you all know by now. And we had a problem come up yesterday that I was unaware of, didn't discover until 3:30, than none of my witnesses had been properly subpoenaed due to an error and miscommunication on my part.

"It is my responsibility to see that subpoenas are served. It's my responsibility to see that they are here and I failed in that responsibility. It was a mistake I made and in conjunction with the clerk's office downstairs and was clearly and totally my responsibility.

"So I'm left in the predicament of proceeding here before you without any witnesses....

"Having said that, I'm winging it this morning. I believe that the testimony this morning will include the state of mind that I operated in, in my business as well as my personal life. And please excuse me, it's very, very difficult for me to be here and to do this. I dreaded this day, but we are here.

"I believe the evidence in the testimony will show that I didn't knowingly steal from these people. That I was forced into a situation from circumstances in my past life, circumstances with civil matters I was involved in and just business realities....

"The testimony will show that until June of '94, each and every person who purchased a water softener from me, received the softener. It was installed properly and they were happy.

"I wasn't Dr. Jekyll and Mr. Hyde that bounced back and forth, just a poor guy trying to make a living.

That's all, and I regret it. You saw these people. They are decent people, but I don't believe that makes me a felon. I care very deeply about it. I believe that when we examine the State's Exhibits that have been put into evidence, you can place a little different perspective on me as a person and that's what I want to share with you.

"I'm so appreciative that you're here for me and for the State and for the people that were here, and you know, I think it's a real privilege to have the opportunity to come into court like this as civilized people and be judged, and I will accept your verdict however you decide.

"I mean, I believe in the system. And that will be my opening statement."

"Thank you," Judge Gilvary offered.

"I'd like to call George Brown to the stand."

Judge Gilvary advised, "You are still under oath, Mr. Brown."

Q. Good morning, George.

A. Good morning, sir....

Q. And the name that was given was Horace Raymond Metz on that letter; is that correct?

A. I believe so, yes.

Q. And my warrant that you filed was in the name of Horace Raymond Metz, also know as Ray Metz; was it not?

A. Yes.

Q. But we discovered that my name isn't Horace Raymond Metz?

A. Yes.

Q. So the source of that name came from Mel Entingh?

A. I can't say that.

Q. Can you tell me where you did get it?

A. No, sir. I thought about it after our discussion yesterday, and I guess based on – it was a conclusion on my part, that Ray is short for Raymond and that was the conclusion that I obviously drew.

Brown thought about it? *Raymond* was just an *obvious conclusion* on his part? The liar had checked my driver's license, containing the name Horace Ray Metz. Every complainant had given him the name Ray Metz.

Q. Thank you. Now, Mr. Brown, I believe yesterday we had testimony that we had an arraignment in Kettering Municipal Court and that you were present at that arraignment; is that correct?

A. I was at Kettering Municipal Court, yes.

Q. We were on record in the courtroom and do you recall that during that arraignment on the record I corrected my name to Horace Ray Metz?

A. That's correct, yes.

Q. That date would have been February 29th of 1996; would it not?

A. It could have been, but one thing that I would like to add is that the social security number and the date of birth were constant throughout my investigation when I ran a check on you, it was – the operator's license check did ultimately come back to Ray Metz, but the social security number, the date of birth and at the time I ran the check, it did come back to the Shawnee Run address, so I was pretty much convinced that I had the right person.

Q. All right. I understand. You had the right person, just the wrong identification form and that's what we are concerned with here this morning?

A. Four letters. Raymond vs. Ray. I mean, it's Horace Ray Metz as you said.

JUDGE GILVARY: Is there any further point you want to make on that?

MR. METZ: There certainly is.

JUDGE GILVARY: All right.

I was going to serve a year in prison over $615, and Brown, Hendrix, King, and Gilvary all *knew* it should not even be in court. And I *knew* that they all knew it. My business rival, Mel Entingh induced prosecutors to include a Caupp count. And he gave Brown *Raymond.*

Q. Let's change course. Let's go back to February 29th of 1996, the day of my arrest. We had testimony yesterday that you came down to visit me in the lobby; did we not?

A. Yes, sir.

Q. And you told me I was going to jail and you left; did you not?

A. I don't recall saying that you were going to jail. I recall saying that that was an option going to jail.

Q. But then later I was brought up to your office and we had a discussion?

A. A brief discussion. Yes, sir.

Q. And at that time you took me personally to municipal court for arraignment?

A. Yes, sir.

Q. I believe it was your testimony that you did that because you like to be a nice guy or something like that; was it not?

A. Well, I think I used the word compassionate after being in the business for as long as I have, I have tried to treat everyone fairly.

Q. All right. When you were called again by – and you were called by Sergeant Buck, right?

A. Yes, sir.

Q. When you were called again by Sergeant Buck or called – yeah, she called you the first time to tell you – when you were called again by Sergeant Buck, were you told that I had threatened to go to the FBI with information that I had about parties in the court?

A. No, sir.

Q. That didn't have any bearing on taking me to Kettering?

A. No, sir.

Q. Okay, thank you very much.

JUDGE GILVARY: You may step down. You may call your next witness.

I had a quandary. If I testified, I knew Hendrix would tear me to shreds. But if I did not testify, the defense would rest.

With trepidation, I decided I had to testify, knowing it made no difference in the outcome. The jury deserved to hear from me.

It was a pitifully inept and incoherent performance. Hendrix tore me to pieces, in a cruel and sadistic way. It was no fun.

Hendrix appeared to be the self-righteous indignant protector of *the peace and dignity of the State of Ohio.* He was being deliberately disingenuous.

And I thought to myself as he abused his position, in front of thirteen civic minded jurors: *You may have your way with me now, you smart-mouthed little punk; hiding behind the power of the State. One day I'll introduce you to real power.*

I made no objections during the trial. What was there to object too, that would carry any weight?

Please, oh please don't rape the psyche, as you must do in order to convict me. But Kolesar was trained to play the game, and it must have been torturous for him to sit mute, and observe firsthand; the debacle taking place. He was in on the *fix,* but wanted to pretend, at least to himself, that he was not a party to it. Sitting in the witness seat, I observed the uncomfortable young attorney at the defense table.

Unsympathetic thoughts came to mind. *You cannot have it both ways, John-boy. You made your choice; learn to live with it. You're either a pathetic smalltime legal whore - or you are not. And you are one; so chill.*

The ordeal was finally over. Later, I ended my closing argument: "I'd just like to thank all of you; each and every one of you. I wish I could get to know you for serving and doing your duty; performing it, and I'm not asking for mercy. I'm not begging for mercy. You make your selective decisions. I can live with that. Thank you."

In Special Prosecutor Hendrix's closing argument, he offered a demented form of logic: "If it please court, Mr. Metz, and ladies and gentlemen, when you accept service as a juror, one thing is, don't check your common sense when you come into this courtroom.

"As a matter of fact, in the American system of justice, we rely on the common sense of twelve individuals, such as yourselves, to go back in the jury room and you'll decide what the facts have shown.

"At this point what I'd like to do is comment on the facts to you and tell you what I would say to you were I given the opportunity to come in the jury room and act as a juror as you will. Mr. Metz has indicated that he thinks that this is a civil matter and not a criminal matter. The Judge will instruct you otherwise. And I will suggest to you, if you didn't know it before, everybody in America now knows that a person can be both charged criminally and civilly.

"When the scene is played out in this horrible string of events out in California, no matter what you think of it, we've gotten an education about the legal system and the difference between civil liability and criminal liability.

"The fact that he is charged with a crime doesn't mean that he can't be charged civilly, and the fact that these people would have a civil remedy against him, doesn't mean he can't be charged with a crime.

"**... He borrowed two thousand dollars from his mother. Remember he said that? What did he do with the money? He went and bought himself a car. With two thousand dollars. I'll suggest to you that he could have paid back the Greens and the Caupps, the ones he tells us he feels worse about.** He doesn't feel so bad about ripping off American General but he feels the worse about the Greens and Caupps because they are individuals who are out money. **With two thousand dollars, Mr. Metz, you could have paid them off and you didn't. You bought a car for yourself.**"

Date of loan from Mother   Nov 28, 1994
Date of Green sale   Jan 16, 1995
Date of Caupp sale   Apr 18, 1995

I borrowed $2,000 from Mother to buy a car, to lower overhead, by ridding myself of a lease. By the time I drove the car to make the Green sale, she had been repaid. I also drove the car to make the Caupp sale.

Hendrix continued, "Mr. Metz is a salesman. He's been selling to you ever since he came in here. He comes in and presents himself as a common man just as everyday and ordinary and unassuming. That's how he drew in these people in their own homes, by coming in being honest and unassuming common. That's the mask he wears....

"In closing, you'll have State's Exhibit #27, which is the brochure which Mr. Metz made up and he gave it out to people and right here he says, 'It is our position that anyone who invades the sanctity of the home, and with con-artist methods deceives the homeowner, is the same as the thief who robs with the gun, and deserves to be treated as such.'

"His own words, ladies and gentlemen, his own words. I submit to you that the evidence has proven beyond a reasonable doubt each and every element, each and every count in the indictment and we ask when you go back in the jury room and find Mr. Metz guilty of all eight counts. Thank you."

My jurors were intent on performing their civic duty. They were denied the opportunity, though no fault of their own. What was done to me over two days, in the Star Chamber proceeding was inhumane. No citizen in our country should endure what I experienced.

That aside, in secular court, February 20, 1997 became *judgment day.*

CHAPTER TWENTY-THREE

Free at Last

Judge James J. Gilvary misread a carefully scripted charge to the jury, designed to create the appearance of propriety. The court stenographer, Lisa Rae Wirkner captured every word.

As the doomed criminal defendant, I fought to keep from laughing as Gilvary joked with naive jurors: "In your deliberations you have no right to discuss or consider punishment. Your duty is confined to a determination of **the guilt or not guilt** – to determine guilty or not guilty regarding the charges against this defendant.

"In the event that you find the defendant guilty, the duty to determine punishment is placed by law upon the court. It is essential to the preservation of the social order that laws be obeyed and violators convicted. **It's equally important that the innocent person should not suffer.**"

It was 985 days since it had all begun; since O.J. Simpson committed the murders Hendrix referred too. I knew; for I had counted them off. Sitting there, nearing the end; I listened attentively as Gilvary created a record he believed only friendly eyes would ever see. And as I listened, I critiqued Gilvary's comments.

Guilt or not guilt was the clumsy misstatement of a gambler who has reached his choking point. Every gambler has one; a time when his bet is so large it takes him out of his comfort zone, and he chokes from the pressure. Such a gambler never wins overall.

Judge Gilvary's misstatement was a *tell*. The misguided fool staked his cherished reputation on getting away with fixing my trial; had gone *all in!*

But Gilvary's bet was more ominous than he imagined. His *life* was on the table. I sat there listening; wondering how he would react if he understood the real stakes.

Gilvary's charge to the jury included the element of *intent:* "It must be established in this case that at the **times in question** there was present in the minds of this defendant, a specific intention to permanently deprive another of his or her or its property."

Thirty-six words in one short paragraph offered the nexus for the *theft by deception* case against me. I had been forbidden to make any statements to the jurors, concerning the meaning of the law, as it applied in my case. *Times in question* were *times of sales.* Gilvary put me in that straightjacket in the final pretrial hearing.

Gilvary possessed judicial knowledge that I had a lawsuit against Lasky's client, demanding damages for business losses; prior to the creation of the criminal case. And Lasky prosecuted cases involving fraud. He made certain the jury never learned this crucial fact.

I became the sacrificial lamb in a hedonistic ritual played out every day, in too many courtrooms across America. I had had the audacity to stand up to the ethically challenged within the Montgomery County courts, and now would pay a steep price for doing so.

The jury left the courtroom at 3:05 p.m. and was out for two and a half hours. Court reconvened with the bailiff's, "All rise. Court is again in session."

Gilvary asked the foreperson, "Have you reached a verdict?"

"Yes, we have," was the response.

Judge Gilvary waited for this moment of personal gratification, and was on his game as he continued, "Would you please hand the verdict forms to the bailiff, please. Would you read the verdict forms, please?"

The bailiff played his role in a somber voice, as I calmly listened, "Yes, I would. Okay, State of Ohio vs.

Horace Ray Metz Case No. 95-CR-2317. We, the jury, find the defendant, Horace Ray Metz, guilty of the offense of theft over three hundred dollars, as to Wilson Green as charged in Count One of the indictment."

"Next form," Gilvary said while smiling slightly.

It was a surreal moment. *Guilty; guilty; guilty; guilty; guilty; guilty; guilty* came the next seven verdicts.

I wondered what my reaction would be when the jurors' verdicts were announced. Would *guilty...guilty* etc. slam into the recesses of the psyche? Would I experience the kind of psychic pain that tortured me down through the years?

Nothing prepared me for what I felt emotionally. And it was thrilling. There was no psychic torture! It was gone; it was *all* gone. I wanted to cry in gratitude; but fought hard to maintain my composure.

Tears at this time would have been misinterpreted. Gilvary could have derived so much gratification; the perverted judge may have had an orgasm.

Gilvary asked, "Does anyone want the jury polled?"

Special Prosecutor Robert K. Hendrix responded, "On behalf of the State, no, Your Honor."

John P. Kolesar parroted, "No."

Gilvary continued smugly, "Very well. Ladies and gentlemen, that concludes your service as jurors in this case, and for the foreseeable future in Montgomery County, Ohio. I do have some certificates and I want to share a few thoughts with you before you leave.

"When I'm finished talking with you, if the attorneys want to talk to you, that's up to you. But you wouldn't want to miss your certificates, so I will, in the meantime, I would ask that every one here just stick around here for a few minutes."

As Gilvary left with the jurors I thought, *I wonder if he's going to tell them what he told me in chambers two days ago, before we began jury selection; when he admitted I was innocent – with a court reporter duly recording it!*

"All rise," from the bailiff interrupted my thought process. Judge Gilvary began, "I'm going to go back on the record."

Special Prosecutors Robert K. Hendrix and Craig King headed for the exit, to talk to the jurors.

"Can I talk to the jurors too?" I asked Gilvary.

Gilvary stopped me, "Mr. Metz's bond – no. You can't talk to them. I'm sorry. You can't talk to them, but your lawyer can, if he wants too."

Gilvary continued on. "Mr. Metz's bond is hereby revoked and he's remanded to the custody of the Sheriff of Montgomery County, Ohio. There will be some paperwork. I'm going to order a presentence investigation and when would we be back in court on that?"

"That would be March 11th."

"Okay," Gilvary said, and repeated himself, "And he's to be held without bond, pending sentence in this case."

"John-boy Kolesar interjected for the record, "We'll move for a bond under Rule 26."

"There will be no bond. Thank you for your request though."

Four deputies quickly surrounded me, cuffed my wrists behind my back, and patted me down. As I was led past the bench, I heard Judge Gilvary whisper – a little too loud – to Kolesar, my supposed legal advisor, "Thank you for helping me out."

Led from the courtroom, laughter could be heard from the room where the jurors were talking to prosecutors about the case.

Not a one of them has any inkling of what has taken place, I thought. *Down through history, some pretty good men have been maliciously cast into prison. Now, I will join their esteemed ranks.*

I had gone to the mountain top; had been able to reach deep down inside, into the very core of my being, to find the courage, the wisdom to live by moral dictates, without fear of the consequences. An incredible sense of wellbeing came over me.

Of all my many failures throughout fifty-five years in this game called life, this was by far my most successful one! I wished the feeling of euphoria could never end.

Laughter faded as I was led away. I was *free at last.*

CHAPTER TWENTY-FOUR

Heart of Stone; Feet of Clay

The sheriff deputies were courteous and professional. I changed out of my civilian clothes into a jail jumpsuit. Then I was taken to a department where I was booked in.

The deputy who had escorted me said to the deputy at the desk, "There was supposed to be a warrant accompanying the booking, but it hasn't arrived yet from Warren County."

My personal possessions were logged. I was fingerprinted and a mug shot was taken. Next I was escorted to Pod D of the Montgomery County Jail; my home for the present.

The deputy at the desk said, "Mr. Metz, I've got an inmate who has thirty days to serve. He's having a difficult time right now. I thought that maybe someone a little older might help him. So, I'm putting you in a cell with him. If there's any problem, let me know and I can move you."

"There won't be any problem, officer."

My missionary work has begun, I thought as I was introduced to my cellmate. The guy was on his fourth DUI and had received thirty days in jail. He was like a caged animal, but I had no problems with him.

As a recovering alcoholic with fourteen years sobriety, I knew more about him than he did about himself. His real prison awaited him on the outside. As my new cellmate confirmed, there are different kinds of prisons.

I had arranged for Attorney John Kolesar to telephone my wife when she got home from work, telling her what had happened. I was able to call Ann that evening.

She was hysterical; was very afraid for me, for us. I kept reminding her, *we walk by faith, not by sight.* God has His hand on our shoulders. With God's help, we would be taken care of. It really hit me for the first time that she would serve a sentence far greater than mine.

I told her where to find our car in a Dayton parking garage, and that she should meet Kolesar to retrieve my briefcase. I instructed her to copy down the jurors' names and addresses, and to return the listings of prospective jurors to Kolesar.

As I talked to her, a fight broke out and deputies stormed into the pod. I had to hang up mid-sentence, and rush to my cell. I was able to call her again later that night, and reassure her I was okay and not in any danger.

"Real nice place!" Ann offered, still afraid for me.

The following afternoon Kolesar came to see me. I was taken into a room with a glass window that faced the pod.

"Hi, John. How are you doing?"

"Better than you are," he said with a sly smile.

"Don't be too sure of that, John."

Kolesar didn't waste any time. "Judge Gilvary wants to make sure that I get the list of prospective jurors back from you."

"Afraid I might tell the jurors they had been duped?"

"I don't think that's the reason. When an attorney checks them out, it's his responsibility to return them to the clerk's office. When you represent yourself, it's your responsibility."

"Well, John, if I had received a bond like I was supposed too, I could have returned them. But don't worry; I've already told Ann where to find them, and told her you needed them.

"John, there are a few things I want to go over with you. Here's a list of things I could think of, off the top of my head that are appealable issues. Little things, like being denied witnesses."

"Yeah, well okay," Kolesar said with a nervous laugh. "I don't have much time."

"Well I do – up to eight years worth. In your opinion, did I receive a fair trial?"

"No, not at all," Kolesar admitted.

"Was denying me witnesses reversible error?"

"Yes."

"Well, you have three days to file a motion for a new trial. File one."

"I can't," Kolesar lamented in misery.

I looked at the pitiful pretender and softly answered, "I know, John. I understand *why* you can't, and I forgive you."

"Someone else will be assigned to handle the appeal. I really don't feel comfortable doing that," Kolesar mumbled.

"Here's what I want you to do, John. I want you to stay on the case until the transcripts are prepared. Once I have the transcripts in hand, I'll release you and hire private counsel. My sister is going to bring you certified funds totaling $7,040. I want you to disperse the funds due each party."

"Ah - I don't know what Judge Gilvary will say about that."

"Fuck him! What's *he* got to do with it?" I owe these people and now that this charade is over, I want to pay them."

"Generally, the judge doesn't want any communication between the prisoner and the victims," Kolesar rationalized.

"That's why I want *you* to do it. I don't really care what Gilvary thinks."

"Ah - I do," Kolesar admitted. "I'll ask him and get back with you. So far as me continuing to represent you for now, that's fine with me."

"I'm curious, John. What did the jurors think? I mean, I had that whole mountain of paperwork on the defense table, and then had no witnesses and didn't use any of it."

"One juror said to me, 'We were waiting for his defense but he didn't have one,'" Kolesar shrugged with his nauseating little laugh.

"That's funny," I said, laughing back. "What else did they say?"

"Another told me that they felt sorry for me. I was the attorney, but you ran the show," Kolesar laughed again.

I feel sorry for you too, you pathetic little whore, I thought. *Just two years out of the idealism of law school and you've already sold your soul. Get your miserable ass out of here, before I vomit.*

As I drifted off to sleep that second night in Montgomery County Jail, my final thoughts were of my kidnapper: *heart of stone; feet of clay.*

CHAPTER TWENTY-FIVE

Good

I learned some new jailhouse lingo, such as *Just-us* and *Dayton, Ohio – where you go on vacation and leave on probation.* I also learned that some inmates had attitudes. One day at lunch, a big tough said to me, "I want your Smokey."

"I'm going to eat the Smokey. But you're welcome to my greens."

"I don't want no greens! I said *I want your Smokey.*"

"And I said I was going to eat it. Tell you what though; if I weren't hungry, I'd stick this Smokey right up your ass!"

The big tough looked at me in shocked surprise and stopped mouthing. The time and place weren't conducive for a rumble. I knew he was about to appear on a domestic violence charge, and couldn't afford a jailhouse fight.

A bureaucrat came to see me to complete the presentencing investigation. He began with arrogance, but mellowed once he discovered I was an atypical inmate.

With his very first question, he wanted to know if I owed any attorneys for representing me. I supposed in Dayton, owing an attorney could keep an inmate out of prison. They like to get paid.

"Mr. Metz, so you feel that this was a malicious prosecution?" he asked at one point.

"It was a malicious *persecution*," I corrected.

"Well, the judge has to be impartial. That's his duty."

"Judge Gilvary had a mission to fulfill. It will be completed with a long prison sentence."

"He can't do that! You're eligible for probation."

"Why do you think I'm in here without bond? This was a theft by deception case involving $7,040. My only prior record involved misdemeanor bad checks over ten years ago, in 1986."

"He has to follow the law, and the law says that you are eligible for probation. My report is going to recommend it."

I finished with, "I guess we'll see."

Kolesar returned with word from the judge. "Judge Gilvary does not want you to make restitution. He said he will make that one of the terms of your probation."

"There's not going to be any probation, John," I explained to the simpleton.

"That's what the judge said. I won't take funds from your sister, to pay the victims. If you do so, on your own, you will make Judge Gilvary mad; and you don't want to do that before sentencing."

"Yeah; the last thing I want to do is piss him off again," I said while laughing. "Let me see if I got this straight. I have been *ordered* by Judge Gilvary *not* to pay the victims. Is that right?"

"More or less, that's what he said," Kolesar agreed.

"I don't imagine that would make the victims very happy, because *there is not going to be any probation.*"

"He's got to give it to you, Ray," Kolesar assured. "It's the law."

Could Kolesar really be this stupid; after three years of law school and a year of practice? I thought to myself. *Sadly, yes,* I answered my own redundant question.

"I guess we'll see. Here's a letter I wrote to Gilvary that I want you to include in your pre-sentencing motion. Thank you for your help, John."

The letter I handed Kolesar was handwritten in ink. I made a copy for my records. It read:

Inmate # 97-4563
Montgomery County Jail
330 West Second Street
Dayton, Ohio 45422
March 5, 1997

Dear Judge Gilvary:

I come before you, by way of this letter, and place myself at the mercy of the Court.

What I ask for, herein, is not for myself, but for my wife Ann, and our aged parents, 79, 86, 90, and 94. There comes a time when prudence overreaches valor. My family wants me, and needs me.

During the recent trial, I did my utmost to dignify your court, before the jury. Not a one had any reason to suspect there were "difficulties" to this case. It was a fair jury of objective citizens, who arrived at the only decision they could, based on the evidence and jury instruction.

They performed their civic duty, and they went home. And that ends their involvement. You need not be concerned about my abusing them, or their right to privacy. I believe in the spirit of the system. And I believe that more responsible citizens would be willing to accept jury duty if they weren't subject to abuse.

Retired Judge Meagher sought closure to old psychic wounds recently. My referencing him led to your sending me for a competency examination.

The emotion and pain that Dr. Hopes reported was genuine. I've gone through "hell" since June 1994, as matters between Mr. Lasky and myself progressed.

In 1961, I was sexually abused by a college professor within the length of two football fields from where the Green's home is located. The attack was over within an hour, and I was back on campus within two.

The professor was reported the next day to the university, and he was dismissed. I failed five exams the following week, and eventually left school.

The attack was one thing; the ensuing cover-up and the double-cross of me later by those to whom I promised my silence, forever changed my life. For thirty years, I kept my word of honor, given as a nineteen year old, and remained silent.

One who graduated from Beavercreek in 1960 with six majors, who attended U. of Cincinnati's College of Engineering in the hopes of attaining an electrical engineering degree, and then becoming a radio astronomer, saw his future crushed by the predatory acts of a man he trusted, and by those who valued reputation more than my life. I became a life insurance salesman at the age of twenty-one and left the business a drunkard, twenty years later.

In civil matters involving Mr. Lasky, the courts abused me as did those who covered up at U.C. those long years ago. And I reacted with the pent up wrath within me. The same spilled over to this case.

As I was led from your courtroom in handcuffs, I felt a peace; a freedom I haven't known in years. I found "closure" to the psychic wounds of the past. I'm so very, very grateful for the peace that's come over me.

Which brings me to the reasons for this letter.

I've attained what I needed from the system. Dr. Hopes wrote, accurately, that I trusted and believed that you'd be fair. I did not state that I'd receive a "fair" trial. I stated that *you* would be fair.

In view of all that's been written, *your* mercy on me, in sentencing me, would seem to transcend the errors of omission of others (in civil matters), and would exact a most compelling dignity upon the court(s) that would surpass the lack of dignity I've experienced from others.

I repaid my parents the $2,000 for the car purchased in November 1994. I am borrowing $10,000 from them to make full restitution to those in this case, and to others situated similarly (I've paid off about $4,000 to date, and owe a total more than $9,000 but less than $10,000).

Judge Gilvary, on behalf of my wife and our parents, I beg
for your mercy, and ask that I be granted probation. I want to
repay my parents before my father dies.
Sincerely yours,
Horace Ray Metz

One day, as I was walking the upper tier during recreation time, I looked down through the glass window
in the interview room, and saw Dr. Bobbie Hopes administering an examination to another inmate. Once
she saw me, she seemed to lose composure, and by
my next lap, she had placed cardboard in front of the
window to block the view.

Maybe word had gotten back to her that I had referred to her in court filings as a *working girl*. I had no
axe to grind with Hopes. On the witness stand, she
would have saved me.

Inmates in the pod gravitated to their own groups to
associate with during meals and time outside the
cells. My group razzed me about going to Lucasville,
Ohio's maximum security palace.

After gaining inmates' confidences, some opened up
to me. An ex-minister from Richmond, Indiana had
come to Dayton and had begun a relationship with a
hooker. Soon he was dabbling in cocaine with her. He
lost his family; he lost his church. Left without in-
come, he lost his hooker. His first attempt to buy cocaine on his own resulted in a drug bust. Filled with
guilt, shame and remorse, he hoped for drug rehab.

I was able to befriend the ex-minister and he claimed
that I helped him. *This missionary work can be gratifying*, I thought.

A young man named Michael Dodge confided that he
was the son of retired Judge Richard S. Dodge and
had gotten into a little trouble. He was terrified about
inmates learning that he was the son of a judge. He
sheepishly said he stole $2 off a mentally disabled
person in a wheelchair.

I pointed out it was not what others thought of him, but what he thought of himself that counted. He was intelligent and from a good family background. He had the resources to make something of his life; get off the drugs and booze.

I wrote Judge Gilvary again on March 8th, and sent the letter directly to him. I made a duplicate of the letter for my records.

Dear Judge Gilvary:

I am writing you, ever so respectfully, with information I thought you should know.

While being booked into jail, one deputy said to another that a Warren County warrant should accompany my paperwork. No warrant was present, and I told John Kolesar about it the following noon (February 21, 1997).

On Sunday, March 2, 1997, I asked a C.O. to check the computer for me.

I was booked into jail on 2-20-97. The Warren County warrant was issued on 2-21-97 and sent to Montgomery County the same day. After my conviction.

I also provided Mr. Kolesar, beforehand, the name of the complainant in Springboro.

How did Montgomery County deputies *know* beforehand, about an out-of-county warrant?

This explains the audacity of not attempting to serve any subpoenas on my witnesses.

Given the fact that I was forced to cross-examine the American General manger, when she was to be *my* witness also, implies that everyone but me knew that I'd have *no* witnesses.

The State has played a hard game, and they "won." George Brown committed perjury. He probably threw away notes that exonerated me, and he didn't use the Springboro matter.

I felt it in everyone's best interests to inform you that I found out about the Warren County warrant *prior* to its issue. I hope that you will accept this letter in the spirit in which I

offer it. Perhaps it's relevant to you; perhaps it's not. This seems to violate the spirit of fairness, to me.
Very truly yours,
Horace Ray Metz

Normally I would have automatically received a bond upon my conviction, based on the crime and the fact that I had honored a Personal Recognizance bond prior to trial. But Gilvary needed for me to be locked up; to prevent me from filing for a new trial within the three days permitted by law.

And so, a warrant was created in Warren County to provide a *justification* to deny a bond. The fact this violated the Ohio Revised Code was immaterial. I was safely locked away where I was helpless.

My letter to Gilvary was to let him know that I knew what they had been up to; in the hope that he would have a change of heart about continuing on. Though I did not disclose my knowledge that Gilvary lacked jurisdiction, *he knew it.*

And more than anything else, Judge James J. Gilvary *knew* that the elements of kidnapping *included* sending a man to prison without any legal authority, to assist others escape criminal detection.

I gave him one last chance to back out of the egregious error I knew he was about to make. I did not expect him to take advantage of it.

Ricky Frazier was the twenty-five year-old son of a female real estate attorney. He had a minor juvenile record for marijuana. As he explained it, he attempted his first big crime, using a magnum to attempt to steal two pounds of cocaine. It had been a set-up, and Frazier had drawn his magnum on an undercover cop. He became petrified when he learned that we both were going to be sentenced by Judge Gilvary on the same day.

"Oh, Mr. Metz, when we go in there together, Gilvary is going to be so mad when he sees you, he'll throw the book at me," the young inmate prophesized.

"It's your lucky day. This is the best thing that could have ever happened for you. I know Gilvary very well. He's going to call my case first, and slam me. To compensate, everyone else he sentences will get off light."

"You really think so?" Frazier asked.

"*I know so.* Trust me. He's one the most shallow and superficial men I've ever come across."

"I hope you're right," the frightened inmate lamented.

"Oh, I know I'm right. You know what that son-of-a-bitch did? He had innocent little grade school children visit the court, during my trial.

"It was horrible! He let them watch while he raped me. He let them watch as he desecrated his oath of office; his oath to God. Then the fool acknowledged it, on the record; for posterity.

"As I sat in the courtroom, I heard a genuine freak; a *spiritual deviant* on the bench."

On March 11, 1997 six or seven inmates were taken to Judge Gilvary's courtroom for sentencing. The anxiety level was high among the group, with one exception. I felt serene knowing that Gilvary, the kidnapper, was about to seal his fate along with mine.

My sister, Karen Lowry and brother, Tom Metz were sitting in the courtroom, and I smiled at them from the jury box where prisoners were seated. Tom was rather hot-headed, and Karen had cautioned him repeatedly; he could not lose his temper in the courtroom, no matter what happened.

By appearing in court, it was the first time any of my family had been involved. I had wanted it that way. My dear wife, Ann decided it would be too hard for her to be there, and stayed away. This was hell for her, but I knew she was with me in spirit.

I also saw Don and Carole Caupp, of Greene County (Count Two victims). It seemed like every prosecutor who had involvement in the case was there - except for the star that had made it all possible, Larry Lasky.

Kolesar came over and told me he had seen the pre-sentencing report and it recommended probation. He still pretended to believe I would receive it.

The bailiff announced *all rise*, Gilvary entered and court began with my case; just as I had predicted. I felt certain that this was a moment that Gilvary had fantasized about for months.

A Ms. Kidwell said,[29] "Good afternoon, Your Honor. This is the docket call for Tuesday, March 11th. The first case is found in the middle of page two for sentencing, for probation report. It's the third one on the page for probation, 95-CR-2317, State of Ohio versus Horace Raymond Metz, eight counts of theft over three hundred. Mr. Kolesar is advisor."

Kolesar and I stood on the right side facing the bench. A swarm of prosecutors stood on the other, representing the State.

Kolesar spoke right up like the good foot-soldier he was, "Good afternoon, Your Honor."

Gilvary acknowledged, "Good afternoon. Good afternoon, Mr. Metz."

"Good afternoon, sir," I answered.

"Anything further you wish to say before the court pronounces sentence?"

Looking directly at Gilvary I said, "Just that my wife lives in Northern Kentucky by herself and she needs me very much. She depends on me. My parents are aging and we spend two days a week with them and they need me at home very much, and I would ask for the mercy of the court."

"That's the first time you've ever used that term."

---

[29] Conversation is taken from the official transcript.

I had a right to expect justice. Asking for mercy is merely posturing for the record, I thought. I replied, "Yes, sir."

"You want me to review some of the other terms that you've used?"

Go for it, dumb ass, I thought. I answered, "No, Your Honor."

"I'm tempted to do so, but there's a lot of other people here that have got other business to do, so I'm going to go ahead with the sentencing.

"On Count One, I'm going to sentence you to a year and a half in the Corrections Reception Center. On Count Two, I'm going to sentence you to a year and a half in the Corrections Reception Center consecutive.

"On Counts Three, Four, and Five, I'm going to sentence you to a year and a half on each count and concurrent with each other and consecutive to the previous counts.

"On Counts Six, Seven, and Eight, I'm going to sentence you to a year and a half on each count concurrent with each other and consecutive with the previous counts for a total of six years."

There it is! I thought. *The asshole has just created what he believes is his escape mechanism! He deliberately created an appealable issue! Counts Three thru Eight all involved one party, American General. They should <u>all</u> run concurrent.*

The work in University of Dayton's law library had paid off. I had known Gilvary intended to escape via a principle called *res judicata.* But I had no idea how he would attempt to abuse it.

From behind me I heard Carole Caupp exclaim, "Good!"

I heard my sister exclaim, "Bullshit!"

Brother Tom, the hot-head, must have attempted to quiet her, because Karen said, "Well that's bullshit!"

"I'm not going to impose any fine. You have a right to appeal the sentence of the court. If you wish to do so,

you should do it within thirty days. If you can't afford
to do it, the court will assist you in this matter. Do
you have anything else to say?"

"No, Your Honor," I replied somberly.

"Good," Gilvary mocked.

Kolesar meekly said, "Thank you, Your Honor."

"You can have a seat, Mr. Metz," were Gilvary's final
words to me.

"Thank you," were my final words to him.

As soon as I was seated, we went off the record, and
Gilvary angrily told a deputy sheriff, "Get him out of
here. I want him out of here *now!*"

The Caupps stood within a foot of me as I was led
away, staring intently. *I wonder how they would feel if
they knew Gilvary had prohibited me from repaying
them their six hundred dollars,* I thought.

A deputy escorted me out the door used by jurors,
and had me sit in a room across the hall. A second
deputy approached us and said, "Take him back to jail
now. Gilvary wants him out of here."

"I'm just waiting for another inmate, so that I can
take two back at the same time."

"Don't wait for anyone. The judge wants him removed *now!*"

Out of the corner of my eye I could see a puzzled
deputy looking at me, as we walked the hallway to the
elevator. As we waited for the elevator, curiosity got
the better of him and he asked, "What in the world *did
you do?*"

"I think the judge is afraid of me," I answered calmly. I hastily added, "Not because I pose any physical
threat, but because I know things about him."

"I've never seen a display such as that as long as
I've been around here," the deputy observed.

"I guess he's having a bad day," I ended quietly.

CHAPTER TWENTY-SIX

A Very Bad Day

Judge Gilvary was having a very bad day, on March 11, 1997. Execution of *The Perfect Crime* had been easier to theorize than to implement. The naivety of its creators – experienced officers of the court in positions of power – was disconcerting.

The desperation that motivated its creation, made its chances of ultimately succeeding improbable. But when created; it must have appeared to be the most ingenious crime ever concocted. It happened this way.

From October through November of 1994, Montgomery County Assistant Prosecuting Attorney Laurence A. Lasky and Miamisburg Municipal Court Judge Robert E. Messham, Jr. created a scenario where I had two evictions under appeal, for the same residence, in the Second District Court of Appeals.

Lasky's client first learned of the second eviction, when served with a counterclaim. No one was in court when Messham scrawled out a heading; and sent it to clerk Maria Lowman for his signature stamp. I alleged Lasky's client was liable for damages caused by their agents, officers of the court; for twice having sued me, and having twice failed to make an initial appearance.

During this time, Federal Magistrate Michael R. Merz ruled; judges could lose their immunity by misusing the signature stamp. This presented appellate judges, Jim Brogan, Mike Fain, and Bill Wolff, Jr. an untenable situation. They conspired with Judge Messham in my case; without knowing of a theft ring he operated.

I noted appellate judges could become co-defendants in my civil suit; and should they disagree with a decision of a jury of my peers, they could always appeal – *to themselves!* It was farcical. Behind the scenes; they should have "encouraged" Lasky to simply pay me off.

In an appellate court Decision, it was acknowledged
I offered to settle for $20,000 to resolve business loss-
es; suffered while battling Lasky, Messham, et al. Pass
the hat and make me whole.

Instead, Brogan, Fain and Wolff turned to Montgomery County Prosecutor Mathias H. Heck, Jr. for resolution. Heck's "BAD BOY" had gotten them into a fiasco;
and Heck could get them out of it. And so, a scheme
was created in the prosecutor's office – in the summer
of 1995.

The Perfect Crime

> The appellate judges could do what-
> ever was necessary to dump my civil
> case appeals and counterclaim; know-
> ing I was destined to become a discred-
> ited convicted felon.
>
> A judge on the court of common pleas
> could do whatever necessary to convict
> me of theft-by-deception – for amounts
> I claimed civilly – because the only
> place to appeal to was the same judges
> who conspired to convict me.

When *The Perfect Crime* was conceptualized, Dennis
J. Langer was Heck's first assistant prosecutor. Langer was about to become a common pleas court judge.
He became the judge assigned my criminal case – that
he helped create as a prosecutor!

Ohio v. Metz, 95-CR-2317 was intended to become
an incestuous "family affair." In essence, the prosecutor's office had charged me; and the prosecutor's office
would persecute me. Indebted appellate judges would
uphold the conviction; by only correcting the sentence.

But matters became complicated. Langer recused after I learned he helped create *The Perfect Crime,* while
a prosecutor. Then the case was transferred to Lasky's
friend, Judge Barbara P. Gorman. She recused once
Maria Lowman was caught stealing.

I had tied Lowman and Lasky to illegal activities in Miamisburg Municipal Court; and Gorman became responsible for fixing Lowman's case. And that is how Judge Gilvary became my judge.

That is also *why* Local Rule 1.19 III(C) existed. It was designed to protect against "judge shopping," no matter who sought to benefit from it.

As the most experienced judge in Dayton, Gilvary had all of the qualifications to fix my case. Furthermore, he had the motivation. He was a personal friend of Prosecuting Attorney Mathias H. Heck, Jr.; and had mentored him since Heck's childhood.

So as matters developed on the way to trial, Judge Gilvary voluntarily agreed to step up; and rescue his friends within the judicial system. Gilvary was a gifted man; who intimately understood the nuances of the law. And he understood the possible ramifications for what he agreed to do.

Judge Gilvary was *solely* responsible for kidnapping me. Like any common criminal, his focus became avoiding getting caught. The Constitution and accompanying Bill of Rights meant nothing to the demented judge. But now that he had consummated his part in a sordid ploy; he lost control of future events.

Learning of the bogus warrant from Warren County, one day prior to its existence, was only the beginning. The sole purpose of the warrant was to provide Gilvary a reason to deny me an appellate bond.

I had written in a pretrial court filing, for Judge Gilvary's eyes, on February 5, 1997:

> Who else besides this Defendant *knew* that skimming of the public funds was going on in Miamisburg Municipal?
> ... Who would be involved? Maria Lowman acted as Judge Messham's moll; his *rubber stamp queen*. She did the banking. Who else? Who knows? How much? Who knows?

It had taken this Defendant one hour and forty-two minutes to trap Judge Messham, Laurence A. Lasky, and Maria Lowman in fraudulent court orders.

Would she/they get caught in skimming? Ha ha. It was a certainty!

Apparently, many officers of the court knew about a skimming operation in Miamisburg Municipal Court. And though I did not know who else was stealing, other than Judge Robert E. Messham, Jr., Judge Gilvary *knew* as he persecuted me on February 18-20, 1997.

The Montgomery County Public Defender's office was embroiled in the theft in Miamisburg Municipal Court. Deputy Director Daniel Kinane was a member of that theft ring. Kinane's involvement had not been revealed to the public. And so, I did not know it.

But Judge Gilvary *knew* it, as he unjustly sentenced me on March 11, 1997. Yes, Judge Gilvary feared me. And he acted out in anger, because he *knew* he was committing a crime far worse than smalltime theft-in-office crimes, as bad as they were. He *feared* he had finally met his match, in condemning me to prison for a crime that did not exist, to cover up the crimes of others. He feared me as he did so without jurisdiction!

He was haunted that somehow, someday, I would discover; at the same time Maria Lowman and I sat in county jail, Kinane faced a pending grand jury indictment on multiple charges of theft in office in Miamisburg Municipal Court.

Spiritual dynamics involving my kidnapping were compelling. And the next happening was a coincidence once defined as:

A coincidence is when God performs a miracle and decides to remain anonymous. —Author Unknown

I was placed in the same pod in the Montgomery County Jail with two young men, who confided in me.

Each was the son of an attorney. Both Michael Dodge and James R. Frazier, Jr. were scheduled to appear before Judge Gilvary the same day I was sentenced.

But Judge Gilvary fears had only begun. Dodge had been represented by Daniel E. Kinane, the Miamisburg Municipal Court thief! Dodge's scheduled appearance in court on the day of my sentencing was aborted. But there was a communications problem.

When Judge Gilvary saw Dodge and me enter the courtroom together, he became alarmed. He called my case out of order. Then he had me removed from the courtroom, and taken immediately back to the jail.

The deputy escorting me was forbidden to wait for another inmate, told, "Don't wait for anyone. The judge wants him removed *now!*"

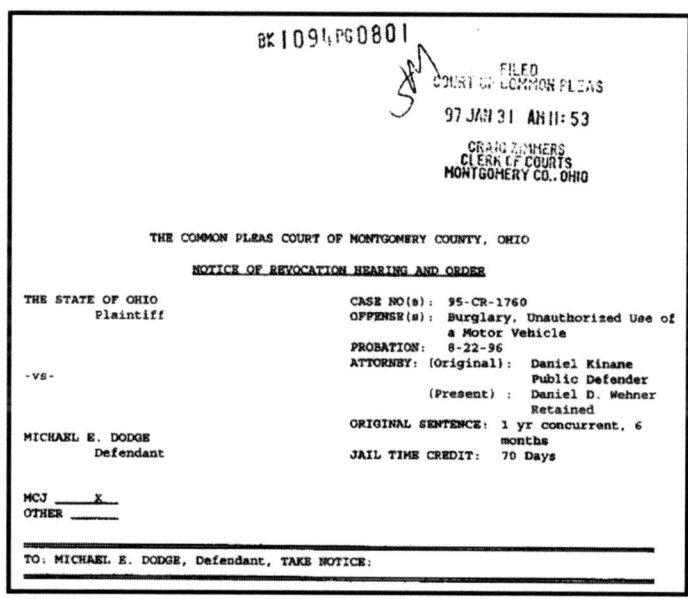

ATTORNEY: (Original) Daniel Kinane – Public Defender

Even though I was now a prisoner, and even though Kinane had been replaced; the cowardly judge feared me. He feared what I might overhear, as other cases were dealt with. He feared that somehow, someday; I would discover Dodge's attorney, described as the *original* on a January 31st document, had been Public Defender Daniel Kinane. Would I put the pieces together? Would I ever be able to prove Gilvary possessed judicial knowledge of Kinane's involvement in a theft ring?

A lot was rattling around, in the troubled mind of my prisoner. Being consumed by fear is a common experience in the prison of the psyche. So Gilvary attempted to "dodge" a potential bullet - by having Dodge's case continued; alleviating the fear of having us appear before him on the same day. And he failed.

I knew nothing of the facts disclosed herein, at the time. But I was aware of one thing. Judge Gilvary was having one hell of a time adjusting to life - in his prison of the psyche.

So long as he feared I would discover the *truth;* I would remain as his warden. And since it was only by facing the *truth,* that he could be freed from the prison he cast himself into; he was doomed to remain in his self-imposed prison.

With me, he had a no-nonsense warden. So unquestionably for the demented judge; March 11, 1997 was *a very bad day.*

CHAPTER TWENTY-SEVEN

Latin for Shit Out of Luck

Back in Pod D, inmates who had kidded me about being sent to maximum security in Lucasville Penitentiary were joking with me, saying *yeah, sure,* when I told them I got six years. It was not until the *cocaine-robber-with-a-magnum-wanna-be* came back and confirmed my sentence; that I was believed. Inmates were shocked at my sentence, many apologizing profusely for ribbing me about Lucasville.

"Hey, it is not you guys' fault. As I always like to remind myself, *if you can't take a joke, don't be one!*"

Ricky Frazier, who confirmed my sentence, sat with me at the evening meal. "Mr. Metz, you were absolutely right. Your case was called first, and he slammed you. I've never heard of treatment like that in a courtroom. The rest of us got off light, just like you said."

"What did you get?" I wanted to know.

Frazier hesitated. "I didn't want to tell you, after you got six years."

"It's okay, Ricky. Things have a way of working out," I soothed. Frazier faced his own prison of the psyche.

"He gave me six months drug rehab!"[30]

"Good for you! Now, you've been given a break. Go and apply yourself in the program, and after you're out, go to Narcotics Anonymous."

"Another guy was even luckier!" Frazier continued. "He burned down an apartment building with his girlfriend's body in the basement. Judge Gilvary only gave him eighteen months!"

---

[30] Actually Frazier was wrong. He got an even better deal. Gilvary overruled his attorney's request for drug treatment, but placed Frazier on probation on March 28, 1997. He was taken off probation on June 22, 1999.

My jailhouse acquaintance referred to Ricky Carter. A cursory review of court records, and a March 26, 1997 article by Rob Modic in the *Dayton Daily News,* is intriguing.

Joycelyn Smith was murdered, and Ricky Carter, her boyfriend was charged with aggravated murder. He burned down an apartment building with her body in it, and was also charged with twelve counts of aggravated arson. The coroner ruled the death a homicide, without being able to determine the exact cause. (Perhaps the reason for the fire?)

In a plea bargain, Carter pled guilty to twelve counts of aggravated arson, Class One Felonies. Judge Gilvary sentenced Carter to three years for each of the arson charges. But the sentences were run concurrently.

In a *separate* plea bargain, Carter pled guilty to "gross abuse of a corpse," a Class Five Felony. He was sentenced to two years for this plea, and it was run concurrently with the arson charges.

Aggravated murder disappeared. It was as though no one was murdered; a corpse just happened to "appear" in the building, causing Carter to burn it down.

When Gilvary sentenced him, Carter faced approximately eighteen months in prison! The case redefined the *bargain* not often found in *plea bargain!* It defied credulity.

On the very same day, Judge Gilvary gave me and an accused murderer incommensurable sentences. It is easily explainable. I posed a serious threat to the reputations of parties within the judicial system. The arsonist-corpse-abuser, probable corpse-creator did not. Additionally, a bribe may have been involved.

In dysfunctional judicial systems, as found in Dayton, these scenarios are repeated routinely. Adherence to the law means nothing; to those entrusted with upholding it. Third World Justice prevails.

I called Ann during the evening of my sentencing. She took the news pretty good. It was her sentence too, as I reminded. I would be sent to a prison in the Columbus area soon, and she could visit me there.

"The worst that can happen is that I'll have to serve four years. That's what a six year sentence means under Ohio law. The worst thing they can do to us is to keep us apart for 1,461 days. That's the worst. Things have a way of working out. And remember, *we walk by faith, not by sight.*"

"Well, it's not the twelve years he could have given you," Ann reasoned.

The day after sentencing, Legal Advisor John Kolesar visited me in jail.

"I have all the paperwork completed to get your appeals started, Mr. Metz," Kolesar began.

"That's good, John." I acknowledged.

"I don't have much time. Just sign above your name on the forms."

"May I take the time to read them?"

"You can; it's just that I'm running behind schedule."

I said, "Very well, I'll sign these and you can be on your way."

I had to file for an appeal to get the transcripts. So I signed the paperwork. Kolesar looked pleased, as he carried out Gilvary's wishes.

"There's one more thing, John. I want you to stay on the case until you have the transcripts secured. I want you to send the transcripts to me in prison, and I will release you from the case and retain private counsel. Do you understand?"

"I understand," Kolesar agreed.

I never saw him again. But attorney-extraordinaire John-boy filed the motions the following day.

The same day, Judge Gilvary filed a Termination Entry, detailing my sentence; providing credit for nineteen days spent in jail to that point. My sister, Karen

Lowry monitored the court records and sent a copy of the Entry to me at a later date.

The Entry was prepared by the prosecutor's office for Gilvary's signature. It incorrectly read:

THE COURT DID FULLY EXPLAIN TO DEFENDANT HIS APPEL-LATE RIGHTS AND THE DEFENDANT INFORMED THE COURT THAT SAID RIGHTS WERE UNDERSTOOD.

In court, Judge Gilvary had said to me, "You have a right to appeal *the sentence* of the court....Do you have anything else to say?"

I had replied, "No, Your Honor."

And so, Gilvary's paranoia caused another slip of the tongue, while sentencing me. His *intent* was; I would appeal *only the sentence* of the court – because he cleverly *created* that appellate issue, by sentencing me incorrectly!

Just as John Kolesar helped him get the conviction, by pretending to represent me; an - as yet - unknown attorney would assist Gilvary in covering it up; by bastardizing the appeal. At least, that was the criminal intent. The problem was; it was too clever!

And like many clever ploys, it had fatal flaws. Protracted dealings with ethically challenged judges made two Latin phrases applicable:

Judici officium sum execedenti non paretur.
Judici satis poena est, quod Deum haste ultorem.

A judge exceeding his office is not to be obeyed.
It is punishment enough for a judge to have God as his avenger.

Res judicata was intended to become, for me, Latin for *shit-out-of-luck*. However, it would be the pious Judge James J. Gilvary who was destined to face the ultimate meaning of *Latin for shit-out-of-luck.*

CHAPTER TWENTY-EIGHT

Con-vic-tions

Prisoners taken from county jail to state prisons never know when they will be transported, for security reasons. I was awakened early Wednesday morning, March 19, 1997, and prepared for the trip to an Ohio penitentiary.

I was shackled to another inmate for the journey in a Montgomery County sheriff's van. There were seven of us in all.

We stopped at London Correctional Institution to drop off a prison inmate who had been "out-to-court" - in Dayton on another charge. From there we proceeded to Corrections Reception Center, south of Columbus.

While I was in route to Corrections Reception Center, Judge Gilvary created the means for limiting my appeal to *the sentence.* From his March 19, 1997 Appointment of Counsel for Appeal:

> IT IS HEREBY ORDERED that attorney **Frank Malocu** is appointed to represent the defendant for the sole purpose of this appeal to the Court of Appeals.

Judge Gilvary knew that I was being transported to prison that day, as he addressed my copy of his Entry to the Corrections Reception Center. I received my copy March 28, 1997.

CRC is accurately described on an official website:

> The Corrections Reception Center (CRC) is the receiving prison for convicted adult male offenders from the southernmost 66 counties in Ohio. As most paramilitary operations, it is driven by policy, rule, and procedure.
>
> As a reception center, CRC is responsible for the evaluation of all newly received adult male offenders. This

evaluation includes educational, psychological, and medical testing as well as classification of inmates to determine appropriate security designation. Reception inmates remain at the Reception Center under maximum/close supervision until transferred to their parent institution or released.

Prison mug shot – CRC

Admission to the maximum security institution included, among other things: being strip searched; taking a shower; getting a hair cut; being finger printed; and posing for a mug shot; before receiving medical attention.

I was incarcerated under the alias the state gave me, Horace *Raymond* Metz, and received a new identity; Ohio Inmate number 346-086. My blood pressure at the time was high. Still, I forced myself to smile for the photograph; for posterity.

Held in maximum security meant sharing a cell with another inmate, and basically getting out, marching double-file to meals; or for a quick shower. Once a week we would get "recreation time," for about three hours.

Inmates at CRC are permitted to correspond with pencils and tablets. No ink pens are permitted.

I wanted to write my family at Easter time, but could not sharpen my pencils. The pencil sharpener was next to the security officers' station. Upon returning from the cafeteria, I hurried to my cell, retrieved my pencils and quickly sharpened them. I rushed back, and as I was about to enter my cell, an officer observing me hit a switch, closing and locking all the doors.

Locked out; I was in trouble. Called before the security station, I was asked in an authoritative voice, *why* I had taken pencils to the cafeteria in violation of regulations. I explained politely, and was ignored.

Not falling into the trap of challenging the corrections officer, I was left to stand at attention in front of the guard station for another half hour. I did so quietly, hands clasped behind my back. Finally, I was permitted to take the pencils to my cell.

And so, I wrote to my family - as a prisoner of war:

Saturday, March 24, 1997 – Day 37
Dear Mom and Dad, and all family members,

A happy holiday season to all, belatedly received. My heart is filled with a humble joy this Easter season. For I'm not alone; all of you are with me, and I with you. And Almighty God's hand is on each shoulder.

Isaiah 7:17 Therefore the Lord himself shall give you a sign: behold a virgin shall conceive, and bear a son, and shall call his name Immanuel.

From a March 5, 1997 letter to Judge James J. Gilvary, in which I begged for the mercy of the court on behalf of my wife and four parents, I wrote: "As I was led from your courtroom in handcuffs, I felt a peace; a freedom I haven't known in years. I found 'closure' to the psychic wounds of the past. I'm so very, very grateful for the peace that's come over me."

Isaiah 26:3 Thou wilt keep him in perfect peace, whose mind is stayed on thee: because he trusteth in thee.

Isaiah 41:10-11 Fear thee not: for I am with thee: be not dismayed; for I am thy God: I will strengthen thee with the right hand of my righteousness. Behold, all they that were incensed against thee shall be ashamed and confounded: they shall be as nothing; and they that strive with thee shall perish.

The New Testament provided me on March 13, 1997, by the Gideons International, offers this preamble:

The Bible contains the mind of God, the state of man, the way of salvation, the doom of sinners, and the happiness of believers. Its doctrines are holy, its precepts are binding, its histories are true, and its decisions are immutable. Read it to be wise, believe it to be safe, and practice it to be holy. It contains light to direct you, food to support you, and comfort to cheer you.

It is the traveler's map, the pilgrim's staff, the pilot's compass, the soldier's sword, and the Christian's charter. Here Paradise is restored, Heaven opened, and the gates of hell disclosed.

The Gideons have placed over 700 million Bibles and New Testaments in hotels, hospitals, penal institutions; with members of the armed forces, school students, and those in the public nursing field.

In the front of my little New Testament is the United States flag, and under it is **Proverbs 14:34:**

Righteousness exalteth a nation:
but sin is a reproach to any people.

The Pledge of Allegiance ends, "with liberty and justice for all."

From *Inside Journal*, "the hometown newspaper of America's prisoners," is an article entitled "Incarceration Rate Slowing." From the article:

The U.S. incarceration rate of one out of every 163 residents is the world's highest. It is six to eight times higher than rates in other industrialized nations.

... the annual rate of increase for the previous 10 years is about 7.8 percent.

From July 1, 1985 through June 30, 1995, the prison incarceration numbers grew by 109 percent. At the same time, our society crumbles, as public officials throughout America are more and more decadent. Our former servants have become our masters.

The answer for America is a shift from the "big brother" ruling class, to the source of real liberty, and individual responsibility.

II Corinthians 3:17 Now the Lord is that Spirit: and where the Spirit of the Lord is, there is liberty.

And so, when on December 23, 1996, I stood before a wretched little man named Judge James J. Gilvary, and calmly observed him tremble uncontrollably, and wrote about it later, my unspoken message was Scriptural.

I Corinthians 4:3-4 But with me it is a very small thing that I should be judged of you, or of man's judgment: yea, I judge not mine own self: For I know nothing by myself; yet am I not hereby justified: but he that judgeth me is the Lord.

Now, when I embarked on the journey that has led me to prison, back on June 13, 1994, I was guided by a *mandate* that I must live by: the Serenity Prayer:

God grant me the SERENITY to accept the things I cannot change, COURAGE to change the things I can, and WISDOM to know the difference.

And, when I embarked on that journey, I had no idea where it would lead, the story it would create and reveal, nor the pain it would inflict on those I love. But here we are, caught up in something that's difficult to understand, impossible to explain, and painful to endure.

Had I known all that would come about, the Serenity Prayer may have led me to the "acceptance" part. But I doubt it would have been the proper route, for me. In any case, I find comfort from Proverbs.

> **Proverbs 24:16** For a just man falleth seven times, and riseth up again: but the wicked shall fall into mischief.
>
> **Proverbs 22:29** Seest thou a man diligent in his business? He shall stand before kings; he shall not stand before mean men.

And, as Judge Gilvary scrambles to cover up his misdeeds, in a futile attempt to cover-up, other Biblical references come to mind.

> **Proverbs 25:21-22** If thine enemy be hungry, give him bread to eat; and if he be thirsty, give him water to drink. For thou shalt heap coals of fire upon his head, and the Lord shall reward thee.
>
> **Romans 13:14** Bless them which persecute you: bless and curse not.
>
> **I John 4:18** There is no fear in love; but perfect love casteth out fear; because fear hath torment. He that feareth is not made perfect in love.
>
> **II Corinthians 4:8-9** We are troubled on every side, yet not distressed; we are perplexed, but not in despair. Persecuted, but not forsaken: cast down, but not destroyed.
>
> **II Corinthians 5:7** (For we walk by faith, not by sight.)

In closing this exercise of faith, the words of Paul bear the question.

> **I Corinthians 10:29** ...for why is my liberty judged of another man's conscience?
>
> **Romans 8:24-25** For we are saved by hope: but hope that is seen is not hope: for what a man seeth, why doth

he yet hope for? But if we hope for that we see not, then do we with patience wait for it.

And alas, I'm imprisoned so that corrupt men can discredit me. The fools assume, as fools do, that my integrity and character is as shallow as theirs is. And they overlook that matters transcend their empty minds, hearts, and souls, to an ideal greater than any of us; the American dream; the American promise. For in the weeks before my arrest in the courts building, I wrote them of the words of Jesus on the cross: **Luke 23:34** Father, forgive them; for they know not what they do.

Assistant Prosecuting Attorney George Patricoff filed a motion in opposition to bond on March 28, 1997.

Counsel for the Plaintiff files this motion with a real and genuine concern for the safety of those who are associated with the instant case or even mentioned in the Defendant's pro se pleadings. One only has to quickly peruse some of his pleadings to get an idea of the twisted thought pattern which haunts the mind of this Defendant. All of his pleadings involve a diatribe of his legal problems which can only be described as libelous, scandalous and inappropriate. He spews forth much venom, hatred and contempt for those whom he feels have persecuted him in the past, as well as, in the instant case. He appears to have a pathological focus on a Forcible Entry and Detainer action occurring years before in the City of Miamisburg, Ohio, for which he holds responsible for his persecution a certain attorney and the associated legal system. In addition, he has weaved in his mind a conspiratorial web of persecution encompassing the whole criminal justice system, castigating those associated with his cases, consisting primarily of attorneys and judges.

Further, it appears that even this court had some concern about the Defendant's mental condition as the court on its own motion had the Defendant evaluated for his competency to stand trial. Not surprising, the forensic examiner found

that the Defendant's responses were deceptive and his conduct was "indicative of defensiveness, attempts to appear
mentally healthy." The tests conducted by the examiner
showed that the Defendant is "hypersensitive to criticism and
broodingly resentful". Further, the examiner states that individuals with test results such as the Defendant's "tend to project their problems onto others, rather than to accept blame
for their own problems or wrongdoings. That they are resentful towards others and hold long term grudges when they
perceive that they have been wronged by others". Finally it
was the opinion of the examiner that the Defendant has a
"paranoid and distrustful orientation toward potentially
conflictual situations and he is experiencing high levels of
emotional distress".

Now that the Defendant has been convicted and sentenced
to a consecutive term of incarceration totaling six years, it is
the Plaintiff's opinion that the Defendant's mental condition
is probably more exacerbated and that he is now a greater
risk of flight and danger to himself and to others, particularly
those associated with his legal problems, both present and
past, as well as those whom he sees as persecuting him, both
real and imagined. If one reviews the pro se pleadings au-
thored and filed by the Defendant in this case, along with the
report and opinion of the forensic examiner who conducted
the competency examination, it is difficult to come to any
other conclusion except that this Defendant is suffering from
a personality disorder and in reality is a time bomb waiting to
explode. As such, the risk of allowing the Defendant to return
to society is too great and therefore he must be restrained
and society protected. Thus, Plaintiff requests a bond in a
minimum amount of $250,000.00

                          RESPECTFULLY SUBMITTED,
                          MATHIAS H. HECK, JR.
                          PROSECUTING ATTORNEY
                          By _____
                          George B. Patricoff, #0024506
                          Counsel for Plaintiff

I wrote a song for my niece, Michele Lowry; who had won a sportsmanship award as a high school senior. She had turned up the *ten of spades* at our Christmas holiday celebration.

I'm An Old Convict[31]

I'm an old convict; with con-vic-tions;
See the best in life, and the bad that's done.
Got a niece that's great; she's a super-sport;
If she told of her unc, get a good report.
As a nice young lass, she's oh so dear;
Though I wish we were close,
Wouldn't wish her here;
'Cause I'm an old convict, with con-vic-tions.

I'm an old convict; hope a soon ex-con;
Only break I get, is the break of dawn.
No campfires warm; no stars at night;
Just a "celli" on the john, and a ceiling light.
Now some might say, *he ain't wrapped too tight.*
Know Michelle would claim,
But that ain't right;
He's an old convict; with con-vic-tions.

Congratulations, Michelle, on your sportsmanship award. You're a credit to your generation, and I'm so very, very proud of you! (As this beautiful song reflects.)

The State of Ohio imprisoned the body, but not the mind. I had been set *free* from a prison of the psyche.

---

[31] "I'm An Old Cowhand (From The Rio Grande)" was recorded in 1936; and first sung by Bing Crosby.

CHAPTER TWENTY-NINE

Time Bomb

There was not a lot to do in solitary confinement. We were sitting in our two-man cell talking. Fortunately, my celli was a seasoned con. He was accustomed to the drill. It made life easier for me, I imagined.

I had shown my celli the motion George Patricoff had filed against me, asking, "Are you sure you feel safe in here with me?"

My celli laughed, and then asked, "Why in the hell are you doing this, Metz? You don't belong here, like I do. You need to go home, to your wife and family."

"There are many reasons. So long as you feel safe, I would rather talk about something else."

My foes cast me into prison. They could not prevent God or His spirit from accompanying me. That was my call. I was cautious about compromising the spiritual aspects of my prison experience. Confiding in a skeptic did not seem prudent.

I am privileged to enjoy life, as a citizen in the best nation to exist since the beginning of civilization, in the best of America's times.

Despite personal challenges in life, I remain forever grateful for my American heritage! Gratitude creates its own sense of duty. And responsibility accompanies privilege like a shadow, creating its own form of courage when duty is embraced.

I believe those of us who can; owe it to our country to enhance the American vision - the search for *a more perfect Union*. It seemed to be a very simple concept. The citizenry had permitted the decaying governmental culture; and only they could correct it.

The *but who* was self-evident. *Them that can; ought.* Though I engaged Gilvary with personal motives, prior to trial, matters transcended me to altruistic reasons.

Sitting there in prison, I felt a sense of honor for having heeded a calling. I imagined it was similar to enlisting in the service, with full knowledge the enlistee was heading into combat in defense of the country he loved. My enlistment was for four years.

And there was nothing heroic about it. I sought no recognition or glory. My country was imperiled, and my background had prepared me to confront those who defiled the most basic, the most sacred tenants of our American way of life.

Sacred tenants defiled as George Patricoff did, by describing me. He began his motion to deny me bond:[32]

> ... with a real and genuine concern for the safety of those who are associated with the instant case or even mentioned in the Defendant's pro se pleadings.
>
> ... He spews forth much venom, hatred and contempt for those whom he feels have persecuted him in the past, as well as, in the instant case. He appears to have **a pathological focus** on...the City of Miamisburg, Ohio, for which he holds responsible for his persecution a certain attorney and the associated legal system.

Patricoff ended with:

> ... this Defendant is suffering from a personality disorder and in reality is a time bomb waiting to explode. As such, the risk of allowing the Defendant to return to society is too great and therefore he must be restrained and society protected.

---

[32] Patricoff said in a tape recorded telephone conversation, in response to my assertion, *They did it for Lasky:* "Well – ah - you know - I don't want to get into that. I don't know anything about it. You know - I can't - you know." Patricoff cautioned me, "Don't think you're Clarence Darrow because you won one." But once I was cast into prison, Patricoff portrayed me as a Charles Manson type.

George Patricoff had a busy agenda. But the reasons for his concern transcended fixing my case; transcended fixing Maria Lowman's case; to other problems. One could be revealed publicly, now that I was helplessly imprisoned in solitary confinement.

Fate is a funny thing. The *same day* Patricoff filed his motion against me, the March 28, 1997 *Dayton Daily News* carried an article by Cathy Mong.

My sister, Karen mailed the article to me, and for an unknown reason, though it violated the strict standards for mail received at CRC, the newspaper article was left in the envelope. The article read:

PUBLIC DEFENDER Lawyer quits office

There apparently were discrepancies in refunds of public defender clients' bond money.

Daniel E. Kinane, deputy director of the Montgomery County Public defender's office, resigned Wednesday after his office reviewed documents that suggest irregularities with $10,000 to $20,000 in bond money.

The money in question was posted by clients Kinane represented during appearances in Miamisburg Municipal Court. Kinane could not be reached Thursday for comment.

The documents were supplied by the court and turned over to the Montgomery County sheriff's office, which began its criminal investigation into the allegations Thursday.

Lynn Koeller, director of the Public Defender's office, said after reviewing the documents with members of the Public Defender's Commission, "I made a determination that I needed his resignation, and he provided it."

Koeller said Kinane also is the subject of a criminal investigation by the county prosecutor's office. It is my understanding the Dayton Bar Association is doing an ethical investigation as well."

George Patricoff, chief of economic crimes and fraud division of the county prosecutor's office, said commenting on the allegation would be inappropriate until some of the 50 or 60 clients included in the report are interviewed.

Sheriff Gary Haines said Miamisburg court officials notified Judge Robert E. Messham, Jr. of Miamisburg Municipal Court of irregularities found in the amount of bond money returned to Kinane and amounts forfeited by the court.

"Dan allegedly told defendants the bond money was forfeited and the money was gone," Haines said.

Messham said no money from the court is involved.

Kinane had been with the public defender's office from 1975 to 1978, and from 1983 until Wednesday. He was acting director from 1994 to 1995.

Kinane took over as acting director in August 1994 after Kurt R. Portmann stepped down after making racial remarks to a black attorney. Koeller was appointed director one year later.

"We're doing such good work here, it's phenomenal," Koeller said. "We were just rising from the Portmann morass and this happens."

This is the second time in one year that Messham and his staff have brought alleged improprieties to light.

In December, former bookkeeper Maria R. Lowman pleaded guilty to one charge of theft in office amounting to $44,000.

After Lowman's case, Haines said, court officials kept digging into its records "and found this discrepancy, too."

According to Patricoff, the same day of the Kinane public disclosure, I suffered from *a pathological focus* on the same municipal court. Patricoff had a *real and genuine concern* for *the safety* of those *even mentioned* in my court filings.

He had valid reason to fear what I would discover. For according to Patricoff on March 28, 1997, Daniel Kinane stole from 50 to 60 clients. And according to the October 11, 1997 *Dayton Daily News*, Kinane pled guilty to theft on August 6th. He made restitution of "more than $11,000."

But according to the *Office of Disciplinary Counsel v. Kinane*, decided in the Ohio Supreme Court November

10, 1999, Kinane stole from *129 clients;* more than twice as many as Patricoff claimed. Kinane was disbarred.

Kinane was sentenced by Judge David A. Gowdown. He received *probation,* with one of the terms being he had to lecture students about *ethics* for 200 hours (including University of Dayton law students). Patricoff "was satisfied" with the sentence.

According to the article in the March 28, 1997 *Dayton Daily News* Maria Lowman pled guilty to stealing $44,000 on December 11, 1996. But her Order of Probation included restitution totaling *$88,503.57.*

The order was signed March 7, 1997, three weeks prior to the newspaper article claiming she pled *guilty* to stealing *half* as much. And Patricoff prosecuted the Lowman case; as well as the Kinane case.

To believe George Patricoff, Maria Lowman acted alone, stealing $44,000. But then she agreed to repay $88,503.57.

To believe Patricoff, Daniel Kinane acted alone, while stealing from 50 - 60 clients. But then he was disbarred for stealing from 129.

To believe Patricoff, I had to remain incarcerated, for the "safety" of those mentioned by me - including him!

The ethically challenged could imprison me, to get me off-the-streets and out of their hair. But the truth remained the same. And *truth* would stand the test of time.

To believe Patricoff, both acted independently. Lowman was caught in July 1996, and Kinane was apprehended later. But it could not have happened that way. The following was extrapolated from the Ohio Supreme Court's summary of Kinane's disbarment.

Daniel Kinane could not possibly have acted alone, in perpetrating multiple thefts. He was the public defender. Events took place in sequential order:

1. Arrest made
2. Bond posted
3. Prosecutor prepares court case
4. Public defender appointed by judge
5. Bond changed to *personal recognizance* - by judge
6. Bookkeeper issues refund of bond – to public defender
7. Case dismissed by judge
8. Defendant told the case was dismissed; and bond equaled fine – by public defender
9. Bond money divided up by the thieves

Judge Messham was intentionally disingenuous in the newspaper accounting; claiming no money from the court was involved. Each of the dismissed cases could have resulted in court costs and/or fines.

To believe Patricoff, Kinane stole $12,000. But it had come from 129 victims. That would create an *average* bond of $93. It was an impossibly low figure.

In conclusion: parties involved in theft in Miamisburg Municipal Court had to include the following:

- Judge
- Prosecutor
- Public Defender/Defense Attorney
- Bookkeeper

Otherwise, the prosecutor and the judge received nothing for looking aside, as case after case was dismissed or simply disappeared. They would have acted out of charity to benefit Kinane; would have been involved in corruption, without being corrupt. That was not the Judge Messham I knew.

For Messham created a perfect alibi for himself, via abuse of his signature stamp. Lasky had shown me how it worked, in my civil cases!

When a bond was changed to *personal recognizance* by Messham; two editions of the same court order were time-stamped simultaneously - whenever one of two things occurred. Messham was on the bench, and an audio recording of the court's proceedings proved the case was not on the docket that day; or, an acting judge presided over court proceedings on that day.

The first edition was signed by someone other than Messham, and would be temporarily placed in the file. If things did not work out according to plan; he could claim he lacked any of knowledge of the corruption. In that scenario, he would pretend to "correct" things.

But once a case was dismissed, and a defendant accepted being told that the bond money covered a fine and/or costs; the first edition would be removed from the file and destroyed. Maria Lowman would place the second edition of the order in the court's file; having affixed Messham's signature via his signature stamp.

The same procedure was used for the dismissal of a case. It was ingenuous. But a question remained.

How many attorneys besides Kinane had similar arrangements with Messham? It remains implausible that such an intricate mechanism was put in place; solely for the benefit of one assistant prosecutor, and one public defender! How much money was really stolen from the public, over the years?

These are questions a *culture of corruption* invites. Imprisoning me to cover-up the criminal activity was the solution a *culture of corruption* invited.

Early into my prison stretch in April 1997, I did not know the details of everything described here. But no matter whatever else prevailed, the *truth* could never be harnessed by the *lie.*

I knew George Patricoff orchestrated the cover-ups involving Lowman, Lasky, Messham, Metz and Kinane; as well as unknown others. He pulled the pin, and held onto a grenade labeled the *truth.*

Patricoff was incapable of letting go. Thus it was the incorrigible chief of prosecuting attorney's fraud division; who held onto a *time bomb.*

CHAPTER THIRTY

Trapped by Res Judicata

Ohio Revised Code was written with the benefit and wisdom of the ages. It was replete with safeguards, to prevent miscarriages of justice, be they intentional or unintentional.

At the same time, safeguards are built in to conserve the limited resources of the judicial system. One of these doctrines of law is named *res judicata;* defined as "a thing adjudicated; a case that has been decided."

In Ohio, that includes appellate issues. In essence, any appellate issues not raised at the first opportunity cannot be raised later.

Res judicata was the legal principle Judge Gilvary counted on to escape scrutiny for his actions at trial. He had cleverly prepared accordingly. His sentence on March 11, 1997 included Counts 3-8 involving American General Finance.

A correct sentence would have been to sentence me concurrently on all six counts. By splitting them into two groups and running the two groups concurrently; Gilvary cleverly created a bogus appellate issue. This made my sentence six years instead of four and a half. It meant serving four years in prison, instead of three.

After intentionally creating an appellate issue, Judge Gilvary appointed Attorney Frank Malocu to write the appeal. All Malocu had to do to satisfy the decadent Gilvary; was limit the appeal to this single issue.

Because of the principle of *res judicata,* lost forever would be my right to appeal on constitutional issues; repeated violations of the First, Forth, Fifth, Sixth, Eighth, and Fourteenth Amendments. Additionally, gone would be any right to move into federal court for these issues.

Attorney John Kolesar wrote me on March 28, 1997, reading in pertinent part:

> I also spoke to Frank Malocu (pronounced Ma-luck), the attorney appointed for your appeal. Frank's office is across the hall from mine and we discussed your case already. I will be providing him with my file. He is an experienced criminal defense attorney, and if there are any reversible errors he will find them.
>
> ... I have also enclosed a draft motion for shock probation, which you should file toward the end of April.

Having Kolesar endorse Attorney Frank Malocu was akin to atheist Madeline Murray O'Hare endorsing a priest. He had absolutely no credibility.

If the young legal whore assured me Malocu would be extremely adapt at prostituting my appeal, he would have had impeccable credibility. *If there are any reversible errors, my ass,* I thought.

With that awareness, on April 1, 1997 I wrote to attorneys, Malocu and Kolesar from my maximum confinement cell, using a pencil and note pad; making a second copy for myself.

> Dear Mr. Malocu:
>
> On Friday, March 28, 1997, I received a copy of the Court's 3/19/97 Order, time-stamped at 11:10 a.m., and postmarked 3/20/97.
>
> At the very time of this filing, I was in a van in route from Montgomery County Jail to CRC.
>
> Without intending <u>any</u> aspersions to you, Judge Gilvary's appointment is suspect, and therefore, is unacceptable.
>
> I am a pro se party, with Mr. John P. Kolesar as my Legal Advisor.
>
> You are hereby ordered to remove yourself as counsel, and to send me copies of <u>all</u> documentation received and/or originated in this case, by your office.

Thank you, in advance, for your kind attention, and prompt performance.

Dear Mr. Kolesar:

Enclosed is a copy of a letter to Frank A. Malocu.

You are hereby instructed that, under no circumstances, are you to file a motion for Shock Probation on my behalf.

Please send me copies of <u>everything</u>, and also, a copy to my sister Karen, for my permanent files.

Thank you for your cooperation. Best regards.

Judge Gilvary filed an Entry pertaining to bond on April 4, 1997:

> ... after due consideration and for good cause shown, the Court hereby <u>ORDERS</u> that Bond be set at $70,000 pending resolution of Defendant's appeal in this case.
>
> SO ORDERED,
>
> JAMES J. GILVARY, JUDGE

A $70,000 bond for a crime of theft by deception of $7,040 amounted to *no* bond. It would cost $7,000 for the ten percent *fee* to a bondsman. Aside from the bond; there was the additional obstacle created by the Warren County detainer.

I was to remain in *his* prison; unless and until I confessed. And while stuck in prison, Gilvary continued to deceive himself; assuming I was helpless.

Malocu wrote me on April 11th. A key player my kidnapper counted on - in getting away with his crimes - had been removed.

Dear Mr. Metz:

Per your request, I have withdrawn from your case. I have enclosed a copy of a Motion and Entry to Withdraw as Appellate Counsel.

Sincerely,

Frank A. Malocu

ENTRY GRANTING MOTION TO
WITHDRAW AS APPELLATE
COUNSEL

For good cause shown Frank A. Malocu is hereby withdrawn as Appellate counsel for Defendant/Appellant, Horace
Raymond Metz.

IT IS SO ORDERED.

_____
JUDGE

For good cause shown, my ass, I thought. I would
never have seen the appeal Malocu prepared, until after the fact.

Inefficient assistance of appellate counsel could possibly have been raised. It is almost always impossible
to prove, because officers of the court are conveniently
presumed to be honorable and competent.

Instead, I likely would have been castigated as an
ingrate, whose sentence had been reduced because of
the astuteness of the very lawyer I complained about!
A "thank you" would have been more appropriate; for
saving me from serving an extra year in prison.

In prison, my resolve remained unwavering. I would
lay on my bunk, in the quiet of night, alone with my
thoughts: *My kidnapper is trapped; is running out of
options. And now, he's about to lose another weapon,
called res judicata.*

CHAPTER THIRTY-ONE

200th Day of Freedom

On April 15, 1997, my 54th day in captivity, I was transferred from the maximum security Corrections Reception Center to Pickaway Correctional Institution that was adjacent to C.R.C. This would be my permanent prison home. I arrived at Pickaway with a balance of 1,407 days to go.

Pickaway Correctional Institution was a hundred-year-old facility. It had once been a mental institution, and had been transformed into a prison when Ohio deemphasized the need for mental health care.

The prison population was approximately 2,200 inmates, with over 500 outside the fences, in an honor camp. The prison's basic classification was "medium security." Honor camp inmates, classified as "minimum security," worked on the prison farm, or went into Columbus to work at places like the governor's mansion.

Inmates ranged from some serving less than a year to others serving life without parole. In Ohio, prisoners serving life can be granted transfers to lower security prisons due to good behavior. I found those inmates to be good neighbors; they appreciated the quality of life found in a medium camp as opposed to maximum security camps. It was their home for life and they made the best of it.

There were three Units within the prison, A, C and D. B-Building housed med-bay and a part of the prison staff. Each unit housed about 550 inmates in bays, where fifty-sixty inmates lived together - on two floors. The lower floor's windows were at ground level.

Upon clearing the sally port, with four new inmates accompanying me, we were ushered to Quartermaster. Clothing was issued, and we changed into our prison blues. I was assigned to A-Unit.

Upon arriving at A-Unit, I was ushered into the Security Office, for a basic orientation. The first inmate I met was Floyd Bishop, who gave the orientation. After Bishop finished, I was sent to the basement floor, to 7-Bay.

My prison home consisted of bunk 36 and a foot locker. My home mailing address became 7-A-36. My identity was Inmate 346-086.

The dehumanizing aspect of prison was a cold reality. But I entered with certain concepts in mind. First, I was a convicted felon; my status was no different than others. I would conduct myself accordingly.

Secondly, the State and the judge took away my physical freedom. They would have the body; but they could never get the mind, or the soul. With those insights, I would serve only *one* sentence; and not *two*.

After the ordeal of solitary confinement in C.R.C., the freedom to walk the grounds at P.C.I. was profoundly pleasant. The yard was long and fairly narrow. It contained a quarter-mile cinder track, softball diamond, and outdoor basketball court. There was also a nine-hole miniature golf layout, a horseshoes layout, and room for volleyball.

The multi-purpose building was modern. Inside, we had a good library - by Ohio prison standards - and a modern gymnasium. There were also classrooms for various purposes. Interestingly, P.C.I. awarded more G.E.D. diplomas than anywhere else in Ohio.

After a week, I met with our unit manager; to receive my prison work assignment. Inmates were allowed to request jobs, from a list of positions available.

When asked what I wanted to do, I offered, "I would like to work in the library."

The unit manager looked at my file, reviewing aptitude test scores, saying after consideration, "Metz, I think you will make a good security office clerk."

"I would rather work in the library. Mr. Sexton said he had a position open," I responded.

"Metz, I think you *will* make a good security office clerk. What do you think?" she asked with an authoritative smile.

"You know, I'll bet I'd make a good security office clerk!" I agreed with a laugh.

"Yes, Metz, I'm sure you will. Bishop told me he wanted someone intelligent to work with him; you'll have to do. Report to him for training, after lunch."

My job amounted to eight-hour shifts, five days a week, doing clerical work for the unit's guards. The pay was set at $22 per month, placed in my commissary account. There was no withholding tax.

Floyd Bishop taught me the job. Basically, he told me, a few inmates ran the unit. The guards provided the security.

Bishop emphasized, it was very important to maintain an accurate accounting of inmate movement, throughout the day. Count times were at 1:00 AM, 5:00 AM, 11:00 AM, 4:00 PM, and 10:00 PM. The count was manually compiled, by security officers going from bay to bay throughout the unit.

If an inmate's bunk was empty, the officer had better know where the inmate was; and for what purpose. For example, he could be at Med-Bay or Out-To-Court; or, more commonly, in the Hole.

Count compiled in each unit was phoned to the Captain's Office, and reconciled with the prison population. Until count cleared, inmates remained on their bunks (supposedly silent), locked in their bay. Normally count-time was a routine matter. But if a clerk screwed up count, it meant a trip to the Hole, and reassignment to an unpleasant job – usually working in the cafeteria.

The job sometimes included more mundane things, like handing out toilet paper. (Though we shared common toilets and showers, each inmate had his personal toilet paper.) The job entailed taking messages to inmates, and handling routine inmate requests. The security office was off limits, except for clerks who worked there.

Another important matter was processing inmates into or out of the unit. Transfers into and out of A-Unit happened daily. There were meticulous procedures to follow.

The job assignment carried negative connotations. Some inmates looked at us as an extension of the system; as *one of them* in the *us-against-them* environment that prevailed. Security office clerks were suspected of being snitches.

But by any standards, it was a cushy job assignment. It gave me a first-hand understanding of the prison security guard. With few exceptions, they were decedent people, with a very, very difficult job to perform.

With no exception, they served a sentence like the rest of us. The main difference was; they served theirs forty hours a week. I got along well with most of the prison guards and others within the prison hierarchy. They were not a party to my kidnapping.

It was a sad matter of fact; those responsible *for me* after conviction; functioned light years ahead of those responsible *to me,* prior to conviction. They earned my respect.

Working with Floyd Bishop was a fortuitous opportunity. We became fast friends. He was from Erie, Pennsylvania, and had been a partner in Ernst & Young for many years, before becoming an officer in Sudbury, Inc.

The Fortune 500 Company once had 23 subsidiaries, mostly in the domestic automotive industry. When

Sudbury went into Chapter 11 bankruptcy, Bishop attempted to buy some of the subsidiary companies. Charged with selling securities without a license, he pled *no contest,* on the advice of his attorney.

Some of the things Floyd volunteered about the legal mess did not add up. Still in all, he was a valued confident while we were in prison together. He was a good man who did something wrong. But 2-15 years was an inhumane sentence for a man older than I.

Over time, Bishop was granted parole, only to have another jurisdiction pick him up on other charges. I learned he died in a federal penitentiary. By the time we parted, I knew there was more to his crimes than Bishop admitted. But he was a very *good* man, who did some very *bad* things, out of desperation. And he paid dearly for them.

On April 29, 1997, only fourteen days after arriving at P.C.I., I was in violation of prison rules. I bought a pack of cigarettes; to give to an inmate, in exchange for making a Mother's Day card for me.

Arriving back in the bay after going to commissary (A-Unit went every Tuesday), a guard came through looking at our merchandise and checking it against our commissary receipt. I lived in a non-smoking bay and was not permitted to purchase cigarettes.

I admitted I had not bothered to read the regulations concerning tobacco possession, since I did not smoke. When I explained that I did not understand that particular rule, and had bought cigarettes as a gift, I was accused of *dealing* (exchanging property for services - prohibited by prison rules).

I was guilty as charged, I admitted. The guard told me I had better learn to draw. He sent the cigarettes to B-Building, and told me that normally, it would end matters. But since I worked in the security office as a clerk, he would have to take further action to avoid any appearance of favoritism. So I would be moved to a smoking bay.

```
┌─────────────────────────────────────────────────┐
│  ─────────────────────────────────────────────   │
│                                                   │
│   Inmate  Attitude  (At  time  of  offense) ___ TRUTHFUL.  │
│                                                   │
│  ─────────────────────────────────────────────   │
└─────────────────────────────────────────────────┘
```

I wept when I saw the word the prison guard had chosen to describe me, in his Conduct Report. For the first time since June 13, 1994, someone in authority found me to be *truthful.* I thought of George Patricoff's characterization of me as a Charles Manson type; as I wept; making sure no one saw me crying.

Having been in my home prison for only two weeks, I had already committed a worse "crime" than I had on the streets! I had a Mother's Day card created, for the mother I loved.

I was moved to 8-bay, next door. After ninety days, I could have transferred back to a nonsmoking bay. But I decided to stay put. Some of the inmates identified with me, and I became a mentor for them.

I wanted to remain close to them. 8-bay became my home address for the rest of my time at Pickaway.

Judge Gilvary never intended for me to serve four years in prison, mandated by his six-year sentence. When he told Attorney Kolesar restitution would be made part of my probation; he meant *shock probation.*

Unlike probation he could have granted at sentencing, shock probation required an inmate to request it. In the process of doing so, the inmate admitted "guilt."

Gilvary needed an admission of guilt from me. After a taste of reality; after spending some time in prison, I would be "shocked" into the reality that if I did not admit "guilt," I had almost four more years to serve.

Gilvary had kidnapped me, and set a ransom. The extortion was the length of the sentence! He demanded my soul. In effect, he attempted to tell me:

> What has been done to you was so
> horrific; you *will* agree it was proper!

The choices Gilvary offered me were: Continue to act like a fool and serve four years in prison. Or, get smart and I will free you in four to six months.

To be sure, there were ample reasons for Gilvary to count on my caving in. One of the questions I am asked most often is: What was prison like? I hesitate to relate stories from *the big house,* because conditions I endured were nothing like many U.S. prisoners face. But I will relate an incident that happened; early on.

Inmates were permitted to make collect telephone calls during free time. A-Unit housed about 550 inmates. There were five phones on each of two floors. We would form a line and wait our turn for an available phone. Once fifteen minutes were up, the phone call would be automatically disconnected.

I was next in line one evening, when a phone became available. Before I could react, a young tough walking by grabbed the phone. I was not about to challenge him, and he knew it.

But inmates behind me began raising hell. It was either face the wrath of a line of inmates behind me; or confront *line-jumper.* Once I backed down, and let him intimidate me, it created an image I could not afford to have in prison.

I spoke up with, "Excuse me, I think I was next."

The inmate paused before dialing, gave me incredulous look and snarled, "Oh yeah?"

"Yes, I was. It would be okay with me, if you jumped the line. But it isn't okay with the men behind me. Please hand me the phone."

My heart was pumping as he asked angrily, "Just what in the hell do you plan to do, if I don't?"

"Well," I began hesitantly as if pondering my answer. "While we're here in prison, I guess I'll let it slide for now. I don't want to go to the Hole over a fight for a telephone. But once we're out of here, I'm gonna look you up!"

"And then what?" the inmate snarled contemptuously at the absurdity of my comments.

"Then I'm going to have my wife kick your ass!" I calmly concluded.

Inmates in line behind me howled in laughter. *Line-jumper* looked stunned, but appraised his options. It seemed he had a sudden awakening.

He had not simply jumped in front of me; he had jumped in front of everyone in line. He would loose face by attacking an older white man; willing to take a beating for everyone. No one said anything.

Finally he handed me the phone, and as he turned to walk away he muttered, "You are really fucked up!"

So to Judge Gilvary, it was incomprehensible I would voluntarily choose remain in prison; even though I had voluntarily gone to prison in the first place.

I had been offered diversion twice. The terms had been enticing. Diversion involved pleading guilty to avoid a trial. If I had done so, I would never have spent a moment incarcerated. Not a solitary moment!

I would have pled guilty, becoming a discredited convicted felon who confessed his "crime." I rejected it.

May 5, 1997, I filed a motion for different conditions of bond. I knew Judge Gilvary would deny it, but certain appellate rights were preserved by making the petition. I received a letter from Kolesar the same day:

> I advise you to file your motion for shock probation immediately, if you have not already done so. According to your previous letter, you specifically requested that I not file any motion for shock probation. I have therefore <u>not</u> done so. Good luck with your appeal.

May 9, 1997, Judge Gilvary filed a Decision, Entry and Order. It read

> This matter came on to be heard on Defendant's motion for different conditions for bond pending appeal filed herein May

5, 1997. The Memorandum in Support of the motion contains no information that would justify a change in Defendant's bond pending appeal. The motion is <u>OVERRULED</u>.

SO ORDERED:

JAMES J. GILVARY, JUDGE

My refusal to apply for shock probation was met with incredulity by other inmates. I was repeatedly told I was crazy. Once a fool; always a fool, I imagined, without further analysis.

The prison experience is such that inmates do or say anything that would lead to release. It is not a pleasant one. The wisdom within prison was that it was easier to fight for one's rights on the outside. The reality was; it was just easier to live without rights on the outside, than on the inside.

A life-without-parole inmate confronted me, "Metz, you weird. You ain't been here long enough to be institutionalized. You is the weirdest individual, I have ever known!"

I replied with a grin, "That's very flattering. Thank you for your kind words. But let me explain something I don't think you understand.

"A judge was nice enough to sentence me to six years, even though he knew I didn't deserve to be so lucky. And then the State comes along and takes away two years of it, for good-time.

"That's not right. The judge knew I was a nice guy when he sentenced me. *He* wanted me to have *six years*. And *nobody* is going to cheat me out of any more of it!"

Shaking his head in bewilderment, the inmate blurted, "You a weird old white man! But you sure do got guts!"

Another inmate asked me, "Mr. Metz, how old was you, the first time you come to prison?

"Fifty-five," I responded.

"No; I don't mean *this* time. I mean the *first* time," he implored earnestly.

"This is my first time," I answered kindly.

"Are you for real?" the young inmate blurted in astonishment.

"Yes, I am. You see, in my family; we thought prison was more difficult to get into than Harvard or Yale. None of us had been to either. We were surprised to learn *anyone* can go to prison! It's so...American!"

Miss Muncy, my case manager instructed me to develop a plan for the parole board. I would have a shock parole hearing. When told I was not interested in shock parole, she informed me refusing to complete the form meant going to the Hole.

And so, I wrote on my form: *I have no plans for shock parole.* Knowing I was certain to receive shock, Muncy reluctantly accepted my "completed" application.

I wrote: *I have no plans for shock parole*

"Heck, Miss Muncy, you people have treated me with more respect than anyone in the legal fraternity did. Respect is so refreshing; I want to bask in more of it!"

And so, I met with a parole board member, who informed me the records sent from Montgomery County were incomplete. My hearing would be rescheduled.

I intuitively knew *someone* would have to appoint another attorney to prostitute my appeal, in order to prevent me from receiving the transcripts. I concluded appellate judges - Mike Fain (a.k.a. Mike F-A-K-E by then) and Jim Brogan were candidates to do so.

I waited patiently until I thought the transcripts would be ready; then on July 15, 1997, I launched two missives towards Dayton. One landed on the Clerk of Courts Craig Zimmers' desk; the other letter landed on Judge Gilvary's bailiff, Steve Davis' desk. They read:

> In the above referenced case, Ohio v. Metz, the following open court and chambers meetings were recorded.... Please identify, by name and address, the corresponding shorthand reporters for each of the above referenced sessions.... Thank you in advance for your prompt assistance herein.

My letters flushed out the unknown attorney. Richard B. Reiling was prepared to file a brief for my appeal, and I did not know he had been appointed to do so! I learned of Reiling's appointment via his response.

> Dear Mr. Metz:
>
> As you are aware this office has been appointed to represent you in connection with the above captioned matter. At this point however, there seems to be substantial confusion as to whether you wish this office to proceed with your appeal or you wish to continue representing yourself *pro se*. Be advised that this office is in possession of a complete transcript of your case and would gladly forward the same to your attention in the event that you wish to pursue your own appeal. As I will be out of the office from August 1 to August 15, 1997, please contact me by writing immediately upon receipt of this letter to give me your decision so I can promptly notify or have a member of my office notify the Court of Appeals. Time is of the essence.
>
> Thank you for your kind attention to this matter. This office will respect any decision that you make in connection with the same.
>
> Very truly yours,
> RICHARD B. REILING
> Attorney at Law

Reiling enclosed a Motion To Extend Time To File Brief, along with an accompanying affidavit. I believed he perjured himself in an accompanying affidavit.

> 2. Affiant further states that on or about May 10, 1997, Affiant notified said Defendant, by letter, of his said representation.

Number "2" of Reiling's affidavit seemed intentionally dishonest. I knew Reiling sent no such letter to me. My kidnappers knew I would have simply demanded that he dismiss himself.

However, I could not *prove* that Reiling never sent a letter to me. I could only prove I never received it. Legal mail was handled separately from other mail; was not handed out in the units. It was signed for.

The prison kept a log of all legal mail inmates received. And I obtained a copy of that log. There was *no record* of a letter from Reiling. But there was a record of an Entry from Judge Gilvary that day! Nothing from Gilvary referred to Reiling's appointment.

I had no intention of permitting Reiling to meddle further in my affairs, but I saw an opportunity to attempt to gain more information about the *fix* that was on. In the faint hope that I could review the appellate brief Reiling had prepared in my case, I wrote his office staff on August 4th.

> Dear Mr. Reiling:
>
> Until I received your letter on July 31, 1997, I was *unaware* that your office had been appointed to represent me on the appeal. I was as surprised as you folks obviously are.
>
> Let me assure you that being a pro se hasn't always been easy, and I was glad to receive your letter!
>
> Since time is of the essence, and since I couldn't reply prior to August 1st, I'm asking for the assistance of staff. Please send me:
>
> 1. A time-stamped copy of the court order appointing you as counsel.

2. A copy of the brief referenced in #3 and #6 of the affidavit enclosed with your letter.

My review prior to Mr. Reiling's return will allow me to communicate in an intelligent manner, after the 15th.

Thank you for your assistance herein.

I hit the jackpot via an August 13, 1997 letter from Attorney Reiling's office. A copy of the appellate brief Reiling prepared was not sent to me. But a form read:

THE ENCLOSED *Appointment of Counsel* IS FOR YOUR INFORMATION AND FILE.

It was an April 30, 1997 Order from the court of appeals. It read:

APPOINTMENT OF COUNSEL

It appearing to the court that appellant, Horace Ray Metz, is indigent and qualified for legal representation at State's expense, and upon due consideration thereof, IT IS HEREBY ORDERED that attorney **Richard B. Reiling, Jr., at BIRT, WALSH, SIMMONS & ENSLEY, 643 Warren Street, Dayton, Ohio 45409,** is appointed to represent appellant for the sole purpose of this appeal to this court....

IT IS SO ORDERED.

FREDERICK N. YOUNG Presiding Judge

JAMES A. BROGAN, Judge

I learned, *seventy-five days after-the-fact,* Attorney Reiling had been appointed by Second District Court of Appeals Judge Jim Brogan. (Presiding Judge Young was uninvolved, as he signed all decisions and entries from other appellate judges.) Judge Brogan had taken it upon himself to see that my appeal was limited to the issue of *the sentence* imposed by Judge Gilvary.

Just how great were the chances it would be prostituted? At the same time the incorrigible Judge Brogan appointed Reiling - a rookie attorney thirteen days shy of having one year in practice - to *fix* the appeal;

Reiling represented David A. Stanley, a former Miamisburg policeman; involving a $5,000,000 civil suit against Miamisburg officials.

Jackpot time! Stanley's civil case was assigned to Judge Gilvary, my kidnapper! *Quid pro quo* is Latin, meaning in essence: You scratch my back; I'll scratch yours.

Stanley alleged he was coerced into retiring; after reporting irregularities within the police department. In the beginning, Miamisburg Municipal Court led others into the clutches of Metz; and in the end, Miamisburg would pay for doing so.

How much of a settlement had Gilvary promised in Stanley's case, for compromising my appeal? It cannot be determined. But one thing was ascertainable.

It was a most fortuitous opportunity for any young attorney; willing to unconscionably betray me. While I intuitively *knew* Reiling agreed to compromise my appellate rights; it could not be proven.

George Patricoff wrote in his Charles Manson-like motion that I had:

> ... a pathological focus on...the City of Miamisburg" and had "weaved in [his] mind a conspiratorial web of persecution encompassing the whole criminal judicial system.

Well, just as with Kinane; Patricoff's *pathological focus* was back again! I wrote Reiling August 14, 1997:

> Dear Mr. Reiling:
> Upon consideration of the circumstances involved in my case, it is respectfully demanded that you withdraw as appointed counsel. I must continue to represent myself as a pro se defendant.
> In that regard, please send me the complete transcript, court filings, and records of the case, in your possession.
> Thank you in advance for your prompt assistance herein.

Attorney Reiling replied to me on August 18, 1997:

Thank you for your recent letter in connection with the above captioned matter.... As you have been determined to be indigent, the State will be billed for my services to date. Please be advised however, that pursuant to your request, this office will take no further steps to represent you in connection with this or any other matter. Best of luck to you.

Reiling was paid $366.32 for work done in my case. In his affidavit, he swore under oath to have prepared an appellate brief; and had been ready to file it. His modest bill was a testament that he limited my appeal to one issue; the *length* of my sentence. By doing so, he would have had to ignore over twenty constitutional appealable issues, involving repeated violations of the 1st, 4th, 5th, 6th, 8th, and 14th Amendments.

A settlement was eventually reached in Stanley's lawsuit. The terms were never made public. It was assuredly lower than he would have received; had Reiling succeeded in "appealing" my case.

Reiling sent those precious transcripts to me. I finally held irrefutable *proof* that Judge Gilvary had judicial knowledge of my innocence – prior to trial.

August 27, 1997, I filed an appellate motion seeking more time to prepare a brief. Judges on the court of appeals had ignored Reiling's motion for his removal from the case, to date. They could not ignore *my* filing. I received a Decision and Entry:

...Upon due consideration of the foregoing, IT IS HEREBY ORDERED that said motions are Granted. Attorney Richard B. Reiling is hereby ordered withdrawn as counsel for appellant. Appellant shall represent himself *pro se* in this matter from this point forward.

IT IS SO ORDERED.

FREDERICK N. YOUNG, Presiding Judge

WILLIAM H. WOLFF, JR., Judge

Trial judge, Jim Gilvary and appellate judge, Jim Brogan enticed a young attorney into whoredom. Just as I had once freed Attorney John Kolesar; I freed the inexperienced, but opportunistic Richard B. Reiling.

I remembered the Biblical story of Silas and Paul being cast into prison; in Acts 16:

> 23: And when they had laid many stripes upon them, they cast *them* into prison, charging the jailor to keep them safely:
>
> 24: Who, having received such a charge, cast them into the inner prison, and made their feet fast in the stocks.
>
> 25: And at midnight Paul and Silas prayed, and sang praises unto God: and the prisoners heard them.
>
> 26: And suddenly there was a great earthquake, so that the foundations of the prison were shaken: and immediately, all the doors were opened, and every one's bands were loosed.
>
> 27: And the keeper of the prison awakening out of his sleep, and seeing the prison doors open, he drew out his sword, and would have killed himself, supposing that the prisoners had been fled.
>
> 28: But Paul cried out with a loud voice, saying, Do thyself no harm: for we are all here.

Paul saved the warden - from himself. I did the same for the soul of one Richard Reiling. But the story goes on, as did mine. And the decisions of Paul in prison provided the model for my next step.

> 35: And when it was day, the magistrates sent the serjeants, saying, Let these men go.
>
> 36: And the keeper of the prison told this saying to Paul, The magistrates have sent to let you go: now therefore depart, and go in peace.
>
> 37: But Paul said unto them, They have beaten us openly uncondemned, being Romans, and have cast *us* into prison; and now do they thrust us out privily? Nay verily; but let them come themselves and fetch us out.

The Perfect Crime had been clever; too clever. But one key factor was overlooked. My cooperation had not been needed to cast me into prison. But once Gilvary had done so, it was impossible to free me without it.

Such cooperation could only be attained by Gilvary caving in; and admitting *his crime* – kidnapping and extortion. Would he willingly take my place in an Ohio prison; to be freed from his prison of the psyche?

Would the coward react much as Paul's captors did, in Acts 16?

> 38: And the serjeants told these words unto the magistrates: and they feared, when they heard that they were Romans.
>
> 39: And they came, and besought them, and brought *them* out, and desired *them* to depart out of the city.
>
> 40: And they went out of the prison...

No, Gilvary would never react as the magistrates did in Biblical times. He would rather take his chances.

As I sat in prison, it seemed ironic to me. I had no way of knowing what the magistrates' fate would have been, had they failed to free Paul.

At the same time; I intuitively knew what lay ahead for Gilvary. His fate was predestined. He would die.

For it was the Romans who wrote, so long ago:

> Judici satis poena est,
> quod Deum haste ultoren.

Like the Biblical Paul, I would sing *praises unto God* from prison. For translated, the Latin phrase reads:

> *It is punishment enough for a judge*
> *to have God as his avenger.*

September 8, 1997 was the day I finally gained control over my destiny. It was my 200th day in captivity.

It was also my *200th day of freedom,* with a life-time left to savor. And I would never turn back.

CHAPTER THIRTY-TWO

Drawing Dead

On Monday, October 6, 1997, I was scheduled for a second parole hearing. (Completed records sent from Montgomery County raised an issue of accountability. Why was I imprisoned?) I walked the one-forth mile cinder track for hours on end, once the hearing was scheduled. If I turned down shock parole, I was stuck in prison for the remainder of my sentence.

It was not simply my sentence to consider; it affected my wife and our extended families. But for me it was a decision that was never in doubt; acceptance of shock parole involved an admission of guilt.

Still, this was not accepted causally. Though I made the best of it, prison was not a desirable place to be. I discussed the legal ramifications with my sister.

Karen agreed with my reasoning; admitting guilt was never an alternative. I did not feel it fair to ask Ann.

It is one thing to decide on a course of action in theory; and quite another to actually carry it out. But I believed there was a purpose in my journey; one that transcended my personal discomfort. And so, I walked and walked the cinder track immersed in quiet reflection; mentally and spiritually preparing myself for the consequential meeting with the parole board.

Finally, I went to the prison's multi-purpose building with other inmates, and we waited our turns to be called before different parole panels, consisting of from one to three parole board members.

As I waited impatiently, I said to the motherly corrections officer, who worked in the lobby of the library adjacent to the hearing rooms, "I wish they would hurry up. My wife and mother are waiting for me in the visiting room."

The officer looked at me and asked in indignation, "Well, what's more important to you – a visit, or the parole board?"

"I don't think you understand. My wife and mother *love* me," I observed with a grin.

When my turn came after a wait of over an hour, the parole board member spent fifteen minutes filling out paperwork. I observed him through a glass window. Finally he beckoned me inside.

"Mr. Metz, the record in your case is now complete, and we can continue with a hearing for shock parole in your case."

"That's fine, sir."

"Tell me a little about how you ripped these victims off."

"I don't mean to be disrespectful, sir, but I do not wish to discuss the case with you. This matter will be resolved through the courts. I will not accept shock parole, if you offer it to me."

The man who erroneously believed my future was in his hands; raised a hand to silence me, responding, "Enough said. I don't need anything more."

He jotted some notes on his paperwork and handed me a copy. "Good luck to you, Mr. Metz," he offered as the brief session ended.

He had printed under Reason:

> *Inmate does not want shock parole – did not wish to discuss the case, said it would be resolved in court.   multiple victims   amount of restitution   prior record.*
> *Shock par den, A1, A2, A4 (Inmate's request).*

On a Parole Board Risk Assessment/Aggregate Score form, I had received four points for "Alcohol Usage Problems – Frequent abuse; serious disruption; needs treatment."

That absurd conclusion was to "pad" my score. I had enjoyed continuous sobriety since December 2, 1983, when I had begun treatment at Green Hall in Xenia, Ohio.

I deserved the four points given me for having been placed on probation for misdemeanor check charges in 1986. But even with padding, a convicted felon with a "risk assessment" of eight points should never have been imprisoned to begin with.

I was not the typical prison inmate. I had only four points; yet I appeared before a confounded parole officer, rejecting proffered "freedom."

Like the Biblical Paul; my posture was: Gilvary put me here; only he can free me - if he deems it prudent. October 6, 1997 was my 228th day of confinement.

This ended all hearings with the parole board. I had just made a commitment to serve *another* 1,233 days.

There was no celebration during the visit with Mother and Ann. But the three of us bonded in a renewed commitment. My family was completely supportive of me; and would remain so!

Refusing shock parole gave me a kind of celebrity status with certain inmates. I was an older white guy who volunteered to remain in prison, to illuminate the injustices too many prisoners experienced. Most, who looked up to me; never learned of my personal reasons for refusing to capitulate to a kidnapper's demands.

Some white inmates I associated with had condescending attitudes towards backs. Though they would try to hide it, I saw their disdain in being forced to live amongst the perceived "dregs" of society.

They viewed me to be a misguided old man, suffering from some kind of persecution complex. There was nothing I could offer to sanctimonious whites. So with few exceptions, I circulated among black inmates who were looking for direction.

Prison is a testament to two social endeavors that have been colossal failures, with devastating societal results; the War on Poverty and the War on Drugs. The first had a liberal genesis that attacked the family unit; the second a conservative one, attacked minorities born outside a traditional family unit, with unconscionable disparate criminal sentences.

An inmate from Cleveland summed up the effects. "My father was a drug dealer who went to prison after I was born. My mother became a crack-whore to support us. So I'm in prison, in my mid-thirties, trying to learn how to live life by principles I never even knew existed."

I saw the fear many felt, as parole approached and they faced returning to the environment that had put them in prison. Whenever possible, I tried to reach out to those inmates.

A young inmate I befriended asked, "Mr. Metz, you refer to us as 'black.' We are African Americans, *Old School.* Why do you do that?"

"I'm glad you ask. You refer to me as, *Old School.* The label is not disrespectful. But if I were to refer to you as, *No School,* that would be very disrespectful. For me, calling another citizen an African American is very, very disrespectful – unless you were born in Africa, came here, and became an American citizen."

"But how is it disrespectful?" the inmate wanted to know.

"It is a very personal thing with me; that conjures memories from a shameful past. Let me tell you a story.

"When I was a little boy, eight years old, we went on a family vacation to Florida. Dad stopped at a Florida gas station. I went to a fountain and began drinking water. The gas station owner yelled at my father in alarm, 'Get that kid away from there before a nigger sees him!'

"I was an innocent little boy, who drank from a fountain marked COLORED. I lost some of my innocence that day. Dad told me not to worry; I hadn't done anything wrong. But I did worry.

"I gained a new awareness, at a very young age. And I was ashamed of white people who used such vile and derogatory language, when referring to another human being.

"Inflammatory racial terms were commonplace when I was growing up. And one of the terms I disliked most was referring to black Americans as 'jungle bunnies.' So for me personally, I am uncomfortable using the term African American. But if that's how you express your pride in your ancestry; I certainly respect it, because I respect you."

"Cool, *Old School,*" the young inmate offered. "I respect you too, Mr. Metz. I'm sure glad I got to know you."

"I feel the same way. And we'll continue on, getting to know each other, and become better friends."

"You want to be friends, Mr. Metz?"

"You *are* my friend; my young black American friend, who is proud to recognize his African ancestry."

"Cool, *Old School.*"

"You're a smart young man. Study things like the writings of Dr. Martin Luther King, Jr.; the lives of men like Supreme Court justices, Thurgood Marshall and Clarence Thomas; or the poetry of Paul Laurence Dunbar."

"Who is he, Mr. Metz?"

"I'm from Dayton, home of the Wright Brothers who invented the airplane. Paul Dunbar was a classmate of Orville Wright. He was the son of former slaves, and became one of the first black poets to gain national prominence."

"How do you know so much, *Old School?*"

"I really don't know that much, but I read a lot. And you can too. There's a whole world out there, just waiting to be discovered. And anyone can discover its treasures."

"What kind of poems did Dunbar write, *Old School?*"

"Let's go to the library, and I'll show you. And while we're there, I'll help you get started on a great new adventure!"

On the way to the library, I explained other things to the young black inmate. The issue of stereotyping was addressed obliquely.

"What do you know about Republicans?" I asked.

"They're racists!" came an immediate response.

"Do you think I'm a racist?"

"Of course you're not, *Old School.* Why would you ask that?"

"Because I'm a Republican," I confided, to the bewilderment of my young friend.

Once in the library, I found a book of poetry. "Here's one I bet you'll like. It was written by Paul Dunbar."

We Wear the Mask

We wear the mask that grins and lies,
It hides our cheeks and shades our eyes--
This debt we pay to human guile;
With torn and bleeding hearts we smile
And mouth with myriad subtleties.

Why should the world be over-wise,
In counting all our tears and sighs?
Nay, let them only see us while
We wear the mask.

We smile, but oh great Christ, our cries
To Thee from tortured souls arise.
We sing, but oh the clay is vile
Beneath our feet, and long the mile;
But let the world dream otherwise,
We wear the mask!

The young black inmate began reading. We would often discuss his discoveries. And like so many things, both good and bad; the more he indulged, the more he wanted too. It was exciting to observe the voracious appetite he unleashed.

My inner circle of older black inmates understood me. But others took issue with the stature gained with some younger blacks. One acted out in anger.

I was lying on my bunk one day, and a frustrated inmate, apparently threatened by my relationships, stood over me.

"Get up, Metz!" he demanded.

I looked up at him, and asked calmly, "What for?"

"I'm gonna beat your sorry ass! That's what for. *Get up!*"

"I'll stay right here," I responded in a calm voice.

"*I said get up, chicken-shit!*" he snarled, shaking in anger.

"If I get up, you're just going to knock me back down on my ass. So why bother? Besides, I might hurt myself while falling."

"*Get up! Damn you, get up!*" He implored.

"This will make a better story to take home to the 'hood. 'I beat up an old white man, while he was lying on his bunk.' Now, either get too beatin' or get the hell away from me," I said with a straight face; but heart throbbing out-of-control.

Other black inmates observing us began laughing, as the frustrated inmate walked away. He was not a bad person. I knew he distrusted all whites, and was very suspicious of my motives in befriending young blacks.

Later, he complained to me, "You put me 'out there' in front of my friends."

"No, you put yourself out there," I corrected. "Look, I share your concern for young black inmates. I only want to help some of them avoid coming back to this hell-hole."

"You really mean it, don't you?" he asked in amazement.

"With all my heart," I said sincerely, as we shook hands, a bond of mutual respect established.

"I want you to understand something else. Most of us are preconditioned, to think a certain way.

"I attempt to get my younger friends to think for themselves, not buy into a way of thinking I espouse.

"So when I ask them if they know *why*, when the prison celebrates Black History Month, a notable like U.S. Supreme Court Justice Clarence Thomas is ignored, it is not being disrespectful or racist. It is not disparaging the celebration. *Who* decides that Thomas, one of only nine citizens to be so honored with a lifetime appointment, does not qualify for inclusion?

"Prison is a place where the human failure of each of us is seen. But it is also a place where the failures of society are just as evident. And it seems to me, as a white man, that the lives of men like Clarence Thomas are so inspirational; so motivating, that young black men would be well served by learning about them.

"To discourage open-mindedness is a disservice. You and I have a common goal. I may be the first and only white man some will ever associate with. Certainly, I could be the first Republican. Removing stereotypes from their mindset is not meant to be disrespectful of you, or any other black man."

We bonded that day, in a unique way. Though we could never look at life through the same window, we saw each other with an enlightened insight. Neither of us felt the other was a threat to his wellbeing.

Prison is a hostile environment. Holidays are an especially difficult time. Prison officials did their best to alleviate loneliness and isolation during these times. Thanksgiving and Christmas dinners were special, by prison standards. The first featured turkey and all the trimmings; and the latter steak.

But regardless of the efforts, *the walls closed* in on many. A few acted out in violence. My first Christmas in prison, two inmates were intimidated by another. One night, they waited until the instigator fell asleep. With four locks from inmates' footlockers placed in a pillowcase, they savagely attacked him.

Beaten unconscious before security guards could be alerted, the inmate was rushed to the hospital. He never returned. The attackers were placed in the Hole, and later transferred to another institution.

Another time, an inmate took exception to the unsolicited celebrity I received. He began harassing me, in innocuous ways. The inmate had a tough reputation, and I ignored his attention. He did things like open the window, allowing a cold draft to hit my bunk. He poured water on the edges of my legal papers, ruining them in the process.

Matters escalated. Finally, he made remarks about my sister - after seeing her picture. He would assert that once freed, he was going to *date* Karen.

His meaning was clear. There are certain unspoken rules of conduct in prison. This violated one of them.

One day he opened the window while Kevin Roser and I played chess. Cold air rushed in. I asked the troubled inmate to close the window. He refused.

I made a comment about visiting him, once I was released from prison. He replied that I would never be welcome in his home. And I pounced.

"I may never get into your home, once I am released. I'll just go up into your wife!"

The stunned inmate was paid back for untoward remarks about my sister. In spades. Roser watched in shocked disbelief.

I quickly apologized; stating that I should not have blurted out the comment. Oh, and by the way, would you please close the window? My friend is cold. Close it yourself, came the response.

I got up, closed the window, and apologized again. *I don't know what came over me. I am sincerely sorry. I assure you; it will never happen again.* The unspoken message was: *Cut the crap about my sister!*

The inmate was out for revenge. Thwarted about referring to my sister, he looked for other means of harassment. My bunk was in the center of the bay, close to the entrance to the showers. Unknown to me; he proposed moving my bunk, supposedly to free the shower area of traffic. A sergeant okayed the change.

Entering the bay for count time, I discovered my bunk had been moved. The inmate confronted me, asserting *he had moved my things*. The move was approved, and there was nothing I could do about it. The hell there wasn't, I responded.

This violated another rule. You never, ever touch another man's possessions without his permission. Ever.

I sought out the sergeant who gave the inmate permission to move my bunk, and raised seven kinds of hell. If allowed to get away with this, his next escalation would be to beat my ass; before he left prison.

The sergeant had been unaware of matters between the inmate and me. Why had I not reported it? This is not junior high school, I reminded him. Because I did not want an ass-kicking, I patiently explained.

The inmate came back to the bay that afternoon, found my bunk in its former location, and confronted me. This move had been approved. I had no authority to move it back. I informed the inmate he had no credibility with the officer, once I explained matters properly. The inmate lost face; was put on notice. Stay the hell away from me, or risk an immediate *Hole shot*. That would count against his impending parole.

That night I fell into a deep and peaceful sleep. My nemesis lay within eyesight; unable to sleep. About one o'clock I was awakened, to find the inmate was being rushed to med-bay. He had an uncontrollable nose bleed. Blood was everywhere, on his bunk and the floor next to it. He was immediately transported to a hospital in Columbus.

Word came back that it was suspected he had had a stroke. Others, who feared the problematic inmate, speculated I was probably happy with his condition.

I explained to the men; I wished the troubled inmate no harm. He was not really a bad person. I hoped he had not suffered a stroke; and wished him well.

The wall close in on all of us, at times, I explained. *We all act out differently, due to our past lives.* I did not judge the inmate for doing so; but only wanted to set acceptable boundaries, as he related to me.

The inmate was fortunate. Extremely high blood pressure caused the nose bleed. But he had not suffered a stroke. He was on best behavior once he returned to the bay. At night I could hear him mutter, "I can't let Metz get too me. I must remain calm. I must remain calm. I must remain calm."

He was released from prison as scheduled; without further incident. I was glad to see him go; for both out sakes!

Kevin Roser was the friend who witnessed my untoward comments to the troubled inmate. On the outside Kevin owned a mortgage company, and was very, very successful. His route to prison involved pleading guilty to securities law violations.

In prison, Kevin was a typical white Republican; out of his element. He lacked any sense of street-smarts.

I was often dismayed at situations Kevin got himself into. He was sent to the Hole for investigation on two occasions; once for allegedly having a shank.

It was a laughable charge, for my prison friend to face. A shank had been planted in his jacket that hung at his bunk. An anonymous letter described exactly where to find it. Though quickly cleared of the charges, Roser had endured two trips to the Hole for a condensing involvement with black inmates; comprehended to be his inferiors.

Prison was especially difficult for inmates like Roser. He tried to fit in with the less educated; the less accomplished, but did not really know how to do so. He failed to see there were many with bright minds, who only lacked formal education. He failed to comprehend the two were not synonymous.

The very best educated people in the nation, given all of life's advantages, had put me in prison. But they were incapable of thinking things through. And that was not particularly bright.

Whatever Roser had done on the streets, he was able to keep his mortgage licenses, and looked forward to picking up his business activities upon release.

He and Bishop added a lot to my prison experience. They were two of only a few white inmates, considered to be friends. All my other prison friends were black.

On many occasions, I saw genuine compassion from prison guards, case workers and instructors; for inmates of all persuasions, attempting to better themselves. A prime example of someone who reached out, beyond her role as a security officer, was Ms. Gossett. She was the daughter of a minister.

Gossett regularly took young black inmates aside, and counseled them. She implored them to "stop being stupid" and "start using their heads." At the same time, I observed she could be hard-assed when the occasion called for it.

One day an inmate came limping into the security office. "Metz, call med-bay! I sprained my ankle."

"You know inmates can't call med-bay. Gossett is downstairs. I'll call for her on the intercom. And please wait outside; you know what she'll say if she sees you in here."

Gossett impatiently asked the inmate, known to be a malingerer, "What's wrong with you now?"

"I need to go to med-bay. I sprained my ankle playing softball."

"That's what you get, out there, acting like a damn fool. I'm not calling med-bay. Get on back to your bunk."

"Ms. Gossett; please, I need to go to med-bay!" the inmate pleaded.

"Shit!" Gossett exclaimed in disdain. "What would you do at home? You'd have a few beers and go to bed.

Now get your ass back in your bay, drink a cup of warm piss and crawl in your bunk."

"Ms. Gossett!"

"And don't be such a damn fool, next time."

The inmate limped off, and Gossett said to me with a grin, "Metz, you don't think he was really hurt, do you? That's how the slackers like to try and play me."

"Hell no, he probably thought he could get out of working in the kitchen in the morning."

"Exactly," Gossett agreed.

If forced to put up with prisoner ignorance every day, as a security officer, there is no way I could have kept my job. I have no prejudices, with one exception. I can't stand a dumb ass. And I especially can't stand a dumb ass with a chip on his shoulder. There were plenty of inmates like that, among the 2,200+ I served time with. It has nothing to do with education.

Prison had its share of whiners and complainers. When an inmate would unjustly whine to me about mistreatment, or about the food, I would often reply curtly, "Next time, stay at the Hilton."

Mentioning food reminds me of the time friends got the better of me. Twice a year Reuben sandwiches were served. This was a favorite meal among inmates.

The cafeteria was set up to serve 5-600 inmates at a time. There were service lines on each side.

The three units were released for meals at staggered times; on a rotating basis. Inmates would eat, leave the cafeteria, and sneak back into the other line.

"Come on, Metz. Let's go back and get another Reuben."

"No. You know I don't do that. I obey the rules. It's not worth risking a trip to the Hole."

"Come on, chicken-shit. It's time you learned how to live a little. I know you want another Reuben."

With trepidation, I acquiesced. Inmates proclaimed their satisfaction with me. I was one of the boys!

Later I was lying on my bunk, and heard a female officer bellow from the hallway, "Metz! Get out here!"

I went to see what she wanted. It seems they had been watching the cafeteria with binoculars. And I had been caught going back through the food line. I was going to the Hole.

"Hands against the wall, Metz." I was patted down. "Put your hands behind your back so I can cuff you."

I believed her until I turned a little, as my hands went behind my back. I saw everyone behind her; working to contain their laughter. The officer burst out laughing. They had pulled a good one on me! And I laughed along with them.

I prepared an appellate brief that would have been filed, under normal circumstances. For brevity, it was limited to eleven Assignments of Error.[33] Any one of the eleven, chosen from more than twenty, standing alone could have overturned my conviction. That is, *if* I had any place to appeal to.

Instead of filing the brief, on October 8, 1997, my sister-in-law, Diane Metz filed a Motion To Withdraw Appeal for me.

Now comes the Defendant/Appellant, pro se, before the Court in a motion to withdraw the appeal in the above-captioned case for reasons set forth in the accompanying memorandum of fact.

MEMORANDUM

The motion before the Court is to withdraw the Defendant's appeal at this time.

On September 8, 1997, the Court recognized the Defendant's *pro se* status and granted the Defendant until October 8, 1997 to file a brief.

---

[33] The appellate brief is available at no charge via email, by writing to me at: raymetz@live.com.

A review of the docket statement and transcripts forwarded to the Defendant by the former court appointed counsel
(without defendant's knowledge) revealed that (1) the transcripts were *incomplete* and (2) the official record had been
tampered with. Shades of civil cases involving the Defendant
that preceded this matter!

The Defendant has found inspiration, wisdom, guidance,
and solace from the Apostle Paul's resolution, when faced
with a similar difficulty while amongst barbarians (Acts 28:3-
5), and was thereby moved to verse and song, as follows, as
referenced: *"... there came a viper out of the heat, and fas-
tened on his hand.... And he shook off the beast into the fire,
and felt no harm."*

Res Judicata

Res judicata, how beautiful her name;
Res judicata, the viper from the flame.
She strikes at the hand that holds the pen,
To kill the words that flow,
From the hearts of noble men.
Though she's sly, and you try,
You cannot win.
He'll shake her off;
You'll pay the cost,
And fall to pieces.
-To the music of "I Fall To Pieces"[34]

Inasmuch as *res judicata* is much easier to avoid than to
shake off, the Defendant finds it imprudent to pursue an appeal brief until such time as he has the means to effectively
do so.

WHEREFORE, the Defendant MOVES the Court to
acknowledge that his appeal is withdrawn without prejudice
at this time.

---

[34] "I Fall To Pieces" was written by Hank Cochran; released by Patsy
Cline in 1961. It became her first #1 hit.

The court responded with humorless insight. *Jurisdictional requirements* were given as the reason my appeal could not be dismissed *without prejudice.*

> This matter came on the be considered upon a motion filed by appellant, Horace Ray Metz, *pro se*, on October 8, 1997, requesting leave to withdraw the above-captioned appeal "without prejudice."
>
> This court cannot dismiss appeals "without prejudice" due to the jurisdictional requirements of filing an appeal within thirty (30) days of the final entry being appealed. Accordingly, appellant must either pursue the current appeal at this time *pro se* or move to have the appeal voluntarily dismissed, with prejudice, pursuant to App.R.28.
>
> Upon due consideration of the foregoing, IT IS HEREBY ORDERED that appellant shall have thirty (30) additional days to either file a *pro se* brief in the above-captioned appeal or request voluntary dismissal, with prejudice, pursuant to App.R. 28. The failure of appellant to either file a brief or request voluntary dismissal within thirty (30) days will result in the dismissal of this action for failure to prosecute.
>
> IT IS SO ORDERED.
> FREDERICK N. YOUNG, Presiding Judge
> WILLIAM H. WOLFF, JR., Judge

On November 21, 1997, my sister-in-law, Diane Metz filed a second Motion To Withdraw Appeal.

> Now comes the Defendant-Appellant, pro se, before the Court in a motion to withdraw the appeal in the above-captioned case pursuant to Rule 28.
>
> The Court's November 3, 1997 Decision and Entry recognizes that there are rules of procedure to be followed that apply to *this* Appellant's cases. That acknowledgment comes as too little, too late.
>
> From the trial transcript on February 18, 1997, in chambers just prior to jury selection Judge Gilvary admitted:

You see, what's happened here since June of '94, is people have been dragged into something that should never have happened. If due process had been followed in civil matters, we wouldn't be sitting here, but they weren't.

That Judge Gilvary chose not to assure Appellant due process in criminal matters, after such an admission, is more than troubling and suggests that he was "ordered" from on high to assure a conviction. That issue shall be resolved elsewhere.

Let it be said that the Court's unauthorized appointment of Attorney Richard B. Reiling; and the keeping of his appointment from the Appellant, has prolonged a false imprisonment by many months. Appellant views this as little more than a blatant obstruction of justice that shall also be resolved elsewhere.

Appellant's demand for withdraw of this appeal "without prejudice" was deliberate. In Title 25 under Rule 28 is a lone case reference; the Second District Court of Appeals 1993 decision in *Davis Montcco Landfill Co. v. Jefferson Twp. Zoning Comm.*, 630 N.E.2d 140. The synopsis reads: "A court of appeals has discretion to deny an appellant's motion for voluntary dismissal."

The case addresses the issue of a frivolous appeal, and that was the basis for dismissing Appellant's civil cases numbered 14863 and 15023 and the motivation for pursuit of criminal charges against him. In short, it was a very stupid thing to do.

Montgomery County has been permitted to establish "local rules." One would like to believe that would foster greater responsibility among practitioners. It seems, however, that given that authority has become equated to becoming "local rulers." That leap leads to repeated problems such as appellant has faced.

Mahoning County patterned its "local rules" after Montgomery County. A fraud and government corruption probe involving the FBI is presently addressing those derelict in duty. As a result Youngstown Municipal Court Judge Kerrigan faces a potential reward in excess of one hundred years in prison and two million dollars in fines. From newspaper accounts, Judge Kerrigan's crimes pale in comparison to what Appellant has been subjected too.

Appellant has no confidence in this Court. No judge presently sitting thereon shall ever be permitted to pervert another matter. Period.

This Court has *no discretion* in the matter before it.

WHEREFORE, Appellant *DEMANDS* that this appeal be dismissed *immediately* upon review of this motion! [Emphasis added.]

On December 2, 1997, the appellate court finally issued a Decision and Entry.

PER CURIAM:

This matter came to be considered upon the filing of a motion to withdraw by appellant, Horace Ray Metz, *pro se*, on November 21, 1997. Appellant has requested voluntary dismissal of the above-captioned appeal pursuant to App.R.28.

Upon due consideration of the foregoing, IT IS HEREBY ORDERED that appellant's request for voluntary dismissal pursuant to App.R. 28 is **Granted**. The above-captioned appeal is hereby **Dismissed** with prejudice and with all costs taxed to appellant.

IT IS SO ORDERED.

FREDERICK N. YOUNG, Presiding Judge

WILLIAM H. WOLFF, JR., Judge

In prison that fateful December 2nd, I celebrated my oldest son, Jeffrey Alan's thirty-first birthday. And it was also the anniversary of my fourteenth year of continuous sobriety from alcoholism.

According to the *Dayton Daily News*, December 2nd became significant for another reason. It was also the day the twin broadcast towers were dismantled at the Voice of America relay station near Mason, Ohio. It was where I had been sexually attacked in the middle of the night in 1961, by Professor Sherrill Wilkes. It was where I wound up, the day I met Judge Gilvary.

One of two Voice of America towers

For all who had paid their entry fee, and had sat at the table, in both the *secular* and *spiritual* world series of poker; the two of us remained. The finalists were the judge and the abuse victim, in the secular world; and the prisoner and his warden, in the spiritual world.

We were playing the highest-stakes poker game imaginable. Unless Gilvary folded in the secular game; he faced a certain death in the spiritual one.

It was Shakespearean! To be freed from the secular prison; I had to confess. But to be freed from his prison in the spiritual world; Gilvary had to confess.

Gilvary had to become willing to take my place, in the secular prison he cast me into. He had to do so; just as I had willingly done so!

Cards had been dealt – except for the final card, *on the river.* And my prisoner was *drawing dead.*[35] Local Rule 1.19 III(C) represented the three common cards on the table. Hole cards gave me a *royal flush.* Judge Gilvary's hole cards gave him *aces and eights.*

---

[35] In Texas Holdem, the final card is called *the river. Drawing dead* meant a player had no chance of winning. Gilvary could hope for a *full house.* But he would still be obliterated - by my *royal flush.*

CHAPTER THIRTY-THREE

Death Row

Once each year, Pickaway Correctional Institution held Yard Day; a summer cookout. Prison employees put it on for inmates.

It was a chance for us to get treats we missed from the outside. Things like hamburgers and hot dogs off the grill, and all the fixings of a normal family reunion. Recreation was planned, just like it would be at home. Inmates enjoyed the day.

I remember standing in the food line, on a weekday in late June, 1997. I did not know the inmate behind me, and as we talked, I offered, "This is a really nice gesture, for us. This is my first Yard Day; three to go."

The inmate replied quietly, "Yes, this is nice. I have been in prison for thirty-five years. And I hope to have more than *three* Yard Days left."

The conversation, with a man I had just met, left me feeling a melancholy sadness. Prison protocol forbids asking what another's crime was, but I could imagine he was there for a long-ago murder.

A man can change, though the consequences of his crime exist forever. Such a man has learned to live in a unique state of freedom.

The State has the physical body for life; but no longer has the mind. Such an inmate has freed himself from a prison of the psyche.

I gained a very different perspective after being incarcerated. Formerly, I was a supporter of the death penalty. Firsthand experience with the abusive power of the State; and living with men serving life-without-parole with quiet dignity, changed me.

As is often noted, *prison changes a man.* I became a more compassionate person.

Dynamics of the dichotomy between Gilvary and me were intriguing. I was willing to accept a sentence in the State's prison, to gain freedom from a prison of the psyche.

But by unjustly casting me into the State's prison, Gilvary turned away from faith in God; desecrating the sanctity of the oath of office he took to Him. He illogically presumed it was *his* courtroom, and in it, the narcissist believed *he* was god.

Fyodor Dostoevsky summed it up very well:

If there is no God, then I am god.

By sentencing me, Gilvary unknowingly condemned himself to *my* former prison of the psyche. He became my kidnapper; fear of disclosure made me his warden!

To accept freedom from the State's prison, on his terms, equated to voluntarily casting myself back into my former prison of the psyche. At the same time it would have set my prisoner free; free to abuse others, without accountability. Hell would freeze over first.

Cicero (106 – 43 B. C.) was the most renowned lawyer, politician and orator in Rome, when the Empire was in decline. He was able to express the workings of a great mind with a special eloquence. For example:

Law is the highest reason, implanted in nature, which commands what ought to be done and forbids the opposite. This reason, when firmly fixed and fully developed in the human mind, is Law....

True law is right reason in agreement with Nature; it is of universal application, unchanging and everlasting; it summons to duty by its commands, and averts from wrongdoing by its prohibitions.... It is a sin to try to alter this law, nor is it allowable to attempt to repeal any part of it, and it is impossible to abolish it entirely. We cannot be freed from its obligations by Senate or People, and we need not look outside ourselves for an expounder or interpreter of it. And there will not be different laws at Rome and at Athens, or different laws now and in the future, but one eternal and unchangeable law will be valid for all nations and for all times, and there will be one master and one ruler, that is God, over us all, for He is the author of this law, its promulgator, and its enforcing judge. Whoever is disobedient is fleeing from himself and denying his human nature, and by reason of this very fact he will suffer the worst penalties...

Cicero wrote about what I refer to as *Universal Laws of Life,* governed by a *Universal Supreme Court* wherein God is *Universal Supreme Court Justice.*

Gilvary may have enjoyed Cicero's intellectual exercises, before he became an ethically challenged judicial whore. But whether or not the demented judge had any inkling of the *laws of life* that governed him - for having taken an oath to God - he was bound by them. Ignorance of laws that govern the universe was of no consequence.

On December 2, 1997, I sat in Pickaway Correctional Institution with another thirty-eight months to serve. But oh, how things had changed!

Gilvary had no further control over me. At the same time, as his warden, I exercised absolute control over the destiny of my prisoner. Confess or die!

By assigning different prosecutors to evolving steps of the process, each could pretend ignorance of the debauchery they collectively perpetrated. Each of them knew the truth, to some degree; and key players knew the whole truth. Prosecutors filed a routine motion in common pleas court, on December 18, 1997.

It took my death row prisoner until January 26th to file a response, for a simple matter. In the interim, he likely consulted with co-conspirators, to no avail. *I'm trapped, just as you once were. What can I do now?*

Hiding behind a deliberately created *ignorance-by-design* strategy did not extend to the trial judge. He was on his own. For me, it was enthrallingly exquisite poetic justice.

George Patricoff had demanded a bond of $250,000 for a theft by deception "crime" totaling $7,040. Gilvary had set bond at $70,000. Now prosecutors forced him to revoke the same bond that had defied the letter and the spirit of the Ohio Revised Code.

> The State of Ohio, through the Office of the Prosecuting Attorney for Montgomery County, and asks this Court to revoke Horace Ray Metz's appeal bond since he has withdrawn his appeal herein and as such appeal bond is no longer applicable.
>
> It is the Order of this Court that the State's December 18, 1997 motion to revoke Defendant's appeal bond is granted as Defendant has dismissed his appeal.
>
> IT IS SO ORDERED.
JUDGE JAMES J. GILVERY

Judge James J. Gilvary had a brilliant mind. He had to intuitively understand the gravity of his perilous position. But still, he would have underestimated the degree of his peril.

By signing the seemingly innocuous order, my prisoner inadvertently accepted his fate! And I transferred my prisoner to death row.

Gilvary's prison of the psyche had no electric chair or lethal injection to carry out the execution; had no hangman's noose or firing squad. No, death would be much less humane. He had become a prime candidate for Cicero's *worst penalties.*

Gilvary was abandoned by those he counted on. Appellate judges Bill Wolff, Mike Fain a.k.a. Mike FAKE, and Jim Brogan weren't there for him.

Assistant Prosecutor George Patricoff could not help him. Assistant prosecutors, Dick Lipowicz and Tom Rauch were long gone from the debacle; and were also useless. Special Prosecutors Bill Schenck, Robert Hendrix, and Craig King remained on the sidelines.

My "defense lawyers," John Kolesar, Frank Malocu, and Richard Reiling were long gone.

Presiding Judge John Kessler, who assigned the case to the kidnapper, never came forward. Likewise, those Kessler assigned prior to Gilvary; Dennis Langer and Barbara Gorman remained mute. The four judges had acted in concert; and all of them knew jurisdiction ended with Gorman. They did nothing.

But most compelling of all, Montgomery County Prosecuting Attorney Mathias H. Heck, Jr. did *nothing*. He did *nothing* to save his life-long friend and mentor.

No one stepped forward to offer assistance to Judge Gilvary. No one! Everyone deserted the judge in his direst hour of need. There was no sense of moral obligation. No sense of honor, or duty was demonstrated; from their collective criminal mindset.

It took an army of judges and prosecutors to illicitly deal with me, and yet ironically, *no one* rescued their would-be rescuer. For me, it confirmed the adage:

There is no honor among thieves.

Yes, Gilvary was all alone; as I conceptualized. In the prison of the psyche, there were no other inmates; there was no visitation. There were only the judge and the sexual abuse victim; the prisoner and his warden.

My prisoner's plight was described in contemporary terms, in an August 4, 1997 filing - from my prison. The motion did not require a response from the Court or prosecutors. It was an assault on Gilvary's psyche.

MEMORANDUM

The matter before the Court is the defense allegation of misconduct of the trial judge.

From the preface of the Code of Judicial Conduct:

This code consists of statements of norms denominated canons, the accompanying text setting forth specific rules, and the commentary, states the standards that judges should observe. The canons and text establish mandatory standards unless otherwise indicated. Applicable canons:

Canon 1   A judge should uphold the integrity and independence of the judiciary.

Canon 2   A judge should avoid impropriety and the appearance of impropriety in all his activities.

Canon 3   A judge should perform the duties of office impartially and diligently.

Canon 4 A judge may engage in activities to improve the law, the legal system, and the administration of justice.

Section 2945.03 of the revised Code, Control of Trial, mandates that the judge "shall control all proceedings" with the objective of "ascertainment of the *truth* regarding matters at issue."

Canon 4 does not provide for the trial judge to *"improve on"* the law, the legal system, or the administration of justice.

It has been written that, "no man is an island." In that respect, no case is an *island* that stands alone. And certainly, no case stands alone with the egregious judicial misconduct as pervasive as is found in this case, going beyond the realm of individual concern, to the whole of societal interest.

No, this case is not an *island.* To more properly place its import in perspective, the Defendant resources Prosecutor Heck's alma mater, the prestigious Georgetown University School of Law.

Writing in the April 1997, edition of the Georgetown Law Journal, Harvard Law School Assistant Professor Carol S. Steiker addressed the issue of "blame" in meting out punishment, and the blurring of the distinction between the civil and the criminal processes. From that fluently written essay entitled "Punishment and Procedure: Punishment Theory and the Criminal – Civil Procedural Divide": [36]

---

[36] Permission to quote was requested via letter to the *Georgetown Law Journal,* without acknowledgment. Since the quotes were pertinent in a court filing I made, permission is assumed under the *fair use* doctrine.

In theory...criminal incarceration occurs in a prison and civil incarceration does not.

... In his essay, "The Expressive Function of Punishment," Feinberg criticized traditional definitions of punishment, noting particularly the words of Flew, Bern, and Hart, for "leav(ing) out of their ken altogether the very element that makes punishment theoretically and morally disquieting." That element, according to Feinberg, is what distinguishes mere penalties or price-tags from true punishments: punishment expresses "attitudes of resentment and indignation" and "judgments of disapproval and reprobation" on the part "of the punishing authority himself" or those in whose name the punishment is inflicted. In short punishment expresses blame, and it is through this expression that we recognize certain action as punishment.

... and according to Driggs, the criminal sanctions present special "political temptations" to government. These temptations go beyond the availability of especially severe consequences like monetary penalties, corporal punishment, and sometimes even death; after all, something approximating these consequences can be obtained through the government's civil powers to tax and fine, quarantine or treat, and conscript into military service. Rather, the criminal process adds to its sanctions the power of what I have called "blaming": These severe sanctions are accompanied not by the reluctance of a sad necessity, but by the self-congratulatory emotion of blame. The convict is held up for hatred as well as confined; the government inflicts pain with a self-conscious attitude of moral superiority. Driggs recognized that this ability to harness the force of blaming represents a particularly threatening aspect of state power, given that the states historically have turned to the criminal sanction both to "disable political opposition" and to express "malice" towards members of identifiable groups...for purely sadistic motives. Thus, we need a special procedural regime to cabin the powerful and frightening "monopoly on the conjunction of blame and force" that the state wields through the criminal process.

... it is important to recognize that what makes the imposition of criminal punishment damaging to individual autonomy is not the fact that criminal punishment often entails substantial loss of property or liberty or sometimes even loss of life....

The thing that makes criminal punishment especially damaging to individual autonomy is the same thing that renders criminal punishment especially attractive to a despotic state: its capacity to harness, reinforce, intensify, and, through repetition, even create attitudes of moral condemnation....

Punishments speak powerfully to the punished.... its capacity to reach inside the self is both potentially valuable and terribly frightening.

... one of the other reasons that special procedural protections are important to blaming is that they limit the state's ability to resort to blaming as a weapon against its political enemies or despised minorities; those procedures must be involved to prohibit a wily state determined to blame from circumventing the criminal process by "rechristening crimes as administrative violations" of some sort. [Emphasis added.]

I reached deep into the inner sanctum of my prisoner's soul. And I confronted him with what he had become, in a second-party manner that was irrefutable.

The damning *blame* Hendrix used in his closing argument would remain in the subconscious:

With two thousand dollars, Mr. Metz, you could have paid them off and you didn't. You bought a car for yourself.

Patricoff's *blame*, found in his Manson-like bond motion, likewise would remain in the subconscious:

[T]his Defendant is suffering from a personality disorder and in reality is a time bomb waiting to explode.

Accustomed to arbitrarily meting out punishment to others in a totalitarian manner; Gilvary had never been exposed to psychic pain. As such, he was amongst the very weakest of the weak. His chances of survival were nonexistent.

And so, paralyzing fear consumed his godless mind. In time, it would spread like an incurable cancer, affecting his aching heart. The soul within my hapless prisoner would cry out in anguish.

In that condition, day after repetitious day, the spirit would weaken, and the will to live would slowly ebb away. He would confide in *no one.* Next premonitions of death would begin to haunt the tortured mind. Physical death would naturally follow.

The prison of the psyche, such as endured by the sexual abuse victim, can be unparalleled in its harshness. Making matters worse, suffering is done in secret; with the victim mostly unaware of the dynamics.

Repetitive trips to the prison's Hole(s) are manifested in the darkest of humanity's baser preoccupations, in fruitless efforts to escape life's realities. In varying degrees, life is a continuous hell-on-earth.

The more fortunate survive; but many others do not. Those not blessed with the strength to endure, too often die a tormented death.

There was only one way for my prisoner to escape a certain fate. *If* he came to terms with himself, and accepted the consequences for his crimes; an appeal - directly to Almighty God - repenting of his sins, would bring clemency; pursuant to *Universal Laws of Life,* as confirmed in John 8:32:

> And ye shall know the truth, and
> the truth shall make you free.

And so, again, the dynamics between Judge Gilvary and me were exquisitely intriguing. In order for the judge to be freed from his prison of the psyche, he had to 'fess up - to kidnapping and extortion - and free me

from the State's prison. But this involved serious consequences for my prisoner.

Gilvary was placed in the position I had been in, pri-
or to conviction. To free himself from the prison of the
psyche, he had to become *willing* to take my place in
the State's prison; as a disgraced former judge.

It was his only hope of avoiding the death sentence.
It was also too much to expect. For he was *god* in his
courtroom! And he revered being seen as such.

Just prior to trial in February 1997, in a motion encouraging a "card shower" for Maria Lowman on Valentine's Day, I ended with:

It's close to *high noon.* I'll see you all at the coral.

The theme song to the 1952 classic movie *High Noon*
was "Do Not Forsake Me." The song was sung by Tex
Ritter; the film starred Gary Cooper, with Grace Kelly.

In the movie, citizens deserted Gary Cooper, in his
hour of greatest need. Here, officers of the court did
the same thing to Judge Gilvary.

Late at night, while lying on my bunk among fifty-
three other inmates, I softly sang two parodies of the
song that had become a part of my American heritage.

Either version will do, I would think as I drifted off,
into a peaceful sleep. *Either version will do...*

I made a vow	I made a vow
While in State's Prison	While in State's Prison
That it would be my	Wouldn't be my
Bunk or his'n	Life but his'n

My prisoner possessed a unique power; could grant
himself clemency. Yes, Gilvary held the hammer Peter,
Paul and Mary sang about.[37] But sadly, he lacked the
wisdom; the character; or the courage to pick it up; as
he languished in solitary confinement on *death row.*

---

[37] "If I Had a Hammer" was written by Peter Seeger and Lee Hays in
1949; rewritten and recorded by Peter, Paul and Mary in 1962.

CHAPTER THIRTY-FOUR

A Street Called Straight

The life of Paul[38] was my favorite story of redemption in the Bible. In prison, it became more compelling.

I support life-without-parole; and oppose the death penalty - except when a condemned man *chooses* to die. As his warden, I respected my prisoner's choices.

I lived as a free man in the State's prison, though I would not be released until February 20, 2001. But Judge Gilvary was not so fortunate. He could not survive until my release.

With that perspective, as his warden, I considered Judge Gilvary with compassion. My prisoner sat on death row, in solitary confinement; after his January 26, 1998 dismissal of my appeals bond - in his prison of the psyche.

As his warden, I spent every possible moment of every day for five months, preparing for the next step in gaining *our* freedom, or preparing for *his* execution.

The next event was filing a motion with the Ohio Supreme Court July 1, 1998. The 1,900+ page, nine volume document, costing $1,680 to print at Kinkos; was a political statement - from a prisoner of war.

---

[38] On the inside flap of his book, *The Mythmaker – Paul and the Invention of Christianity* by British scholar Hyman Maccoby, is written: "Who was the founder of Christianity? The answer seems obvious – Jesus Christ. Yet for Talmudic scholar Hyan Maccoby, this answer is wrong. In *The Mythmaker* – a work of revolutionary import to New Testament scholarship – Maccoby contends that Jesus was no more the founder of Christianity than the historical Hamlet was the author of *Hamlet*. Rather, Christianity was the invention of St. Paul, who used elements of Judaism, Gnosticism, and pagan mystery cults as his material, fusing them around the story of Jesus' crucifixion."

Finally, on June 30, 1998 my sister and brother-in-law, Karen and Ted Lowry, filed a Petition To Vacate Or Set Aside Sentence And Conviction.

Filed in Gilvary's Court in Dayton, it provided the basis for filing the 1,900+ page Affidavit of Disqualification of Judge James J. Gilvary with the Ohio Supreme Court. The implicit message to Ohio Supreme Court Chief Justice Thomas J. Moyer: disqualify him - or I shall.

The following morning Karen and Ted drove to Columbus, and filed the motion. Then they personally served a copy on Gilvary in Dayton; delivered a copy to *Dayton Daily News* reporters; and then served a copy on Special Prosecutors in Xenia.

It had been a busy morning for them. Excerpts from Karen's letter to me described my prisoner's reaction.

> ... The look on Gilvary's face when we gave him the case was priceless. I wonder if they can hold someone in custody for laughing too much.
>
> ... At this time we proceeded to the third floor. Ted is carrying one of the boxes on his shoulder. We get in the elevator and go to the third floor.
>
> We walked down the hallway passing several people and enter Judge Gilvary's outer office. The person who works for him is not behind his desk. Gilvary must hear us from his office and comes out and greets us pleasantly. I told him I had a delivery for Judge Gilvary, pretending to not know who he is. He says that would be me. We hand over the nine volumes of the case to him.
>
> He asks what this is, and I replied, "This is a case that was filed with the Supreme Court of Ohio this morning. We are personally dropping off a copy for you." He asks what it is about and looks at the front cover and OHHHHH! I asked if I got a receipt and he said no. We thanked him and took off out of the office. As soon as we got in the hallway we burst out laughing. We handed this over to him on July 1, 1998 at 1:12 p.m. What a Fourth of July celebration for him.

Before changes in the Ohio Revised Code, a motion for Post Conviction Relief could be filed at any time in the trial court. With *truth in sentencing laws* passed during the time of my conviction; that right was taken away from those convicted; severely limiting the time to only 180 days from the time a trial transcript was requested for an appeal.

The court of appeals dismissed my appeal on the 181st day. While ink was barely dry on the new law; opportunists found a way to pervert it. It was *one day* beyond the new time limit for Post Conviction Relief.

In the prison law library, I read in excess of 100 Affidavit of Disqualification petitions filed in the Ohio Supreme Court. Almost all were overruled by Chief Justice Thomas Moyer.

July 2, 1998, the day after Karen and Ted's filing, an Entry was filed in the Ohio Supreme Court:

> Horace Ray Metz has filed an affidavit seeking the disqualification of Judge James J. Gilvary from further proceedings in the above-captioned case.
>
> ... For these reasons, the affidavit of disqualification is found not well-taken and is denied. The case shall proceed before Judge Gilvary.
>
> Dated this ___2nd___ day of July, 1998.
>
> THOMAS J. MOYER
> Chief Justice

Moyer predictably overruled my petition, which clearly showed a conspiracy between appellate judges and the trial judge. Surprisingly, he ruled in *one day!* Perhaps he was a speed reader par excellence.

The intent of the filing with the Supreme Court was not to gain a disqualification of Gilvary. I could have referenced Local Rule 1.19 III(C) that stripped Gilvary of jurisdiction. Moyer would have sustained it.

But I would have lost control over matters; would no longer have been Gilvary's warden. My fate and his fate would have depended upon who the case went to.

History told me truth and justice would not have become a sudden priority; would not have prevailed.

The purpose of the filing was to get the *Oh shit!* reaction from Gilvary that Karen and Ted observed in laughter, when they dumped a nine volume pleading on him. I had struck the psyche again!

I ripped Chief Justice Moyer's ass anyway. In a war of words, a relentless attack is mandated. And this extra effort would pay big dividends, in the near future!

From a letter of complaint sent to Moyer:

> The charges made against Judge Gilvary et al. are serious. The material presented supports those charges, the least of which is that every party to the case, going into trial *knew* I had committed no crime.
>
> That the Supreme Court would rule on that document, in the manner described herein, within twenty-four hours of its filing, suggests in and of itself...bias and prejudice.
>
> Any mayor's court would do better.

Ohio Supreme Court Justice Thomas J. Moyer never read the 1900+ page creation. Prosecutors and newspaper reporters never read it. But one person read it; was compelled to read it, even though he abhorred it. The nine-volume filing became my prisoner's version of the dreaded Hole; became Patricoff's *time bomb.*

Psychologically, Gilvary was incapacitated; incapable of avoiding a thorough reading of what his warden had to say. And he read it in bits and pieces; as he served his sentence in stark lonely isolation, on death row.

I began the *Affidavit of Disqualification:*

> No apology is made for the John Grisham read; no apology is expected from the Court for conduct of officers of the court who made this necessary.
>
> In life, Nicole Brown Simpson prepared for her inevitable fate by placing incriminating evidence of abuse in a safe deposit box, assuring the apprehension of her eventual murderer. After-the-fact, she "spoke" from beyond the grave.

In freedom, Horace Ray Metz prepared for his inevitable fate by placing incriminating evidence of abuse in a tape assimilation, filed as a pretrial exhibit, assuring the apprehension of his eventual kidnapper. After-the-fact, he "speaks" from beyond the prison walls. The reviewer should listen to the tape that accompanies this filing.

... Like most with criminal intent, Gilvary made mistakes. His crime was far from perfect, and moreover, was recorded! A casual reading of the material provided herein *may* lead to the conclusion that:

> *Judge Gilvary forgot more law*
> *than*
> *pro se Metz will ever know.*

... It has often been observed, "He who represents himself has a fool for a client." To counter that posture while acknowledging the "fool" part, Metz would note that in courtroom conflict, although God is sworn too repeatedly, by jurors; by witnesses; and by officers of the court, all too often God is "left" on the courthouse steps on the way in, to be "picked up" on the way out.

Metz entered the fray as a *pro se,* but he was not alone in his courthouse battles. He was assisted throughout by *angels* of God. The **callous scofflaw** shall be provided the opportunity to become a **believer.** To those ends, Metz offers his own words to Elvis Presley's singing of a Hank Snow classic standard, as written in August 1977 and inspired by Elvis' death.

(Now And Then There's) A Fool Such As I

> Pardon me, if I cry a little,
> When I praise my Lord;
> Don't be angry with me
> If I do.
> Been a fool many times,
> When I ignored His word;
> But He stood by me,
> Through and through.

Been a fool many times, Lord,
When I ignore Your word.
You taught me how, to love somehow,
I'd forget what I learned.
I'm a fool, but I'll love You, Lord,
Until the day I die.
Now and then there's a fool
Such as I...am over You!

This was the hook that assured my prisoner would read every torturous line; from beginning to end. Did I *know* of Local Rule 1.19 III(C)? It was the one fact that could seal my prisoner's fate. Fear motivated my prisoner; as he searched in vain: *did he know?*

I had a lot to tell my prisoner. A lengthy memorandum accompanied the affidavit. It began:

> The issue the Defendant/Appellant, hereby referred to as "Metz", places before the Court is an affidavit of disqualification of Common Pleas Court of Montgomery County Judge James J. Gilvary.
>
> It would appear prudent to remember the words of an avid *poker player,* President Harry Truman, that were recorded when he decided not to seek another term:
>
> > *There is a lure in power. It can get into a man's blood just as gambling and a lust for money have been known to do.*
>
> With a supposition that such lust disabled those who imprisoned Metz, thereby making them gravely ill; and with whatever compassion such a posture engenders, Metz believes that the evidence as presented herein *in part,* supports the claim he has been falsely imprisoned in a manner that equated to kidnapping as defined in section 2905.01 of the Ohio Revised Code, and is being held hostage against his will.
>
> The Code provides that aggravated kidnapping, where the victim has not been released unharmed prior to the criminal's detection and apprehension, is a felony of the first degree and is punishable by a prison sentence of up to twenty-five

years. The release of a kidnap victim in a safe place and un-harmed, reduces the crime to a second degree felony that carries a lesser penalty. The murder of a kidnap victim is a capital offense, punishable by death.

Metz believes that the criminal activity he discovered in the courts, beginning in 1994 and continuing to the present, and the ensuing cover-up with tentacles that reach to a Supreme Court justice and the Ohio governor, have placed him in peril because of (1) the heinous crime perpetrated against him and (2) the fear of public disclosure that the perpetrators may have. Metz believes that the evidence is sufficient to convict the following principal parties of the crime of kidnapping:

1. James J. Gilvary   Common Pleas Court Judge
2. Mike Fain   Appellate Judge
3. James A. Brogan   Appellate Judge
4. Mathias H. Heck, Jr.   Montgomery County Prosecutor
5. William F. Schenck   Greene County Prosecutor
6. Craig Zimmers   Montgomery County Clerk of Courts

As an imprisoned *pro se,* supposedly without means to sustain, the words of Patrick Henry, spoken before the pre-Continental Congress in Williamsburg, Virginia during a discussion on cession from England, are recalled and embraced as Metz's own:

> I know not what course others might take, but
> as for me, give me liberty or give me death.

… Judge Gilvary enjoyed the right to be presumed an impartial trier of fact, by virtue of his willingness to remain on the case. That *right* remained, at all times, subject to an accompanying *responsibility* to uphold his oath of office and to adhere to the mandates of the Code of Judicial Responsibility. Judge Gilvary shirked that responsibility…. Judge Gilvary's court was *for sale.*

HIGH STAKES POKER

Perhaps the renowned Russian novelist Dostoevsky would have been impressed with Metz's bet: twelve years of his life on the table with nothing in "his hand" except his faith in God and his belief in his country – against the power of a vengeful state and the tyranny of an out-of-control judiciary. Metz's sanity could be questioned. Metz was certain that it would be. He was holding a ***royal flush*** against ***aces and eights***.

With good time, my six-year sentence meant serving the Russian's exact four-year sentence! Dostoevsky's prison experiences were fictionalized in a novel entitled *The House of the Dead*. His novel brought reforms to harsh Russian prison conditions. He described his time in captivity more vividly in a letter to his brother:

> I consider those four years as a time during which I was buried alive and shut up in a coffin. Just how horrible that time was I have not the strength to tell you…. It was an indescribable, unending agony, because each hour, each minute weighed upon my soul like a stone.

Also included in the affidavit of disqualification:

> As for the *illusion* of a long sentence, Judge Gilvary routinely compromised himself after-the-fact. Consider the *Dayton Daily News* article entitled "Over objections judge grants shock probation" of April 17, 1997 that reads:
>
> > … Judge James J. Gilvary…granted shock probation Wednesday to John Vanderpool, 37, after he served about nine months of a seven-to-25 year sentence on a guilty plea to voluntary manslaughter in the Jan. 1, 1996, fatal shooting of William Wilhoit, 26, outside Butch's Bar, 61 Horton St.

Lois Osborne of Dayton responded to this outrage (the public couldn't know that it was a set-up involving the prosecutor) with a Letter to the Editor of the *Dayton Daily News* on May 28, 1997, that reads:

> **Early release of killer a mockery of system**
> Montgomery County Common Pleas Judge James J. Gilvary's decision to release John Vanderpool after he served only eight months of a 7-to-25 year sentence for voluntary manslaughter is a mockery of the justice system in the United States.
> Any judge who would release a killer back on the streets after eight months should not be reelected to the bench.
> Montgomery County needs a judge who will set a better example for the community. Felons need to know that the citizens of Dayton will not tolerate this violent behavior.

A May 15, 1997 Speak Up opinion printed in the *Dayton Daily News* reads:

> I would like to know how Montgomery County Common Pleas Judge James J. Gilvary would feel if his son were murdered and the murderer was back on the street in eight months because of shock probation.

Another case prompted this June 16, 1997 *Dayton Daily News* Letter To Editor:

Judge Gilvary too lenient on hit-and-run driver
My son Michael Miller was killed in a hit-and-run accident on Dec. 31, 1996. William D. Deerfield failed to stop for a red light and after killing my son, he fled on foot. After a month, he was caught and charged with aggravated vehicular homicide and involuntary manslaughter.
Montgomery County Common Pleas Judge James J. Gilvary sentenced Deerfield to serve only three years for the death of

my son. Where was Gilvary's mind when he slapped Deer-field's hand for taking my son's life?

We don't need a judge like that in our court system.

Peggy Miller Trotwood

Also included in the affidavit of disqualification:

... *If* Judge Gilvary were to be disqualified *because* he for-feited jurisdiction prior to trial, it would follow that the as-signed judge would find the conviction to be <u>void</u>, upon a timely motion for summary judgment to follow-up the (simul-taneously filed to this affidavit) Petition to Vacate or Set Aside Sentence and Conviction Pursuant to O.R.C. 2953.21. No hearing would be necessary.

... There is a long-standing precedent for such a form of po-etic justice, as is indicated by the Latin phrase:

Quid turpi ex causa promissum est non valet.

Translated: A promise arising out of immoral circumstances is invalid.

... There is one God, Whose angels directed Metz to this pathway. The April 13, 1997 *Dayton Daily News* had an atten-tion-grabbing headline:

Attorneys given chance to go up against God

The article referenced the ACLU's intent to challenge the constitutionality of Governor George V. Voinovich's insistence that the state motto be inscribed in granite in front of the newly remodeled Statehouse. The inference could be drawn from the headline that ACLU attorneys opposed Gov. Voino-vich, who is "god."

Of course that's silly, as Ohioans know that the late (?) George Burns is "god," and Governor Voinovich is just anoth-er lawyer who frowns a lot (lately). The motto in debate reads: "With God, all things are possible."

Left out of the discussion is any conjecture as to what God's position might be in the confrontation, other than the implicit suggestion from some quarters that ACLU attorneys are little more than pagans. As *His employee,* Metz shall offer insight, ala John Denver in the movie, "Oh God."

Newspaper accounts attribute that Gov. Voinovich got the idea some time ago while in India, where he saw the slogan "Government's Work is God's Work" inscribed on a public building. (*Dayton Daily News;* August 3, 1997.)

Gov. Voinovich may well have come home with other ideas, for Ohio emulates India's recognition as the eighth most corrupt nation in the world; behind Indonesia, Mexico, Pakistan, Russia, Columbia, Bolivia, and Nigeria. (*The Vindicator;* August 24, 1997.)

From border to border; from east to west and north to south; from the lowliest of public employees to the highest office in the state, Ohioans are besieged and bewildered by government scandal after scandal, involving a breach of public trust amoral in the extreme. Official scorn for the letter and the spirit of the will of the citizen (a will that is bent, but remains unbroken) violates the sanctity of America's natural heritage, and is further subjected to the *universal laws of life* that are common too, and yet transcend, any particular faith.

This suggests that divine guidance has *not* been a sought-after part of the leadership equation, and moreover, that "endorsement by slogan" carved in stone mimicking Moses' Ten Commandments is being sought as a means of (self) deception; that reduces the "we'll take the cash, You take the credit" pretenders, to be brazen mockers of God.

What has been God's historic action when He is so mocked? Given the subject matter herein and considering the religious and career backgrounds of the governor, finding an answer in the Christian's Holy Bible is apropos. That answer is found in Job 12:17:

> He leadeth counselors away spoiled,
> and maketh the judges fools.

... Metz likes to remind that Rome wasn't destroyed in a day. American civilization is crumbling as societies tend to do when the citizen is lax in attention. Left to their own devices, politicians inevitably become corruptible and therefore, are corrupted. The servants *serve* themselves.

Metz believes that man's successes are directly related to his efforts to live in harmony with the universe; to acknowledge and appreciate there are *universal laws of life* that transcend any particular religion; that exist of their own volition as part of a grand scheme beyond man's limited comprehension.

Metz believes that man's failures are directly related to living without seeking harmony with the universe; to ignoring and disavowing that there are *universal laws of life;* to existing as though man made the laws that count, no matter how pagan; no matter how administered.

Man's efforts to live in harmony with his universe were exemplified in a June 5, 1997 *Dayton Daily News* article entitled "Standards – Summer gets stretched 1 second." From the article:

> ... The season will get an extra "leap" second on June 30, the National Institute of Standards and Technology reports.
>
> ... Leap seconds are used to keep in time with the spinning of the Earth, which has slowed slightly. This is the 21st such adjustment since 1972....

Metz spent the longest summer in years in prison, where he saw a Wizzard of Id cartoon depicting a prisoner behind bars, asking of a passerby, "What time is it?" The response was, "Why?"

WHY! Metz marvels at the cleverly devised system of man that provides for his keeping of time, in harmony with nature; with the universe. The system begins with the second; a minute has 60 seconds; an hour has 60 minutes or 3,600 seconds; a day has 24 hours or 1,440 minutes or 86,400 seconds; a year has 365 days or 8,760 hours or 525,600 minutes or 31,536,000 seconds. Every four years man adds an extra day, or 86,400 seconds, and calls it *leap year.*

And with all of that, science has determined it to be necessary, on occasion, to increase the length of a year from 31,536,000 seconds to 31,536,001 seconds, to maintain perfect harmony; perfect order!

... A four year sentence equates to 1,461 days, or 126,-226,230 seconds. Science added <u>one</u> second.

... There are times when the pen moves across the page, as if of its own volition.

... The patriot writes of flag and country; the tyrant of fairness and equality. The analyst writes of the elephant and the donkey; the dreamer of pen and the sword. The Romanist writes of the birds and the bees; the philosopher of the bird and the worm (If the early bird gets the worm, what does the early worm get?). The Christian's apostle wrote of the dog and the sow (II Peter 2:12); the Jew's wise man of the dog and the fool (Proverbs 26:11). The humorist writes of the fairy tale; the songwriter promises that "fairy tales can come true, it can happen to you...if you're young at heart."

Through it all the human condition remains much the same, as history repeats itself ad infinitum. Things are never quite as good as they seem, nor quite as bad as they seem. The glass is *always* half full and half empty; the cup that *runneth over* wasteth. Perception alters reality in the eye of the perceiver; an altered perception creates its own reality. Reality becomes at the last an illusion, as William James noted:[39]

> Nothing is at the last sacred, but
> the authority of your own mind.

---

[39] Quoting from memory in prison was perilous. The correct quote came from one of my favorites; Ralph Waldo Emerson: *Nothing is at last sacred but the integrity of your mind.* The context of the message was the same. For in Gilvary's mind, he was a god in his courtroom; as my continuation suggests.

Those whose reality involves invoking their will on others, via the misuse of force and power, risk being held accountable to those who endow the same. Life provides a man for all seasons; life is accommodating and life accommodates. A sense of humor helps those who shoulder the yoke of engagement in opposition to those who abuse.

... I may never get to your heaven. Don't despair; you'll be in mine.

One Time Soon

I'm gone to see my Savior,
One time soon; one time soon.
I'll be face to face with Jesus,
In heaven's holy room.
There'll be joy; there'll be laughter;
No sorrow and no gloom,
When I go to see my Savior,
One time soon; one time soon.

I'll walk arm in arm with Jesus,
Down the lane; down the lane.
There'll be eternal sunshine;
No clouds and no rain.
I'll meet Peter, Paul and Mary;
And John the Baptist too,
When I go to see my Savior,
One time soon; one time soon.

I'll speak to Pontius Pilate
On that day; on that day.
And to he who drove the nails
Through Jesus' hands of clay.
I'll rejoice with saints and sinners,
As I move from room to room,
When I go to see my Savior,
One time soon; one time soon.

Yes, I'm gone to see my Savior,
One time soon; one time soon.
I'll be face to face with Jesus,
In heaven's holy room.
There'll be joy; there'll be laughter;
No sorrow and no gloom,
When I go to see my Savior,
One time soon; one time soon.
**-Written with original music by Horace
Ray Metz; Denver, CO; 1977**

... The depravity of Judge Gilvary's actions is best described in James 1:18:

A double minded man is unstable in all his ways.

... Metz frequented the law library at University of Dayton, and sensed a spirituality while amongst the students. Metz would leave the campus with a sense of melancholy reflection "of what might have been" had his college education not been summarily aborted.

And always, he made an escape from a case of "what ifs" by a laugh at himself; remembering the story of the grave digger wanna-be:

It seems that in days gone by, an immigrant made his way to Ellis Island, from the Old Country. The day after he arrived, he learned of a grave-digger job way out on Long Island.

With a newcomer's determination to succeed, he walked the whole way to the job site. He was asked to fill out an application. In broken English, he explained he could neither read nor write.

It was explained to him that both accomplishments were essential for the job, as the grave digger would be provided written instructions on where to dig. He was cast aside, with no rush of applicants for the job.

Undaunted, on his way back to New York City, he spent his last nickel on a delicious looking red apple. As he walked along, he polished his prize apple, postponing the pleasure of eating it.

A passerby noted the apple's quality and offered the immigrant a dime for it. Sensing opportunity, he sold it, walked back to the apple-seller and purchased two more.

He polished and sold them; repeated the process; repeated it again and again. Soon he had a modest fruit stand; then a larger one.

Eventually he went to a bank to borrow $1 million to build a large warehouse; whereupon he was asked to fill out a loan application. It was explained how he could neither read nor write.

The banker was enthralled by the immigrant's story, and exclaimed, "Only in America! Good gosh, man, just think where you'd be if only you had an education!"

And the immigrant smiled knowingly and nodded his head, as he replied, "Yes; a grave digger on Long Island."

... Considering Miami University President James C. Garland's column in the January 31, 1997 *Dayton Daily News,* I envision the day when Ohio's university presidents hire the likes of Sally Struthers to do commercials.

With teared eye, she'll say, "Won't you please help, governor? Let Ray Metz out of prison so that one of our downtrodden creatures can be educated."

And I'll respond, "Not so fast, little lady. A bunch of 'educateds' is why I'm here."

... To Metz, subjecting innocent law students to a sermon on "ethics" from Daniel Kinane was akin to the university's president subjecting them to a sermon on Christianity by atheist Madeline O'Hare.

Much better to subject Kinane to sitting anonymously in the University of Dayton Law Library, for two hundred hours, searching in silence for something misplaced; looking for the spirituality that Metz sensed as a humble and formally uneducated *pro se* defendant, seeking the wisdom, beauty, and strength of a history of law based on the unique bedrock foundation of the United States of America's Constitution and Bill of Rights.

Then, Mr. Kinane might have had something profound to say to aspiring lawyers.

The assault on the psyche of my prisoner, via the 1,900+ page court filing, was unrelenting. As he suffered in silence, I decided to rub salt in the psychic wounds. He had depended on prison being so heinous; I would not be able to withstand it.

Now the tables were turned. And I let him know just how miserably his desperate ploy had failed.

While in maximum security at Corrections Reception Center, spending twenty hours a day in my cell, I detailed a part of the 1997 President's Day; for posterity. Solitary confinement is unpleasant. But I made the best of it, as this part of the affidavit demonstrates.

NOTED FOR CLARIFICATION

In Cincinnati, Ohio, on October 24, 1996, police officer Ed Johnson arrested Sylvia Stayton, charging her with disorderly conduct and obstructing official business. She retained an attorney and demanded a jury trial.

In early February 1997, only days prior to my trial in Dayton, Stayton was found guilty on the Obstruction charge, and not guilty on the Disorderly charge. She was sentenced in early March, 1997, after I was incarcerated - fined $500 fine and $200 in court costs.

Her internationally known crime was unique:

In front of a veteran Cincinnati policeman, Stayton put *a nickel* in an expired parking meter. And as that was not enough to earn a trip to the pokey, put *a dime* in the adjoining meter!

Stayton was audacious enough to claim that, if her meter had expired, she hoped someone would do the same thing for her! She encouraged and promoted lawlessness – while using the subterfuge of random kindness to a stranger! The 63-year-old grandmother became known as *meter feeding granny.* She died in July 2004, with her dignity and character intact.

WLW-radio played a parody of Marty Robbins' classic ballad "El Paso," bringing additional notoriety to her crime spree. They must not have appreciated that the city was in the midst of an endemic crime wave.

For right about that time, Jeff Friedlander, blind since birth, was ticketed in downtown Cincinnati for jaywalking. Friedlander was hit by a pickup truck and knocked down as he crossed the street.

Officer Chauncey Prude determined he was unhurt, gave him a ride to his workplace; but then wrote a $100 ticket for his failing to cross the street within the walk-lines.

Again, the Cincinnati case drew national attention. Prosecutors decided to drop the case, even though Mr. Friedlander "technically was in violation," according to the chief assistant city prosecutor.

END OF CLARAFICATION NOTES

Monday, February 17, 1997
President's Day
Cincinnati, Ohio

Heading west on McMillan, on his second trip around the block, he spotted *his* parking space, seven car lengths ahead. Unconcerned that another might snatch the lone empty space, *his* space; he patiently waited for traffic to move.

"Convenient-parking-space-attainment" had not been a career goal when he'd entered University of Cincinnati, those many years ago. Life compensates. It has been written that there are various gifts. For some, doors are opened; for others, parking spaces mystically appear, as needed.

Approaching his destination, he alerted the car behind with his right turn signal: leave him room to park his beauty, or be prepared to set in traffic.

Noting with satisfaction a savvy and courteous driver to his rear, he adroitly slid the pink 1985 Buick Regal out of traffic, and into the la-la land of *parking meter granny.*

Stepping up to the parking meter, he carefully considered the options. If he refused to insert money, and simply walked away, it was likely the penalty would be a ten buck ticket. If he inserted a coin, he risked up to six months in the slammer; for there were twenty minutes of unexpired time on the meter, and no one to witness that he'd just parked.

Sensing the *doors-are-opened* crowd disenfranchised *parking-space-mystics* (soreheads), he stood pondering his dilemma; all the while he risked a *loitering-by-meter-with-change-in-pocket* rap.

With nary a lawyer in sight, he sought divine guidance. *Parking meter granny,* by his reasoning, had been a mother first. What had his mother taught?

He tried to remember. Something like: "Son, don't stiff the meter maiden." Proverbs 22:6 reads:

> *Train up a child in the way he should go, and*
> *when he is old, he will not depart from it.*

And so, with the innocence of a child, and the Wisdom of Solomon, he pulled change from his right jeans pocket, and ran the meter to the limit. Grinning to himself at a new inspiration, he rammed home another nickel and dime, in solitary tribute to *granny,* to motherhood.

Lightheartedly, with a bounce to his step reflective of instinctive self-assurance, he tripped up McMillan towards Clifton Avenue in the glorious President's Day mid-thirties sunshine, humming the tune to, "This land is *your* land; this land is *my* land...this land belongs to *you* and *me*.[40]

---

[40] Lyrics to "This Land Is Your Land" were written in 1940 by Woody Guthrie, using existing music; and recorded by him in 1944.

He passed the new College of Law Building on Clifton, and turned into campus on the sidewalk that circled up the hill in front of McMikkan Hall. His pace slowed; the humming stopped; the day's work had begun. He was "back on campus" for a time of solitude; of reflection; of meditation.

He savored the day and the setting, as he meandered through the maze of buildings. He sat for an hour at the top of the football stands, and then made his way to the College of Engineering rectangle. He paused in quiet reflection, as he stared at a third floor office window, of the building to the east, noting sills badly in need of white paint.

Finally, he went off campus into the adjoining Burnet Woods.[41] He found a park bench and spent another two hours in quiet solitude and reflection, preparing himself for what lay ahead. Déjà vu. It was his last day of freedom. Trial would begin tomorrow.

After showing my prisoner I was fine and dandy, while in maximum security in the beginning the four-year prison stint; I indelibly showed him, once again, how inhumane and egregious his crime against me was. I took him back to Burnet Woods, when I was a nineteen-year-old college freshman.

Spring of 1961:

Off Tylersville Road, next to the Voice of America Relay Station, where a message of hope, a message of freedom was beamed across the heavens, mine was taken from me....

Sitting as gingerly on a park bench as he could in the quiet of night, a street light shinning down on him, Metz opened his Bible as he sought guidance and solace in his hour of despair. The Good Book opened and his eyes were drawn to a simple and precisely perfect passage found in Proverbs 24:10:

If thou faint in the day of adversity; thy strength is small.

---

[41] A 90-acre park next to University of Cincinnati.

Next I tormented my prisoner with quotes from pre-trial motions; pleadings he callously chose to ignore:

> The defendant doesn't know where he shall find the strength and the fortitude necessary to face his accusers in court. The psychic pain that the defendant is enduring is unimaginable. Old wounds have been reopened.
>
> This defendant doesn't want your millions. This defendant wants your inhumanity. He wants Aldridge and Wilcox to be freed from the tyranny of the system. He wants a frightened little Centerville girl, unjustly tried as an adult, to be freed.
>
> In the name of heaven, what are you people about?

The sheer magnitude of my filing was not its 1,900+ page length. The magnitude on the psyche of my prisoner was the scope and depth of the criminality it encompassed; and far more importantly, what it left out. For Local Rule 1.19 III(C) was what gave absolute credence to my charge of kidnapping.

I had danced around the kidnapping issue repeatedly; and laid out the entire scenario, in detail. A crucial fact was omitted, that would drive Gilvary mad. *Could he know; would he ever find out?* I never once hinted that I knew of the existence of:

Montgomery County Local Rule 1.19 III(C).

Judge Gilvary knew the significance of the Rule. He possessed a high intellect. It was his courts' rule!

My prisoner possessed *judicial knowledge;* he alone would be held responsible for kidnapping. Given the tone and thrust of what was included therein, along with the remainder of the filing; my 1,900+ page filing created a mountain slide on the psyche of my prisoner - as measured by Dostoevsky's *weight of a stone.*

I paused in preparing the affidavit of disqualification; for there was more. I was the warden; but was also the catalyst whose efforts imprisoned the demented judge.

Having endured decades in my prison of the psyche, and having escaped that life sentence *because* of the actions of my prisoner; there existed an underlying sense of compassion that could not be shaken.

The compassionate man felt compelled to forewarn the demented judge of his pending fate. But as a convicted felon serving time in prison, I was limited in how I could do so. It had to be done abstractly.

Upon careful contemplation, two philosophical questions came to mind. Would those who abandoned Gilvary in his hour of need, ever come to realize their roles in his demise? The answer to the first philosophical question was easy: it mattered not; dead is dead.

The second philosophical question: Was death an inevitable consequence for Gilvary's deeds? The answer was self-evident, given his sheltered life, without exposure to enduring psychic pain.

Given his ego, an all-forgiving God would never be sought. Nearing the end; he would no longer be able to fool himself. Faced with being exposed for what he had become; one escape remained. Death was a certainty!

And so it was; I formulated an abstract warning. A parable about a man and a dog named *Spot* was created - describing Gilvary's dilemma. The parable was sandwiched between the two philosophical questions.

A Philosophical Question

If a man were alone in the forest, and a mighty Redwood fell and crushed him...and no one heard the sound...would he still be dead?

A Parable

Once upon a time there lived a man alone, in a clearing at the edge of a great forest, with his faithful dog Spot. Year in and year out they lived in harmony with nature and with each other, as close as man and mammal could be.

But alas, man possessed an ego that mammal did not, and an imagination that could be creative, that mammal also did not. And that combination caused man problems. Ego told man that he was not only master of Spot; master of his own personal little universe; man was master *of* the universe, and *he* had been placed in dominion over the great forest found next to his home of many, many years.

Whereupon, the ego-driven man decided to explore that part of *his* universe, and he thereby trekked deep into the forest where no man had ever trod before; the ever faithful companion tagging along behind.

And it came to pass that man over-estimated his prowess, and as night fell deep in the forest where no man had ever trod, he became disoriented. Fear, that follows ego like a shadow, overcame him. Fear is a lack of faith; faith is the antidote for overcoming fear. But the ego-driven man's faith was in himself and was thereby limited to the powers he possessed.

The ego-driven man's perception of reality was the illusion that *he* was the center of the universe, and he was bound with that limitation. He forgot that he was but a speck for a time in the overall scheme of things in God's universe.

In that condition man ignored his resources – his faithful companion of so many, many years that possessed powers of instinct that could have led them to safety. Left to his own devices, man panicked.

He was blinded to the reality that a simple search for truth and meaning could reveal the pathway to safety. Relying solely upon himself, day after day, man walked in circles in the deep forest where no man had ever trod before. Lost and alone, his trusting companion following dutifully behind, man foraged off the land as best he could.

As days turned into weeks he became weaker and weaker, and as hunger preoccupied his every thought, man began to look at his faithful companion in a new way. And each time he did so, he'd look away, shaking his head side-to-side ever so slightly, in despair and dismay. For man has a conscience to look after ego.

Finally, seeing no recourse, in desperation as starvation approached and survival instinct prevailed, man built a fire and slay his only means of escape; his true and faithful companion of so many years. He devoured his prey and filled his stomach.

With his needs temporarily satisfied, man leaned against a tree and picked his teeth in a state of quiet reflection, as he observed the remains of his dastardly deed.

Riddled with guilt and shame, he called on ego's defender named Rationalization, and mused to himself:

Wish ol' Spot were here.
He sure would enjoy these bones!

A Philosophical Question

If a man were alone in a forest, amongst the mighty Redwoods...and no one observed his deeds...would Emerson's *every act rewards itself* be valid?

Excruciating fear tormented my prisoner in the isolation of death row. Though he tried, bordering on obsession, he could not shake it off.

Yes, fear followed my prisoner like a shadow. Fear is caused by a lack of faith. *Spot* represented the faith he turned away from; always available, if only called upon.

But sadly, my prisoner's faith had been misguided; was placed entirely in himself and his co-conspirators. And now he was alone; all alone deep in the forest.

It was not a place where *no man had ever trod before;* just a place where my authoritarian prisoner had never been. The nine-volume filing was created to establish dynamics for my prisoner's final opportunity to redeem himself. And it abstractly described his ultimate fate.

The State filed a Motion To Dismiss on July 8, 1998. Assistant Prosecuting Attorney Laura Ulrich wrote an intelligent and well reasoned argument; one that was legally correct.

As I read her motion, I wondered what she was doing; associating with the slime in the prosecutor's office. I wondered how she felt, making a reasoned argument in a case where I had obviously been royally screwed. Did she have a conscience? It mattered not.

A petition for post-conviction review is not a constitutional right and in a post-conviction proceeding the convicted defendant has only the rights granted by the legislature....

(2)   A PETITION UNDER DIVISION A(1) OF THIS SECTION SHALL BE FILED NO LATER THAN ONE HUNDRED EIGHTY DAYS AFTER THE DATE ON WHICH THE TRIAL TRANSCRIPT IS FILED IN THE COURT OF APPEALS IN THE DIRECT APPEAL OF THE JUDGMENT OF CONVICTION OR ADJUDICATION

... The court granted his motion to dismiss the appeal on December 2, 1997.
... Therefore, he had until November 29, 1997 to file his petition for post-conviction relief. Since that date falls on a Saturday, he had until Monday, December 1, 1997 to file his petition....
Thus, the State submits that the Defendant's petition for post-conviction relief was untimely filed and cannot be considered by this Court on its merits.

Judge Gilvary filed an Entry July 13, 1997:

Defendant shall respond to the Plaintiff's **Motion to Dismiss** on or before July 31, 1998 at 4:30 p.m.
SO ORDERED.
JAMES J. GILVERY, JUDGE

July 31, 1998 would be Judge Gilvary's 526th day in a prison of the psyche, where he resided in the harshest kind of solitary confinement imaginable. With the knowledge that his life was on the line, I wrote an impassioned plea for common sense, as the mandated response; filed by my sister, Karen on July 31, 1998.

The Defendant would now acknowledge the wisdom of the Court for demanding a response from the Defendant on the crucial issue of dismissal, for the State asserts claims that the State abandoned and cannot reassert to the detriment of the Defendant, pursuant to Ohio Revised Code 2901.04.

MEMORANDUM

The State's Motion To Dismiss, as filed on July 8, 1998 by Ms. Laura Ulrich by and through the Montgomery County Prosecutor's Office, while a refreshingly well reasoned and well written position of law, is nevertheless fatally flawed.

Were the issues raised therein relevant to the instant case, the Defendant would not have filed. The State waived the right to Ms. Ulrich's claims at sentencing, and has failed to make any attempt to overcome that waiver.

After the Court imposed sentence, the following discourse took place:

> THE COURT: Do you have anything else to say?
> THE DEFENDANT: No, Your Honor.
> THE COURT: Good.

The Defendant *did not* exclaim that a six-year sentence for owing three parties a total of $7,040 was ludicrous. Nor did the Defendant, then or at any time thereafter, contend that he should have been sentenced under the more lenient "new law." Nor is the Defendant making such a claim herein; nor shall he ever make such a claim.

This is an important issue. For standing at the bench and representing the State at sentencing was a *multitude* of prosecutors. None from the multitude assembled objected to the sentence, as imposed.

No one spoke up and said, "Excuse me, Your Honor, but you've mistakenly sentenced the Defendant under 'old law,' and the State objects on the grounds that this grants the Defendant unlimited time in which to file a petition to vacate, is a misuse of prison resources, violates the intent and spirit of 'new law,' and far beyond all of that, amounts to cruel and unusual punishment. Therefore, the State respectfully demands that the sentence be corrected, here and now."

As the Defendant has stepped off his sentence, day-by-day, he is aware that many felons have petitioned the courts for re-sentencing under "new law," and in every instance the State has vigorously opposed those efforts.

Additionally, during the time the Defendant was preparing, seven days a week for over sixteen months, in order to have his conviction overturned, the State never objected to the Defendant's fate; or to the State's own.

To the contrary, Assistant Montgomery County Prosecuting Attorney George Patricoff filed a scathing motion in opposition to an appeals bond that falsely portrayed the Defendant to be a Charles Manson-type.

At the same time Mr. Patricoff negotiated a plea bargain for former Miamisburg Municipal Deputy Clerk Maria Lowman, who was sentenced to six months in county jail for theft in office of $44,000, and, expressed his satisfaction with a public defender sentenced to probation for theft in office of $12,000 from the same court.

Additionally, Special Prosecutor William F. Schenck expressed publicly that he recommended a short jail sentence for a Wright State University dean for a large theft in office, and probation for another.

So be it.

The authority afforded the Defendant to file under Ohio Revised Code 2953.21 is contained in the language of "old law."

> (A)   Any person convicted or adjudged delinquent claiming that there was such a denial or infringement of his rights as to render the conviction void or voidable under the Ohio Constitution or the Constitution of the United States,

>*may file a petition AT ANY TIME in the Court
>which imposed sentence.*

The Defendant would logically and correctly contend that <u>if</u> the Court sentenced under "old law," with *no objection* from the State, and *no remedial effort* undertaken by the State from February 20, 1997 until June 30, 1998, the Defendant was, is, and shall forevermore be afforded the protections according to the law he was sentenced under, pursuant to the strictest interpretation of the *mandates* of Ohio Revised Code 2901.04, Rules of Construction, that reads

>*(A) Sections of the Revised Code defining offenses or penalties shall be strictly construed against the State and liberally construed in favor of the accused.*
>
>*(B) Rules of criminal procedure and sections of the Revised Code providing for criminal procedure shall be construed so as to effect the fair, impartial, speedy, and sure administration of justice.*
>
>*Committee Comment to H 511*
>
>*This section codifies the rules that penal statutes must be STRICTLY CONSTRUED AGAINST THE STATE AND LIBERALLY CONSTRUED IN FAVOR OF THE ACCUSED. See Harrison v. Ohio, 112 Ohio St. 429, 147 N.E. 650 (1925) aff'd 270 U.S. 632; State ex rel. Moore Oil Co. v. Durben, 99 Ohio St. 406, 124 N.E. 232 (1919). In addition, the section provides a rule for the construction of procedural measures, based on the premise that THE PRIME OBJECT OF PROCEDURAL STATUTES AND RULES IS TO PROMOTE JUSTICE both to the accused and to the state. Thus, procedural measures are not to be construed in terms of strictness or liberality, but rather, to effect the fair, impartial, and sure administration of justice.* [Emphasis added.]

On page 4 of Ms. Ulrich's Motion To Dismiss she writes, "It is equally clear that the language provided by Am. Sub. S.B. No. 4 is *mandatory* concerning the timing restrictions for filing a post-conviction petition."

While this out-of-context position is correct as far as it goes, it is conditioned as put forth herein, as the legislation Ms. Ulrich referenced includes *changed* sentencing, and further, details the intent of the legislation so far as sentencing in non-violent criminal matters such as theft by deception, which the State has acknowledged repeatedly in Theft In Office cases referred to herein.

The Court chose to ignore this – as well as other mandated obligations – and the State failed to object.

For these reasons the petition as filed by the Defendant on June 30, 1998 is a proper and timely means to remedy one of the most troubling and sinister "railroad" persecutions *ever* enacted.

WHEREFORE, the Defendant respectfully demands that the State's Motion To Dismiss be OVERRULED, and that the matter before the Court proceed to an orderly and lawful conclusion based on the merits of the Defendant's claims.

Ulrich was correct as to the *letter* of the law. I was correct as to the *spirit* of the law. And my prisoner, on death row, had to decide whether to live or die.

Judge Gilvary, who was forever and ever, *one judge too late* to preside in my case, had to decide if the same Ohio Revised Code – waived for him – would be waived for me.

I felt Judge Gilvary might need more encouragement. Simultaneous to the above motion, I filed a Motion For Summary Judgment, reading in part:

The Defendant was projected into the role of Paul (after his conversion) by the State, as detailed throughout the memorandum that accompanied the Affidavit of Disqualification of Gilvary. In turn, the Defendant projected Judge Gilvary into the role of Saul (prior to his conversion), as shall be detailed.

The conversion of Saul on the road to Damascus is found in Acts 9:

1 And Saul, yet breathing out threatenings and slaughter against the disciples of the Lord, went unto the high priest.

2 And desired of him letters to Damascus to the synagogues, that if he found any of this way, whether they were men or women, he might bring them bound unto Jerusalem.

3 And as he journeyed, he came near Damascus and suddenly there shined round him a light from heaven:

4 And he fell to the earth, and heard a voice saying unto him, Saul, Saul, why persecutest thou me?

5 And he said, I am Jesus whom thou persecutest: IT IS HARD FOR THEE TO KICK AGAINST THE PRICKS.

6 And he trembling and astonished said, Lord, what wilt thou have me to do? And the Lord said unto him, Arise and go into the city, and it shall be told thee what thou must do.

7 And the man which journeyed with him stood speechless, hearing a voice, but seeing no man.

8 And Saul arose from the earth; and when his eyes were opened, he saw no man: but they led him by the hand, and brought him into Damascus.

9 And he was three days without sight, and neither did eat nor drink.

10 And there was a certain disciple at Damascus, named Ananias; and to him said the Lord in a vision, Ananias, And he said, Behold I am here, Lord.

11 And the Lord said unto him, Arise, and go into the street which is called STRAIGHT, and inquire in the house of Judas for one called Saul of Tarsus: for behold, he prayeth.

12 And hath seen in a vision a man named Ananias coming in, and putting his hand on him, that he might receive his sight.

13 Then Ananias answered, Lord, I have heard by many of this man, how much evil he hath done to thy saints, at Jerusalem:

14 And here he hath authority from the chief priests to bind all that call on thy name.

15 But the Lord said unto him, Go thy way: for he is a chosen vessel unto me, to bear my name before the Gentiles, and kings, and the children of Israel:

16 For I will shew him how great things he must suffer for my name's sake.

17 And Ananias went his way, and entered into the house; and putting his hands on him said, Brother Saul, the Lord, *even* Jesus, that appeared unto thee in the way as thou camest, hath sent me, that thou mightest receive thy sight, and be filled with the Holy Ghost.

18 And immediately there fell from his eyes as it had been scales: and he received sight forthwith, and arose, and was baptized.

As Saul was blinded on the road to Damascus (*"when his eyes were opened, he saw no man"* –Acts 9:8), it came to pass that Judge Gilvary was blinded on the journey to trial, by written statements of the Defendant, as indicated by comment just before sentencing:

> THE COURT: You want me to review some of the other terms you've used?
> THE DEFENDANT: No, Your Honor.
> THE COURT: I'm tempted to do so.

As Saul was blinded "for three days" (Acts 9:9) and *"they led him by the hand"* (Acts 9:8), [to] *"the street which is called STRAIGHT"* (Acts 9:11),

It has come to pass that Judge Gilvary's third day is upon us and the Defendant shall take *"him by the hand"* – the hand that holds the pen – and shall offer him the way *"which is called STRAIGHT."*

THE FIRST DAY OF BLINDNESS – March 5, 1997:

Dear Judge Gilvary:

I come before you by way of this letter, and place myself at the mercy of the court.

What I ask for, herein, is not for myself, but for my wife Ann, and our aged parents, 79, 86, 90, and 94. There is a time when prudence overreaches valor. My family wants me, and needs me....

My plea for mercy was ignored and I was sentenced to six years in prison.

THE SECOND DAY OF BLINDNESS – May 5, 1997:

The Defendant filed Defendant's Motion For Different Conditions For Bond/Stay Pending Appeal.

The Court's Charge To Jury included: *"It is essential to the preservation of the social order that laws be obeyed and violators be convicted. It is equally important that the innocent should not suffer."*

Judge Gilvary ended the second day of blindness by a May 9, 1997 filing: *"The motion is OVERRULED."*

THE THIRD DAY OF BLINDNESS – The present:

And now the third day is upon us, and Judge Gilvary, *"hearing a voice, but seeing no man"* (Acts 9:7), as the Defendant "speaks from beyond the prison walls" via the tape assimilation filed with the Affidavit of Disqualification (see Vol. 1 of affidavit, page following the cover page).

Judge Gilvary (and the State) should listen to Larry Lasky on October 18, 1994, say, "You do what you have to do, but I'm just gonna tell ya somethin', you threaten me, you're gonna come up short."

Next Judge Gilvary (and the State) should listen to Maria Lowman say, on October 18, 1994, "Yeh, but see, he [Lasky] knows the law; you do not."

... The Defendant believes that *"people that have been dragged into something that should never have happened"* (Judge Gilvary's words prior to jury selection) shall be better public servants – and better people – for having experienced the Defendant's case(s).

The Defendant believes this to be particularly so for Judge James J. Gilvary. For **very, very few are afforded the opportunity to undo the wrong they've done, as Judge Gilvary, ala Saul, is being provided. The Defendant wishes him well.**

WHEREFORE, the Defendant respectfully moves the Court for a summary judgment that includes a finding that the conviction of February 20, 1997 is *void*. [Emphasis added.]

With full knowledge of what he was doing, on August 28, 1998, Judge Gilvary called the bet via a Decision, Order and Entry. In retrospect, I have often wondered what went through his mind, as Judge Gilvary sealed his fate; when he signed his own death warrant.

Gilvary was far too intelligent; much to savvy, to be completely oblivious to the cold hard facts of life. Yet the coward ruled, ala Pontius Pilate:

... Thus, it is the Court's finding that the Defendant's petition is untimely filed.... Accordingly, the State's motion to dismiss is hereby **SUSTAINED**. Further, as a direct result of this decision, the Defendant's motion for summary judgment filed on July 31, 1998 is moot.

SO ORDERED,

JAMES J. GILVERY, JUDGE

"The opportunity to undo the wrong [he'd] done" was moot to Judge Gilvary. He rejected redemption.

Ironically, it was the thirty-fifth anniversary of Dr. Martin Luther King, Jr.'s immortal *I Have a Dream* speech. Dr. King spoke eloquently of a time when men might be judged *by the content of their character*. And in time, my prisoner might be judged similarly.

Still, it was nothing personal with me. As his warden, it remained a civic duty to see the death sentence was carried out; as my prisoner acquiesced - on the record!

Yes, it was Shakespearean. To the end, Judge James J. Gilvary defiantly rejected *a street called Straight*.

CHAPTER THIRTY-FIVE

Who Do You Like in the Derby?

Now that Judge Gilvary had sealed his fate, with his August 28, 1998 ruling, I began preparing for his execution in earnest. It involved an all-out assault on his psyche.

Judge Gilvary provided leadership to his community in a variety of ways. He was very active in the Catholic Church. An article in the June 26, 1993 *Dayton Daily News* was entitled:

Gilvary Will Lead Abuse Unit

According to the article, the Archdiocese of Cincinnati chose Judge Gilvary to be the chairman of a six-member permanent Child Abuse Review Board. Archbishop Daniel E. Pilarczyk established the board.

The article went on to note the esteemed judge had experience involving child abuse cases. "I'm trying one right now – and it's not the first one I've tried."

Judge Gilvary knew the following things about me and my case:

- I was innocent of the crime I had been convicted of;
- The "trial" I received was replete with violations of the 1st, 4th, 5th, 6th, 8th and 14th Amendments;
- Gilvary had been appointed – while lacking jurisdiction – to assist in a cover-up of criminal activity within the courts;
- Though eligible for probation, Gilvary sent me to prison to further that cover-up;
- Gilvary sentenced me to a long sentence, using it as extortion to induce me to admit

"guilt" via application for shock probation, or as a condition for shock parole;
- Gilvary ignored chances to release me, his kidnap victim;
- Gilvary knew I had been sexually assaulted while in college;
- Gilvary sent sex offenders to prison; some of whom were incarcerated with me.

As warden, I wanted to make my prisoner's stay on death row as heinous as possible. I needed an assault on the psyche that would be a direct hit; one bound to pierce the psyche in a debilitating manner!

Fate is a funny thing. And I received unexpected assistance, from an independent source.

About ten inmates were regulars in the prison law library. Inmates had access to five IBM Selectric typewriters, used solely for legal matters. Time was allotted to the typewriters in one hour segments.

One day an inmate asked me; if I would give up my hour. He had an urgent court filing to prepare for another inmate, and time was of the essence. I conceded, as we looked out for one another whenever possible.

"As a matter of fact, Metz, this is going to your trial judge," the grateful inmate offered.

"No shit! What's it about?"

He was assisting a sex offender named Kirby A. Goodrich, who had been sentenced by Judge Gilvary. The legal eagle introduced me to Goodrich.

Goodrich exclaimed in exasperation, "I paid the little whore fifteen dollars for a blow job. How the hell was I supposed to know she was thirteen?"

When asked why he pled guilty, Goodrich responded as I expected. "Well...there were other matters involved, that I faced."

Goodrich paid a retainer of a thousand dollars or so to Attorney Mike Long, who induced a plea bargain. According to Goodrich, Long claimed he and Gilvary were close friends, who even had a mutual interest in thoroughbred horse racing. Long promised to use his friendship with the judge to induce a short sentence. In essence, Goodrich was duped by Long.

Goodrich pled guilty, expecting a short sentence and Gilvary stroked him with 8-20 years. He was very, very pissed off. The prison legal eagle was attempting to get the sentence reduced.

I casually mentioned to the legal eagle; there might be a much better chance of prevailing, should Gilvary be disqualified. And I knew Chief Justice Thomas Moyer would give careful consideration to such a petition.

I slyly explained how I had recently reamed Moyer's ass out for ruling on mine in one day – over the same judge. The legal eagle was delighted, and filed an Affidavit of Disqualification in the Ohio Supreme Court.

I was not interested in the lurid details of the case. As a category, most of the sex offenders in prison gave me the creeps. Goodrich was no exception.

I knew nothing about the case, and had no involvement in petitioning Moyer. In fact, I never learned anything about the pleading filed; until Moyer ruled.

But I wanted a copy of the any response by Judge Gilvary, and a copy of Moyer's decision. It was agreed I would pay a dollar per page, for the information.

I paid three dollars; via boxes of Debbies. It amounted to paying for ingredients of a lethal injection.

Judge Gilvary was forced to explain his interests in horse racing to Ohio Supreme Court Chief Justice Thomas J. Moyer. After careful consideration, that took longer than the one day in my case, Moyer ruled that legal eagle's request to disqualify Gilvary was:

... found not well-taken and is denied.

A copy went to Montgomery County Prosecutor Mathias Heck, Jr.

COURT OF COMMON PLEAS
MONTGOMERY COUNTY COURTS BUILDING
GENERAL DIVISION

JAMES J. GILVARY
JUDGE

41 NORTH PERRY STREET
P.O. BOX 972
DAYTON, OHIO 45422-2150
(513)496-7951
FAX (513) 225-5466

November 4, 1998

Richard A. Dove
Associate Director For
Legal and Legislative Services
The Supreme Court of Ohio
30 East Broad Street
Columbus, Ohio 43266-0419

In Re: <u>State of Ohio v. Kirby A. Goodrich</u>
Case No. 94-CR-431
Your File No. 98-AP-124

Dear Mr. Dove:

    I received your letter of October 26, 1998, on October 28, 1998. In his affidavit of disqualification, relator charges that Michael Long told him that I was a "good friend" and that we had a "horse racing relationship." I have been practicing law in the greater Dayton area since 1955. My guess is that Mike came on the scene around 1960. I have known him since he started practicing law here. On perhaps two occasions in the late 1960s or 1970s, we were part of a group of ten or twelve couples who went to the races at Keenland, Kentucky. I have probably talked to Mike on the street 4 or 5 times over the past 25 years about the sport of thoroughbred racing. We have no "horse racing" relationship other than a love of that sport. We have not spent a total of an hour together discussing any subject over the past 25 years, and that includes Case No. 94-CR-0431 on this Court's Docket. We have never had a "financial interest" of any sort. Any "advice" in picking winners would be limited to meeting each other walking down the street on four or five occasions in the past 25 years and asking "Who do you like in the Derby?" The present case with Mike Long is the first contact I have had with him since I took the bench in 1991.

    My knowledge of Mike Long and my interest in horse racing had nothing to do with my accepting Mr. Goodrich's plea of guilty to multiple counts in this case.

James J. Gilvary, Judge
Common Pleas Court
Montgomery County, Ohio

Explaining his interest in horse racing to the Ohio Supreme Court - The last time I would see Judge Gilvary's signature.

My prisoner, alone in stark solitary confinement, in his prison of the psyche, day after weary day, had to *believe* this latest assault had been instigated by his warden. Reality, for my prisoner, was the appearance that Kirby A. Goodrich and I had bonded in the State's prison; an abuser and an abused. Devilishly satisfied, I imagined Gilvary cursed me; while cursing his fate. The spiritual dynamics were compelling.

Gilvary mocked me, while covering up criminal activity of others within the judicial system. He mocked me, knowing I had been sexually abused. He mocked me as he sentenced me; to live with sex offenders. He did so, while acting as an overseer of sexual abuse incidents for the Catholic Church.

I foresaw the dire implications for Gilvary. He had taken Lasky's seat across from me at the poker table, in the casino called *Life*. From the beginning, Lasky had gone *all in*. He said to me on October 18, 1994:

It's what we say in Vegas. You gotta pay to play.

I had written to Lasky the following day, October 19, 1994, in an attempt to reason:

Any more cheap shots like yesterday,
and I'll respond with a *vengeance*.

In a November 27, 1995 civil appellate motion, I noted that *Attorney* beat *Vengeance* at Keenland in the third race on October 27th. It was the first race for both two-year-olds, and *Attorney* had an inside bias; due to the condition of the track that day.

In a December 21, 1995 civil appellate motion, I noted that *Boomerang* beat *Attorney* in the fifth race at Churchill Downs on November 24th. Two days later, I further noted, *Vengeance* won at Turfway Park.

On January 12, 1996 Lasky complained in an appellate court filing, "[T]his is not a 'voodoo' court in which a litigant can magically interpret hidden messages from racing forms and use them to protract litigation."

In a response entitled "Voodoo" Court Motion, I noted that *Great Pretender* beat *Voodoo Spell* in the first race at Aqueduct on December 27, 1995. *Have Faith* came in third.

I further noted:

> While Mr. Lasky is correct in that race results are not a basis for decision-making in matters before the Honorable Court, they could be used as an indicator for proper conduct, henceforth; much like a weather report induces one to leave home with a raincoat, boots, and an umbrella when a pending storm is forecasted.... I predict a hurricane.
>
> You folks haven't seen anything yet.

On January 29, 1995, I wrote appellate judges, Jim Brogan and Mike Fain a letter following an oral hearing; after they upheld a second eviction against me from Miamisburg Municipal Court. From the letter:

> ... And what were those words from the bench in the beginning of the hearing? "God save..." God has a heap of work to do, in the legal profession and the court system. As *His employee*, I'll do my part.

Vengeance fell within God's domain. Writing Lasky concerning it equated to: *I'll sick God on you!*

Insights were based on Deuteronomy 32:35:

> To me *belongeth* vengeance, and recompence; their foot shall slide in *due* time: for the day of their calamity *is* at hand, and the things that shall come upon them make haste.

> Romans 12: *19 Revenge forbidden.*
> 19 Dearly beloved, avenge not yourselves, but *rather* give place upon wrath: for it is written, Vengeance *is* mine; I will repay, saith the Lord.
> 20 Therefore, if thine enemy hunger, feed him; if he thirst, give him drink: for in doing so thou shalt heap coals of fire on his head.

As *His employee,* I understood my role as the prisoner's warden. Clemency was always an option. But jurisdiction for a petition of clemency was strictly limited;
was between my prisoner and his God.

I had forgiven Judge Gilvary, and informed him so;
via a written court filing from prison in July 1997:

> The Defendant believes *"people that have been dragged in-
> to something that should never have happened"* (Judge
> Gilvary's words prior to jury selection) shall be better public
> servants, and better people; for having experienced the De-
> fendant's case(s).
>
> The Defendant believes this to be particularly so for Judge
> James J. Gilvary. For very, very few are afforded the oppor-
> tunity to undo the wrong they've done, as Judge Gilvary, ala
> Saul, is being provided. The Defendant wishes him well.

This particular motion was declared moot by Judge
Gilvary – in man's secular court. But it could never be
erased from the mind, the heart, or the soul of either
of us.

Therefore, the petition remained to be ruled on – in
the *Universal Supreme Court* governed by *Universal
Laws of Life,* where God served as *Universal Supreme
Court Justice.*

My prisoner turned away from God, by desecrating
his oath. His only hope of a favorable ruling on my petition was to return.

It was beyond man's power to intercede further in
his behalf. I could not; nor could any priest or church
official Gilvary sought out. Sadly, I knew he lacked the
character and the courage to humble himself before
God. In that condition; he remained helpless.

As warden, as *His employee,* my role was to assure
the execution was carried out. It was a responsibility I
took seriously.

I laid on my bunk the night after receiving a copy of
Judge Gilvary's letter to Chief Justice Moyer. Unable

to sleep far into the night, I remembered the reasoning in Lasky's appellate motion, concerning voodoo.

And in the quiet of night, amongst fifty-three sleeping inmates; I laughed until I cried, as I entertained enchanted thoughts:

Who do voodoo? Who do voodoo? Who do voodoo?

Fate is a funny thing. Four years after promising Larry Lasky I would come after him with a vengeance, should reason not prevail, something boomeranged on the judge; who had inherited Lasky's seat at the table. Gilvary was the Great Pretender, whose self-delusion and aloof pretentiousness had been vanquished.

Being the warden had become enormously rewarding! There was no reason to doubt Gilvary's version of his and Attorney Mike Long's relationship. And there was ample reason to conclude Gilvary would *believe* I was behind the allegations. I had simply gotten lucky.

The assault on my prisoner's psyche was as complete as it could possibly be. The pious, liberal Judge James J. Gilvary was inspired to defend himself; to a prim and proper conservative, Ohio Supreme Court Chief Justice Thomas J. Moyer.

Alas, my prisoner would never enjoy another visit to Keenland; would never again ask, *Who do you like in the Derby?*

CHAPTER THIRTY-SIX

The Terror of Loneliness

Judge Gilvary was similar to a person who never received his inoculations to protect against disease. Unaccustomed to psychic pain, my prisoner was helpless. My next step would be to allow time to pass; so psychic wounds could fester into a more serious malady. Before long, my prisoner would be unable to fend off the mighty Redwood *when* it fell across his psyche.

In contrast to my prisoner's misery, I was serene in my role as his warden. There was a civic duty to perform, and I would perform it perfunctory.

I was looking forward to the execution. It was *winner take all* at the poker table, in the casino called *Life*.

Included in the legal mail I received from my sister, Karen in July 1998, with the Ohio Supreme Court filing, had been a copy of the tape recording filed as an exhibit; in Gilvary's court on December 27, 1996. (It was taken to Gilvary; with the Supreme Court filing.)

Audio tapes were not permitted into the prison unless they came directly from a retailer. I pointed out to the guard searching through the nine-volume filing that this recording was a part of my case, and had been properly filed with the Supreme Court.

The tape was in a sealed envelope that was stamped with a Supreme Court case number. He allowed me to keep it.

It was surreal. I could walk the prison track, or lie on my bunk, and hear the golden voices of Lasky, Lowman, and Messham et al. I could look at the American flag flying majestically, and listen to Lee Greenwood sing "God Bless the USA," or hear Conway Twitty and Loretta Lynn sing "God Bless America Again"; listen to Johnny Cash sing "Ragged Old Flag."

I could hear Gene Autry tell of "The Solitary Man" – the story of Jesus and the mockery of a trial.

Contents: Tape recording filed as exhibit on 12-27-96
in: Ohio vs. Metz
95-CR-2317

This tape exhibit and its accompanying trial court motions are
made exhibits in:
Affidavit of Disqualification of Judge J. Gilvary

See exhibit page E-323; Memorandum Page M-835

98AP 079

Tape filed with Affidavit of Disqualification – Ohio Supreme Court

Flag seen as I walked the
track on the prison yard
in Pickaway Correctional
Institution

I would remind myself daily; I was one of the luckiest men to have ever walked the earth; I was an American citizen. And as such I had a sacred responsibility to do whatever I was led to do, so that the America I loved could find her soul again.

Songs on the Tape

1. "The Solitary Man" by Gene Autry
2. "Town Without Pity" by Gene Pitney
3. "Maria" from West Side Story
4. "Who Am I" by Elvis Presley
5. "Happy Trails To You" by Roy Rogers and Dale Evans
6. "Oh Come All Ye Faithful" by Al Martino
7. "It Wasn't God Who Made Honky Tonk Angels" by Kitty Wells
8. "Back Home Again" by John Denver
9. "Ragged Old Flag" by Johnny Cash
10. "It Is No Secret" by Elvis Presley
11. "God Bless America Again" by Conway Twitty and Loretta Lynn
12. "I Believe" by Elvis Presley
13. "Walkin' In The Sun" by Glen Campbell
14. "Waterloo" by Stonewall Jackson
15. "Who's Sorry Now" by Connie Francis
16. "God Bless The USA" by Lee Greenwood
17. "In The Jailhouse Now" by Sonny James

In 8-Bay, four of us formed an especially tight-knit group: myself, Kevin "P-Nut" Parnell, George Favors, and Jim Bush. I respected these men I bonded with, and promised my friends I would remember them; in my book, someday.

A white man and three black men formed an uncommon bond. It was well known; they had my back.

Favors provided me with memorable prison wisdom. George liked to proclaim with toothy grin, in a disarming manner, "It's your lie; tell it the way you want too."

One day P-Nut and I were going to play a prison card game named Casino. We decided to cut cards to determine who would deal. As Parnell pulled a card from the deck, I pointed at his hand and commanded, "Call the card!" "Five of spades," Parnell blurted out. He turned over the five of spades. Later he signed a written statement, documenting what took place.

> October 2, 1998
>
> Met and I played Casino on his locker box, on his bunk. One day neither of us wanted to deal first, and we agreed to draw cards. The deck was fanned, face down. High card would deal.
>
> As I pulled a card from the deck, Met pointed towards my hand and exclaimed, "Call the card!"
>
> "Five of spades," I said. I turned up the five of spades.
>
> A few days later Met asked me what I thought had happened. I replied, "It was just like we had done that before, and I _knew_ what the card was."
>
> This was the only time we cut cards in such a manner.
>
> P-NUT
>
> Kevin Parnell
> #351-212

P-Nut called out, "Five of spades."

Once again, I _knew_ God was with me, and I with Him. I was acting out a spiritual obligation mandated by a spiritual principle; _faith without works is dead._

Prison creates its own sense of community. I cultivated a rapport with inmates I lived amongst. I always had the pen, the paper, or other small item needed. I was generous sharing commissary with inmates who received no outside funds, and who had no hustle to earn money.

I had an empathetic ear, and offered guidance when appropriate. I liked to think some of the younger lives were touched in a positive way.

I was encouraged and inspired by prison friends. Society perceives a convict by the crime he committed; but I got to view the very human element, aside from the crime.

And no matter what else; in most men, there was a good side to observe. From the two thousand plus imprisoned with me, I could have pulled forty-one at random, and assembled a group with more integrity than those who persecuted me. *Any forty-one!* It says volumes about "well educated" officers of the court.

Another of the 8-Bay inmates was Bobby "Starr" Wingard. Starr's route to prison was an unusual one. One night he was sitting at the bar minding his own business, in a tavern he had never been to before. At a nearby table, a drunk hit a woman in the face with his fist, knocking her to the floor.

Starr went to help her up, and as he bent over her, the drunk broke a beer bottle over his head. Starr grabbed the guy's wrist and stuck the bottle in his throat.

As he sat the woman on her chair, another of the drunk's crowd came at him with a pool stick. Starr broke it in half and stuck the end into the guy's stomach, giving it a few thrusts, in and out for good measure. A third came at him, and Starr broke his kneecaps with two kicks.

Starr was charged with "excessive use of force." In court, he was offered five years probation – the judge remarked it was unbelievable; that a little man like Starr could inflict such havoc on three huge toughs.

Starr's work took him all over the world as a deep sea diver. Probation meant he could not leave Ohio; he would lose his high paying job. Starr chose prison instead, stepping off an eight-month sentence for "falsification," whatever imaginary crime that was.

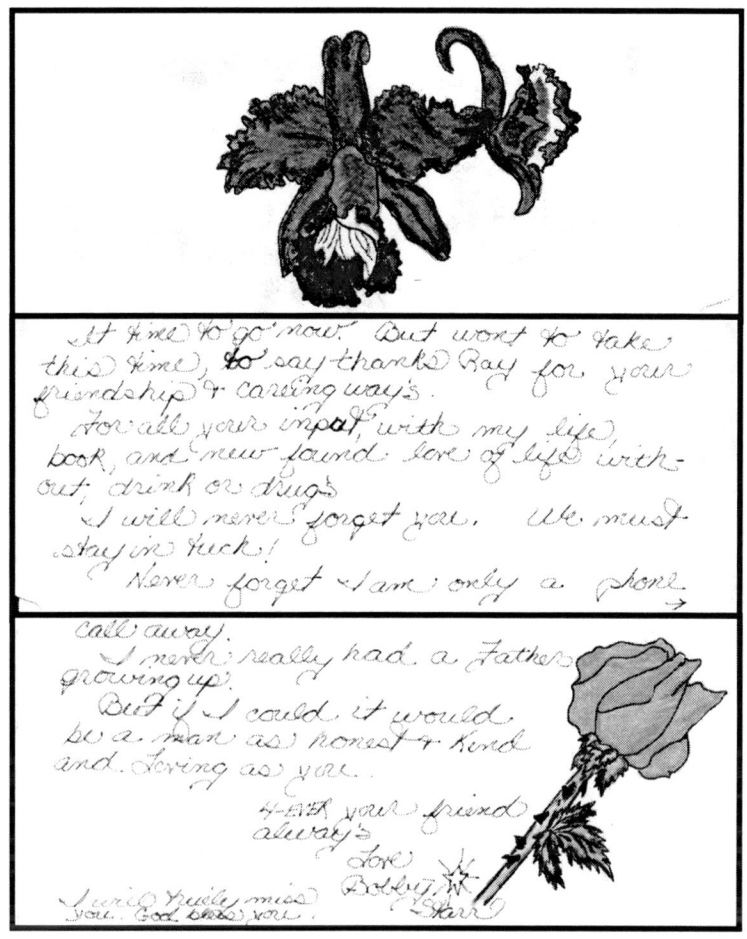

My heart went out to a war hero; his heart came back to me.
Prison artwork of Bobby "Starr" Wingard.

Starr was over forty years old. He joined the Army at age fifteen, and had become a sniper. He shared many of his war experiences with me.

Demons from the Vietnam War still haunted him. I would lay awake at night listening; as Starr literally went through hell, suffering unimaginable nightmares as he cried out in a restless sleep - *every single night.* One night he dreamt he was diving out of a window to escape enemy attack, and broke his wrist after he dove off his top bunk.

Bobby "Starr" Wingard served two prison sentences. One was unjustly imposed by the State of Ohio. But a worse one was imposed by fate; a life sentence in the prison of the psyche. It was a double injustice for a very decent human being.

Prison can break a man; can harden a man's heart, and make him angrier; bitterer. Or, prison can make a man, giving him the blessed gift of compassion, and a new appreciation for freedom; and for life.

My prison experience was a spiritual one, filled with fellowship and meaningful relationships. It made me a better man.

My prisoner was not as fortunate. From graduating high school as class valedictorian, Gilvary sought the approval of others. He lived for it, much as the drunk's dependency on the next drink.

By now the potential consequences of detection for his crime was beginning to sink into his psyche. He was guilty of kidnapping and extortion.

Unconcerned at the time; with what he had done, he now feared public disclosure. As warden, I understood Gilvary's dilemma. Solitary confinement on death row is akin to *hell on earth.*

His greatest fear, bordering on obsession, was that I would learn of Rule 1.19 III(C), divesting him of jurisdiction. He could never imagine I had known about it; from the day we first met.

It was unimaginable, because I had created a history of being predictable, at the poker table. It appeared to my opponent; each time I found something untoward, I immediately documented it in court filings.

Alone with his fears, his plight was described in words of a song I had written in the 1980s, and put in the 1,900+ page Affidavit of Disqualification.

Life Sentence

Now listen, brother, to a tale I tell;
'Bout a man-made prison; 'bout a place called hell.
No bars of steel; no walls of stone;
Just a jug of wine, drinkin' all the time;
Livin' all alone; livin' all alone.

No guards with guns; no warden there;
No judge who sentenced; no jury fair;
No parole board, to hear a plea;
Just a jug of wine, drinkin' all the time;
Live in misery; live in misery.

A prison of turmoil and strife,
Confined there by the *laws of life*.
Stripped of all joy; all dignity;
Just a jug of wine, drinkin' all the time;
Such a pity; such a pity.

There's no escapin' on one's own;
Many have failed; many forlorn.
There's one way out; it's hard to see.
Just a jug of wine, drinkin' all the time;
There's one way free; one way free.

Beaten by life; by the jug of wine;
On bended knee; there's a God to find.
Learnin' the rules, of life's great game;
No jug of wine, drinkin' all the time;
No life of shame; no life of shame.

I was this prisoner, I sing about;
Now I am free, and there's no doubt;
Lovin' the life; been given me.
No jug of wine, drinkin' all the time;
God set me free; God set me free.

Walk from that prison; walk tall and free;
Live a life of sobriety.
Praise the great God, Who set you free.
No jug of wine, drinkin' all the time;
Live with dignity; live with dignity.

A prison of the psyche involves many visits to the prison's *Hole(s)*. I wrote of drinking. But the addiction could be any other; that enslaved a man's soul.

In Gilvary's case, the willingness to abuse power, for the gratification found in the adulation of others; was a difficult one to deal with. To be true to the words of my song, Givary must turn to his God.

Given the realities, he was bound to turn to himself, since he viewed himself as god in the courtroom. And it is precisely what Gilvary did. But things did not go as planned, for this human and illusionary version of man-god.

To Gilvary's great dismay, I had the transcripts. I had his *confession,* transcribed by an independent court reporter, as spoken:

> You see, what's happened here since June of
> '94, is people have been dragged into some-
> thing that should never have happened. If due
> process had been followed in civil matters, we
> wouldn't be sitting here, but they weren't.

This was not supposed to happen. It exacerbated his fearful state. To Gilvary, this outcome was unfathomable.

In fact, soon after his careless confession, made on the record, Judge Gilvary made certain it could never happen again. He installed a tape recording system in his courtroom and chambers, eliminating the need for an unbiased court reporter.

In the future, the decadent judge could control editing needs, if necessary for self-preservation. He was viewed as a "judicial innovator," instead of a thief who controlled a video recording of any future crimes.

But no matter what my prisoner did, to protect himself from future gaffs, he was stuck with the historical impact of what was done in *Ohio v. Metz.* And so, he remained a cowardly, lonely prisoner with no avenue of escape.

By attempting to perpetrate *The Perfect Crime* with appellate judges and the prosecuting attorney, it was assumed every possible contingency had been anticipated. They were egregiously in error.

They had depended on the mistaken belief that what was being done to me was so heinous; I would be incapable of withstanding it. They assumed, like most inmates, I would do anything to get out of prison.

But I discovered fulfillment and purpose in prison. Friendships were formed. To be sure, it was a difficult environment. To be sure, it was not always easy. But I was at *peace* with myself. And I joyously endured the hardships that accompany prison life. It was just the opposite of what my oppressors had planed; the opposite of what my prisoner experienced.

I became inspired by an old Elvis Presley standard.[42]

> Are you lonesome tonight
> Do you miss Him tonight
> Are you sorry you drifted apart
> Does your memory stray
> To that bright sunshine day
> When He reigned as Lord of your heart
> Does your life seem empty
> Heart filled with despair
> Do you gaze at your mantle
> See the crucifix there
> Shall He come back again
> Be your Lord, be your Friend
> He's Jesus; He's waiting tonight
>
> *A warden's spoken word:*
> I know you're lonesome tonight
> Shakespeare said the world's a stage
> And each must play his part
> Fate had me playing in court with you
> A judge without a heart
> Act one was when we met
> You loathed me at first glance

---

[42] "Are You Lonesome Tonight?" - recorded by Elvis Presley in 1960.

You read you lines so cleverly
And took a gambler's chance
Then came act two, you did not change
Acted deranged
And why I'll always know
Judge, you lied
When you took your oath to God
And He had no cause to doubt you
But you'd rather go on telling your lies
And go on living without Him
Now the stage is bare
And you're standing there
With emptiness all around
And if you won't turn back to Him
Then God will bring the curtain down
    Is your heart filled with pain
    Shall He come back again
    Tell me, judge, are you lonesome tonight

Fate is a funny thing. Things had boomeranged on Judge Gilvary. It happened, just as noted in the *Daily Racing Form* Official Chart for Churchill Downs' fifth race on November 24, 1995; duly noted in a Second District Court of Appeals civil case motion of December 21, 1995, involving Larry Lasky. The motion read:

> The running line from the *Daily Racing Form* reads: "*Attorney, well placed to the stretch while racing four abreast between foes, came up empty in the drive.*" The race was won by *Boomerang.*

Without legal authority to become involved in my criminal case, Gilvary recklessly agreed to "rescue" associates within the Dayton legal community. This implied that he sought their approval, to the extent that he egregiously violated his oath to God. I recognized this superficial side of Judge Gilvary immediately.

Admitted to the Ohio Bar August 26, 1954; Gilvary came to adulthood during a World War II generation.

As such, he had been identified by sociologist David Riesman, in *The Lonely Crowd: A Study of the Changing American Character,* a 1954 analysis of the post-war American society.

Riesman defined the perfect candidate to become involved in a sleazy cover-up within the judicial system. Conclusions from his book, applicable to Gilvary:

> "Behavioral conformity" is achieved through "an exceptional sensitivity to the actions and wishes of others," Riesman wrote. With that, the sense of *self* changes as one gravitates from group to group. "The other-directed person has no clear core of self," therefore he resides in *"the terror of loneliness."*

The *walls were closing in* on Judge Gilvary, in the isolation of his prison of the psyche. He was a man attempting to run away from himself, and there was nowhere left to run.

The day was fast approaching when the bewildered judge would be confronted with himself; a time that would leave him mourning with a profound sense of sadness and shame, at the enormity of his disgrace; a time when he would accept another way to escape *the terror of loneliness.*

CHAPTER THIRTY-SEVEN

The Mighty Redwood

I began making final preparations for the execution. Only clemency from God could stave off the inevitable.

US Senator Mike DeWine was from Greene County. DeWine's former law partner was Greene County Prosecutor William F. Schenck. His wife, Barbara was the State Director for Senator DeWine.

Bill Schenck had been invited to Washington, to act as advisor for Senator DeWine; during the impeachment trial of President Clinton. He expressed satisfaction; a question he raised had been answered by US Supreme Court Chief Justice William H. Rehnquist, who presided as judge over the Senate trial.

It was time for William F. Schenck to serve his country again. On March 6, 1999, I wrote him.

> By separate letter, I have contacted your wife and Senator DeWine, seeking his assistance in attempts to have a federal investigation of the courts, clerk of courts, and prosecutor's office in Montgomery County, similar to the federal probe in Mahoning County.
>
> An Ohio State Patrol officer visited me in prison, upon request of prison authorities, and informed me that there is federal jurisdiction for the criminal activity I have evidence of. I believe that prosecution could be attained under the federal RICO act.
>
> Recognizing that while you filed an appearance as special prosecutor in my case, yet never participated in the trial or proceedings; I am suggesting a way for you to avoid personal liability.
>
> The Montgomery County Local Rules of Court are explicit. Quoting:
> Rule 1.10 Rules of Construction.
> IV Effective Date.

These rules *shall* take effect on July 1, 1993. They govern *all* proceedings in actions brought on or after July 1, 1993.

Rule 1.19 The Assignment System
III(C) Transfer Of Assigned Cases To A New Judge.
If the case is transferred from the *originally assigned* judge to a new judge, *the* new judge *shall* hear all motions and proceedings to the case.

Shall is a mandate. On April 16, 1996, Dennis J. Langer became the *originally assigned* judge. He recused and Judge Gorman was assigned. On July 29, 1996, Deputy Clerk Maria Lowman, who had participated in criminal activity in civil cases I had in municipal court, was fired for theft in office.

Gorman removed herself from my case via procedure peculiar to civil cases, and was assigned Lowman's case. On August 26, 1996, James J. Gilvary became a third judge in my case, with *no* jurisdiction.

As the special prosecutor who agreed to take my case, and as the representative of the State with ultimate authority (and responsibility), should *you* file a motion in Gorman's court to void the conviction, I am confident that she would respond responsibly.

You should reference the 1975 case of *Cuyahoga County Board of Mental Retardation, Appellee, v. Association of Cuyahoga County Teachers of the Trainable Retarded, et al., Appellant,* 47 OApp2d, 28 100 3d 168, 351 N.E.2d 777:

> The oath of office of a judge, required under Section 7, Article XV of the Ohio Constitution and specified in R.C. 3.23 requires that a judge will "discharge and perform all the duties incumbent on him as such judge"***
> ... the trial judge was prohibited from hearing this case; that he was under a compulsory duty to disqualify himself, and that his breach of that duty rendered his subsequent actions null and void.

... the attempt of a trial judge to exercise his authority as a judge in violation of his mandatory duty is of absolutely no effect.

... the duty of the trial judge under Section (3)(C)(1)(d)(i) of the Code of Judicial Conduct, similar to that provided under U.S.C. Section 455 (1975 Supp.) controlling the disqualification of federal judges, is one placed solely upon the individual judge.

Unquestionably, Langer, Gorman and Gilvary have judicial knowledge of their own rules of court. In answer to what difference this made in my eventual fate, I refer you to the 1,900+ page Affidavit of Disqualification of Gilvary filed with the Ohio Supreme Court on July 1, 1998, and served on you that same day.

Little wonder that Ohio Supreme Court Chief Justice Thomas J. Moyer was able to rule on such a detailed motion within twenty-four hours. It was oxymoronic. He who was never qualified could not be disqualified!

There's a certain poetic justice to be found for our Democrat friends in Dayton. President Clinton's artful use of the word *is* saved him from a legal definition of perjury. Here, explicit intent of the word *the* make my captors eligible for the charge of kidnapping, in an effort to escape criminal liability in other matters.

After you've had time to consider the alternatives, my sister, Karen Sue Lowry shall contact you in person, for your reaction and/or response.

Very truly yours,
Horace Ray Metz
copy to: *Dayton Daily News*
        Sam Donaldson

Sam Donaldson was sent a copy, to encourage proper attention. Next I wrote to Barbara Schenck.

Dear Mrs. Schenck:
Enclosed please find a letter to Senator DeWine.

Inasmuch as you and your husband are personal friends of Senator DeWine, I am requesting that you bring the correspondence to his *personal* attention.

My sister, Karen Sue Lowry, shall contact you in the future to seek your assurance that Senator DeWine personally saw my letter to him.

Thank you for your assistance in this matter.

Very truly yours,

Horace Ray Metz

enclosure

copy to: *Dayton Daily News*
         Sam Donaldson

Bill Schenck liked to boast of his high success rate in prosecutions. He rarely lost in court. There are likely two good reasons; prosecutorial lying and cheating.

He probably trained Rob Hendrix, who persecuted me as a Special Prosecutor. I believe this to be probable, because Hendrix was a liar and a cheat.

So what happened was very satisfying. I asked Bill Schenck's wife to assure that his friend, Senator Mike DeWine helped me in getting the FBI to investigate her husband, et al.

I thought while contemplating the delicious irony; *Let the weasel squirm his way out of this one. Squirm, squirm - right to Gilvary!*

Dear Senator DeWine:

I seek your assistance in having federal authorities contact me, in order that I can turn over evidence of criminal activity within the courts, clerk of courts, and prosecutor's office in Montgomery County.

Essentially, the *only* reason I am in prison is because of the criminal activity I uncovered. Prison officials arranged for an Ohio State Patrol officer to visit me, and I was informed that there is federal jurisdiction for the crimes committed.

Federal prosecution would likely be under the RICO Act. To date, I have been stonewalled in efforts to see a United States attorney, marshal, or someone from the FBI. Should

your office wish to review evidence in my possession, I would
make it available.

Thank you, in advance, for any assistance you may be able
to provide.

Very truly yours,

Horace Ray Metz

p.s. William F. Schenck filed an appearance as special
   prosecutor in my case, although he never personally
   appeared.

copy to: *Dayton Daily News*
         Sam Donaldson

My sister, Karen visited Barbara Schenck's office.
Mrs. Schenck assured Karen she would personally see
that Senator DeWine saw my letter. She showed Karen
that it was right on her desk, to be dealt with.

Karen left Senator DeWine's Xenia office, and went
directly to the prosecutor's office in the Greene County
Courthouse.

Karen saw a telephone message from his wife with
Karen's name on it, lying on the desk of the secretary
who talked with her. The message was to Greene
County's version of *Slick Willie!* Contradictory state-
ments by the person who answered for Schenck; told
Karen the Greene County/Montgomery County Special
Prosecutor - William F. Schenck *hid from her!*

Karen asked Billy-boy's secretary to have Special
Prosecutor Schenck telephone her, and of course, she
never heard from him. Alas, he was nothing special!

I intuitively *knew* that a very, very perturbed weasel
would make a beeline for the culprits in Montgomery
County. My letter to him ended up going right where I
planned - piercing the psyche of my prisoner.

The one thing Judge Gilvary feared most was that I
would learn of Rule 1.19 III(C). His greatest fear, his
great obsession - became his reality.

I received a letter from Senators DeWine and Voinovich, dated April 12, 1999.

MIKE DeWINE
UNITED STATES SENATOR
OHIO

GEORGE VOINOVICH
UNITED STATES SENATOR
OHIO

United States Senate

WASHINGTON, DC 20510-3504

CASEWORK HOTLINE: (800) 205-OHIO (6446)

April 12, 1999

Horace Ray Metz
Pickaway Correctional Institution
P.O. Box 209
Orient, Ohio 43146

Dear Horace:

Thank you for your recent correspondence regarding criminal activity within the courts, clerk of courts and Prosecutor's office in Montgomery County. As your United States Senators, we appreciate that you brought this matter to our attention.

We have merged our casework offices because we believe services offered by a joint casework staff will be more efficient and cost effective to the constituents of the State of Ohio.

After carefully reviewing the information provided, our office has forwarded your concerns to the Federal Bureau of Investigation. As soon as we receive any information, we will promptly be back in touch with you again.

In the meantime, please do not hesitate to contact our casework office at 1-800-205-OHIO (6446) with any additional questions or comments.

Very respectfully yours,

MIKE DeWINE
United States Senator

Sincerely Yours,

GEORGE VOINOVICH
United States Senator

RMD/GVV/hb

37 WEST BROAD STREET, ROOM 970
COLUMBUS, OHIO 43215
(614) 469-6774 / FAX: 469-7419

PRINTED ON RECYCLED PAPER

Letter from Senator DeWine's office

Things were moving expeditiously towards execution day, for my prisoner. Ohio's US senators requested that the FBI get involved in my *"concerns"* involving *"criminal activity within the courts, clerk of courts, and Prosecutor's office in Montgomery County."*

Sunday, April 8, 1999 was my 787th day in captivity. A security officer came to 8-Bay about 9:30 in the morning, and told me to report to the Captain's Office.

It is something every inmate dreads, and too many have to experience.

"Mr. Metz, have a seat," a captain began in a kindly manner. "I am sorry to have to tell you, I received a call about an hour ago. Your father passed away at 12:15 this morning. You have my condolences. If there is anything you need, or that we can do for you, please let me know. Would you like to see the chaplain?"

With tears welling up, I told the captain there was nothing he could do, and thanked him for his kindness. My father's death came as no surprise, as his health had been failing. I had a strong faith, I explained; I would be alright.

As an inmate in good standing within an Ohio medium security prison, I would be permitted to view Dad's body, the captain informed me. The cost would be $70 for two guards to escort me to the funeral home, where I would have a private viewing.

I did not want to go. I did not want my last memory of father to be of me standing, alone and in shackles, in front of his casket. My family understood and supported my wishes.

The day of Dad's funeral, I was given permission to skip class in a prison computer course I was enrolled in. I spent the morning alone, reminiscing.

In that moment, I had no control over the thoughts that came to mind, and made no attempt at such control. I compared Dad's eighth-grade education to that of Judge Gilvary. I thought of how much smarter Dad was; as a gambler, and more importantly, as a man.

During a visit when I lived in Denver from 1975-83, I took Dad to the Family Restaurant in downtown Littleton.

Two brothers owned the place. And I introduced Dad to one of them. Everything was *on the house.* We had a few beers; and a couple shots of Canadian Club with our lunch, and enjoyed the owner's hospitality.

Then Dad asked, "Louie, are you a Greek?"

"Yes, Mr. Metz, I am."

"I used to work for a damned Greek; drove an ice cream truck for him during the Depression. Tightest son-of-a-bitch I ever worked for!"

I had forewarned Louie about Dad. And I rolled my eyes in exasperation, as Louie laughed along with Dad.

"No more booze, Louie!" I pleaded to no avail.

I finally got Dad out of there. But we had to sober-up before going home to face Mom. So I took him to the race track.

It was the first time my father had ever been to the track. And we sat in the grandstand at Centennial, in the sunshine of a glorious Colorado day. We watched three or four races. During the post parade for the next race, Dad spoke up.

"What's the least amount you can bet?"

"Two dollars."

Dad reached into his billfold and carefully extracted two dollar bills. "Bet it on that steel grey. I grew up on a farm, and that's a damned good looking horse!"

Of course, the horse won easily, and paid $16.40 to win. "Go get my money, boy," Dad said indifferently, as if he had known all along the horse would win.

As he took the money from me, and carefully put it in his billfold, he looked up at me and said with a big grin, "I'll be the only son-of-a-bitch in America, that's ahead for life!"

That was my Dad. It is the way I remembered him; and cherished the memory of that day - *ahead for life.*

Mother intended to place an obituary in the *Xenia Gazette,* and not in the *Dayton Daily News.* I insisted that we place an obituary in the Dayton paper also. I explained to Mother that it was a *spiritual* matter, for me. She readily agreed with my wishes.

My letter of March 1997, from county jail, wherein I begged for mercy from Judge Gilvary on behalf of my wife and aged parents, ended with: *... before my father dies.*

> **METZ, Horace A.**
> age 88 of Waynesville died Sunday April 18, 1999 at Quaker Heights Nursing Home, Waynesville. He retired from GM/Frigidaire in 1971 after serving for over 30 years. He was also a member of the Sharon United Methodist Church in Kingman, OH. He was preceded in death by four brothers; Dave, Jim, Nick and Jake Metz and five sisters; Mary Parthemore, Edith Howe, Mildred Kendig, Ann Winget and Sarah Shipley. He is survived by his wife Lucille; three sons and daughters-in-law Ray and Ann Metz of KY, Gerald and Shirley Metz of Jamestown, and Thomas and Diane Metz of Kettering; daughter and son-in-law Karen and Ted Lowry of Waynesville; 15 grandchildren; 19 great grandchildren; and several nieces and nephews. Graveside services 11:30a.m. Wednesday at the New Burlington Cemetery. Rev. Charles Ellison will officiate. Stubbs-Conner Funeral Home, Waynesville is serving the family. If desired, contributions may be made to the New Burlington Friends Church c/o Jean Jones, 9149 Compton Rd., Waynesville, OH 45068.   4/20/99   D.D.N.

Dad's obituary in *Dayton Daily News*

Unlike my father, Judge Gilvary was a pathetic gambler. *The Mighty Redwood* – Local Rule 1.19 III(C) - had fallen across the psyche of my prisoner. It was simply a matter of time. The end was near for my unrepentant prisoner.

CHAPTER THIRTY-EIGHT

I'm Sorry for You, My Judge

Unknown to me at the time, five days after Father's funeral, Judge Gilvary entered Miami Valley Hospital in Dayton, suffering a "sudden illness." This was *two weeks* after Senators DeWine and Voinovich wrote me that they had referred my concerns to the FBI.

Ohio's state motto reads:

With God all things are possible.

The motto is from Matthew 19:26. When the Ohio Statehouse was remodeled, the motto was engraved on the plaza at a cost of $47,000.

Bronze insert of Ohio motto on Statehouse plaza - Columbus

The ACLU challenged the use of the Biblical phrase under separation of church and state. They lost in court and then in appellate court.

It occurred to me that no one would have objected, if Jesus' admonition to Saul on the road to Damascus had become the state motto (Acts 9:5):

It is hard for thee to kick against the pricks.

The ACLU's assertion that the Ohio motto promoted Christianity, in lieu of other religions, was preposterous. A proper lawsuit against the latent *hypocrisy* of government officials; pandering to the power of faith in God, within a culture inviting desecration of oaths to Him, may have succeeded.

In prison, I had the opportunity to read newspapers from across the state. Ohio ranked high in the nation, in wide-spread corruption of public servants. It was everywhere.

Without the protections of the Bill of Rights, there can be no American dream. A tyrannical government can take away the citizen's pen at will.

We are then reduced to a government similar to Russian Tsar Nikolay's (1825-1855) form of despotic rule, and its suppression of independent thinking; including its intricate development of informers and spies. Opposition to censorship and serfdom had invited harsh measures in Russia.

Fyodor Dostoevsky (1821-1881) was convicted of political crimes in 1849, and sentenced to death. His sentence was commuted and he served four years in prison in Siberia. Subsequently, his novel entitled *House of the Dead* led to a reform of Russian prisons.

In my criminal case, desecration of the oath illustrates, *without* God anything becomes acceptable. Concerning my fate, Gilvary displayed contempt for the oath he took *to* God; demonstrating repeated contempt *of* God. Gilvary even sentenced me to serve the renowned Russian's exact sentence – four years!

Dostoevsky summed up Gilvary's denial of God well:

If there is no God, then I am God.

Judge Gilvary had dug a hole for himself that could only be corrected by him. He had to have this stark realization after learning of my March 6, 1999 letter to Greene County Prosecutor William F. Schenck. The letter reminded him unequivocally, with decisive case precedent; he was *solely* responsible for kidnapping.

In the letter, I asked Schenck to arrange a federal RICO investigation, knowing full well he would do no such thing. But he would alert Gilvary of my efforts to involve the FBI. And that was what I really wanted!

Gilvary desperately needed to proclaim: "It has been brought to my attention, according to precise dictates of Local Rule 1.19 III(C), I lacked jurisdiction over *Ohio vs. Metz.* Therefore the conviction is set aside, and the case is dismissed."

But in order to do so, he would have to *kick against the pricks.* And that would remain unimaginable. Yes, life was closing in on the esteemed Judge James J. Gilvary. His plight reminded me of a song I wrote in 1980.

He Don't Know Where He's Goin'

He don't know where he goin'
And he don't know where he's been
Confused and bewildered
Alone in his sin
Fightin' life at ever' turn
And life is closin' in;
For he don't know where he goin'
'Cause he don't know where he's been

Learned always take the high road
Leave the low road behind
Walk the straight and narrow
And you'll have peace of mind
For if you take the low road
Fog of life comes rollin' in
And you won't know where you're goin'
'Cause you won't know where you been

The road of life gets rocky
And steep along the way
The path of least resistance
Beckons ever' day

But if you take the low road
You'll live your life in sin
And you won't know where you're goin'
'Cause you won't know where you've been

And he don't know where he's going'
'Cause he don't know where he's been
Confused and bewildered
Alone in his sin
Fightin' life at ever' turn
And life is closin' in
For he don't know where he's goin'
'Cause he don't know where he's been

I received a letter from Senators DeWine and Voino-vich dated May 4, 1999. I believed death was at hand for Judge Gilvary. Enclosed was a letter to Senator DeWine from the Justice Department. They would look at my claims of criminal activity in Dayton, Ohio. The letter read:

Dear Horace:

The U.S. Department of Justice, Federal Bureau of Investigation has forwarded the enclosed correspondence in response to our inquiry regarding your case. We trust this information is satisfactory to you.

Again, thank you for contacting us regarding this matter. We appreciate having the opportunity to be of assistance. If we can be of further service to you in any way, please do not hesitate to contact us. Our casework hotline number is 1-800-OHIO (6446).

Very respectfully yours,	Sincerely Yours,
MIKE DEWINE	GEORGE VOINOVICH
United States Senator	United States Senator

Following A. Robert Walsh's letter from the Justice Department, I had the intuitive urge to sing Mickey

Gilley's "Room Full of Roses".[43] For reasons unknown to me, I had the overpowering urge to keep singing the words over and over. And so I sang.

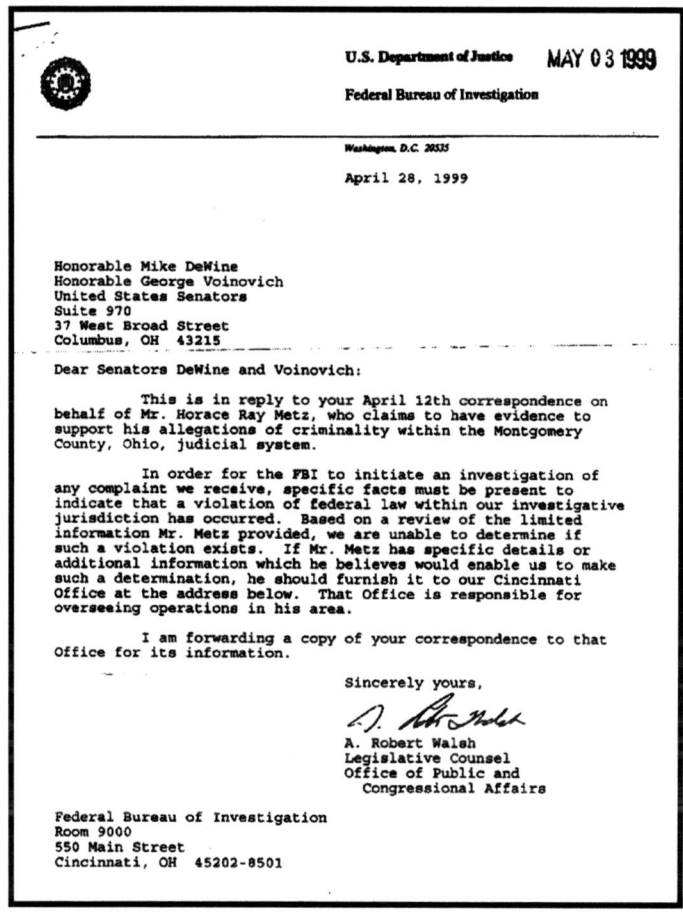

U.S. Department of Justice   MAY 0 3 1999

Federal Bureau of Investigation

Washington, D.C. 20535

April 28, 1999

Honorable Mike DeWine
Honorable George Voinovich
United States Senators
Suite 970
37 West Broad Street
Columbus, OH 43215

Dear Senators DeWine and Voinovich:

This is in reply to your April 12th correspondence on behalf of Mr. Horace Ray Metz, who claims to have evidence to support his allegations of criminality within the Montgomery County, Ohio, judicial system.

In order for the FBI to initiate an investigation of any complaint we receive, specific facts must be present to indicate that a violation of federal law within our investigative jurisdiction has occurred. Based on a review of the limited information Mr. Metz provided, we are unable to determine if such a violation exists. If Mr. Metz has specific details or additional information which he believes would enable us to make such a determination, he should furnish it to our Cincinnati Office at the address below. That Office is responsible for overseeing operations in his area.

I am forwarding a copy of your correspondence to that Office for its information.

Sincerely yours,

A. Robert Walsh
Legislative Counsel
Office of Public and
  Congressional Affairs

Federal Bureau of Investigation
Room 9000
550 Main Street
Cincinnati, OH 45202-8501

Letter from Department of Justice

This went on day after day, as I waited for matters to manifest. I would softly sing, *If I sent a rose to you, for*

---

[43] "Room Full of Roses" was written and recorded by George Morgan in 1949. The song was released in April 1974 by Mickey Gilley, went to No. 1 on the *Billboard Magazine Hot Country Singles,* rocketing Gilley to stardom.

every time you made me blue... while walking the prison track; sing in the shower; and sing in an inaudible
whisper late into the night, while lying on my bunk. *If
I sent a rose to you...*

The letter from Senator DeWine was dated Tuesday,
May 4, 1999. Judge Gilvary died seventeen days later.

Perhaps my intuitive song from prison equated to
Paul's long ago singing God's praises from prison. In
any case, a yellow rose was placed on Gilvary's bench.

An obituary article in the May 22, 1999 *Dayton Daily
News* read:

Judge James J. Gilvary dead at age 69

Judge James J. Gilvary of Montgomery County Common
Pleas Court died early Friday morning at Miami Valley Hospital following a brief illness. He was 69.

Born in Sidney and raised in Dayton, Mr. Gilvary had a dis-
tinguished 45-year career that emphasized public service and
deeply held religious values.

"Judge Gilvary's career as a preeminent trial lawyer and
outstanding judge was marked by a keen mind, honesty and a
high purpose," said County Prosecutor Matthias H. Heck, Jr.
Heck had known Mr. Gilvary since his childhood when Heck's
father hired Mr. Gilvary in 1958 as an assistance county prosecutor.

Mr. Gilvary was the first assistant to announce his departure in 1960 after the senior Heck lost a bid for re-election to
the county prosecutor's office.

Mr. Gilvary won his first and only contested election that
led to a newly created judgeship in July 1991. Five months
later Mr. Gilvary was one of three judges and 10 other elected Democrats who stood with his former boss's son as the
younger staged a show of support for his successful bid for
the county prosecutor's seat in the democratic primary.
Judges rarely engage in political support.

Judge Barbara P. Gorman, administrative judge of the general division of the common pleas court, said, "He cared

about people in the community, and he spent a lot of time trying to make things better."

Chief U.S. Judge Walter H. Rice said, "He was a marvelous attorney; he was ethical; he was moral and tremendously skilled. And he had an absolutely marvelous, exquisite sense of humor."

Judge Gorman said a yellow rose was placed on Judge Gilvary's bench Friday afternoon and the lights in his courtroom will remain lit in his memory next week.

Mr. Gilvary graduated as class valedictorian from both Chaminade High School and the University of Dayton. He received his law degree from Case Western Reserve University in Cleveland where he was a scholarship student.

He was the law director for the city of Kettering from 1956 to 1958 before joining the county prosecutor's office.

Retired Judge Walter H. Porter recalled that in 1965 he invited Mr. Gilvary to join what became Dayton's powerhouse legal firm, Smith & Schnacke, where the two became close friends and fishing companions. Smith & Schnacke later merged with Thompson & Flory.

"He was a very positive guy about the things he believed in," Porter said.

Judge John W. Kessler was co-counsel with Mr. Gilvary in 1980 when they defended Timothy Eugene Burggraf, a co-defendant in the slaying of a Kettering couple. Burggraf was convicted. But Kessler, now the senior judge in the general division, said the trial became a clinic for him.

"I learned so much about how to try a case," said Kessler, who became the first director of the county's public defender office. "Jim was the quintessential prepared lawyer. He never missed a detail and he understood not only the law, but the nuances of all the cases."

Kessler was elected to the bench that year. Five years later, Mr. Gilvary defended Good Samaritan Hospital and Health Center against a civil case in Kessler's courtroom. A 25-year-old woman claimed the hospital's mental health unit released her prematurely and she subsequently killed her 13-week-old daughter with an overdose of Tylenol.

The jury returned a $1.8 million judgment against Mr. Gilvary's client.

Ten years after that verdict, Mr. Gilvary, as a judge, presided over a larger verdict - $2.95 million – against a local obstetrician-gynecologist who delivered twins and then was accused of leaving part of a placenta in the mother, an error that led to her death.

Steven K. Dankof, who spent his first summer internship working for Mr. Gilvary at Smith & Schnacke in 1975 and later joined that firm, was one of the attorneys who won that verdict in 1995.

"He was a bright man and very hard-working," Dankof said. "He was a people's lawyer, representing the little guy. Albeit he was very hard-working, he had a good sense of humor."

Dankof recalled Mr. Gilvary as an avid fisherman and racetrack visitor. He also enjoyed watching professional golf tournaments. "He loved his alma mater, the University of Dayton, and he was a member of Holy Angels Church. He was a daily communicant at Emmanuel Catholic Church," Dankof said.

In 1982, Mr. Gilvary represented a group that sought zoning changes to bar an abortion clinic in Kettering.

Mr. Gilvary proved himself not only as an able judge and attorney, but as a judicial innovator. Two years ago, he had his entire courtroom and office equipped with video cameras with voice-activated microphones to routinely record all his trials, hearings and docket calls rather than relying on a court reporter who typed transcripts of the proceedings.

Mr. Gilvary served 18 years on the board of trustees of the University of Dayton. The last three years, 1987-1990, he chaired the board of trustees.

In 1993, UD gave him an honorary doctor of humane letters. "What struck me most about Jim Gilvary was his commitment to the excellence of our academic programs and a real concern that our students develop the traits of character – moral sensitivity, compassion and service to their communities," said Brother Raymond L. Fritz, the university's president. "He was a man of integrity, a man of strong convictions."

At the university's Friday afternoon trustee meeting, a prayer was offered on behalf of Mr. Gilvary, a university spokeswoman said.

Judge Patrick J. Foley of Montgomery County Common Pleas Court said Mr. Gilvary "didn't waiver from his principles. They could be unpopular, but he wouldn't waiver. He had guts."

Judge John P. Petzold of Montgomery County Common Pleas Court, the current president of the Ohio Bar Association, said Mr. Gilvary "typified the highest caliber of what I feel a lawyer and judge should be about."

Mr. Gilvary served on a statewide ethics committee of the Ohio Bar Association and on the local committees. He served as president of the Dayton Bar Association during 1977-1978.

During that period, Mr. Gilvary took issue with an article about attorney fees published in the Dayton Journal Herald, then owned by Dayton Newspapers, which also published the Dayton Daily News. Mr. Gilvary wrote that the story unfairly portrayed attorneys as "money-grubbing, legal mercenaries."

"I have always been of the opinion that a community where both major newspapers are controlled by a single owner, the only way one can hope to obtain anything approaching an objective dialogue on any controverted issue is to establish another newspaper," Mr. Gilvary wrote. "I don't have the resources for such a project."

The target of Mr. Gilvary's letter was Mary Ann Sharkey, now director of communications for Gov. Taft, who will select Mr. Gilvary's successor.

Mr. Gilvary entered Miami Valley Hospital on April 26 and underwent surgery the next day. Complications developed in the following weeks, but he appeared to be recovering this week, Gorman said.

A few days before Mr. Gilvary's illness sent him to the hospital, he made a casual visit to the chambers of Judge George J. Gounaris senior and presiding judge of the common pleas court. Gounaris, who was being treated for an illness that was causing some uncomfortable side effects, recalled that meeting.

"He asked me how I was doing, and we reminisced about when he was at Chaminade and I was at Fairview," Gounaris said. "We knew each other at UD. At the end of our meeting, he told me he loved me and I told him I loved him, too. We got up and hugged."

Mr. Gilvary's family will receive visitors at 5 p.m. Monday at Holy Angels Church, 218 K St., followed by a Mass at 6:30 p.m.

Mr. Gilvary is survived by his wife, Julie; three children, Claire, Joseph and Mary; and several grandchildren.

I read the obituary written by reporter Rob Modic, on my prison bunk during count time. When we were released for dinner; I skipped the meal in the cafeteria. I went to the cinder track on the yard, and walked in quiet contemplation; reflecting somberly over Judge Gilvary's death. I thought of singing "Room Full of Roses" again and again.

Judge Gilvary, whose "tell" had been those *trembling hands* in open court on December 23, 1996, served 820 days in his prison of the psyche; before he died.[44] It had been *hell on earth.* I thought of the bet Gilvary called, sentencing me to serve Dostoevsky's four years.

> Perhaps the renowned Russian novelist Dostoevsky would have been impressed with Metz's bet: twelve years of his life on the table – with nothing in "his hand" except his faith in God and his belief in his country – against the power of a vengeful state and the tyranny of an out-of-control judiciary. Metz's sanity could be questioned. Metz was certain that it would be. He was holding a *royal flush* against *aces and eights.*

---

[44] I inadvertently learned Gilvary died of blood clots. The unconfirmed cause is harmonious with my universal *"heart of stone"* observations.

For all his reputation, Gilvary-the-gambler lacked the intestinal fortitude for the realities of playing high-stakes poker. He overplayed his hand.

I thought of the letter Dostoevsky wrote to his brother, about his four years in the Siberian prison. It described Judge Gilvary's prison of the psyche.

> I consider those four years as a time during which I was buried alive and shut up in a coffin. Just how horrible that time was I have not the strength to tell you.... It was an indescribable, unending agony, because each hour, each minute weighed upon my soul like a stone.

My Royal Flush
Local Rule 1.19 III(C)

Gilvary's Aces and Eights
Local Rule 1.19 III(C)

Ah, yes, those aces and eights! I thought. On June 25, 1876, George Armstrong Custer and 265 men lost their lives in the Battle of Little Big Horn, known as Custer's Last Stand. Custer's friend, Wild Bill Hickok (1837-1876) was in Deadwood, South Dakota at the time. Hickok began having premonitions. He felt he was marked for death; there was no way to avoid it.

It was 4:10 p.m. Twenty-five year old Jack McCall slipped up behind Hickok and fired once from an old .45 Colt revolver. The bullet went through the back of Hickok's head and came out under his right cheekbone. When the undertaker arrived, Wild Bill's fingers still crimped from holding his last poker hand – a pair of black aces and a pair of black eights, with a kicker.

From then on *aces and eights* would be known as *The Dead Man's Hand.*

I slowly walked the cinder track for three hours. Dusk approached and a loud speaker announced the yard was closed. Inmates went inside for the night.

An inmate serving what amounted to a life sentence saw me, and proclaimed in a loud voice overheard by all, "There's *Judge Killer!*"

In the end my prisoner accepted death, rather than face the music. While that would not have been my choice, I understood it. He died with his public dignity intact.

H.L. Mencken wrote about gambling:

> The taste for gambling, like that for sports, is a kind of feeble-mindedness – maybe even insanity. It can be justified only by a resort to the most preposterous sophistry. Whenever it has seized a man of any visible talent – for example, Dostoevsky or C.C. Colton – he has ended crazy. It is the silliest of all the vices.

Laying in the quiet, with fifty-three sleeping inmates, I reflected on all that happened between Gilvary and me. *Mencken may have been right about gambling. It may be the silliest of all the vices. Gilvary's dead and I'm stuck in prison. But it was one hell of a poker game!*

My duties as a warden were almost over. I supposed a warden needed to fill out paperwork, after an execution. So as I lay in the quiet of night, unable to sleep; I composed a tribute in memory of Judge Gilvary, based on a song written by a man idolized in childhood.[45]

Then I went to the restroom where there was adequate light, sat on a commode, and put words of the song to paper. My final thoughts were of my erstwhile opponent. *He never stood a chance. I'm sorry for you, my judge.*

---

[45] "I'm Sorry for You, My Friend" by Hank Williams; February, 1952.

I'm Sorry for You, My Judge

To prison for too long a time,
A judge, he sentenced me.
From prison wrote a motion for
The judge to set me free.
The crooked judge, I wished him well;
Showed him the way called Straight;
The same as Christ had offered Saul;
He said I filed too late.

There is a time when mortal man
Is blinded by his sin.
It comes to me; it comes to you;
We must have God to win.
The brotherhood of mankind
Is all we have to share;
A helping hand to extend;
A heart that shows we care.

When you take an oath to God;
To God you give your soul.
A wayward man, a broken vow;
He can make you whole.
From prison of another kind,
God can set you free.
Ask Him and He will do for you,
What He has done for me.

It is too late for the judge;
God has called him home.
No more a black-robed thug;
His earthly powers gone.
Those who morn their loss of him,
Defend him to the end.
To each I say, *He had his way,*
I'm sorry for you, my friend.
And I'm sorry for you, my judge.

CHAPTER THIRTY-NINE

In Absentia

I had written Judge Gilvary via a court filing: *No case is an "island" that stands alone. And certainly, no case stands alone with the egregious judicial misconduct as pervasive as is found in this case, going beyond the realm of individual concern, to the whole of societal interest.*

The prodigious battle between Judge Gilvary and me was a war of the ages, for the soul of the individual; for the soul of a community; for the soul of a nation. Much like Fyodor Dostoevsky, I stood against an oppressive state, and Judge Gilvary was enlisted to defeat an "enemy" of the oppressors.

Judge Gilvary was a well educated man. Yet he recklessly squandered his gifts; by thoughtlessly rebuking his oath to God and country.

In the secular world Gilvary invited the least useful of human responses. He was a man to be pitied.

However in a mystical context, he was an extraordinarily intriguing man. Behind the public facade, was a spiritually impoverished man; with a Shakespearean quality about him. Approval of his peers meant more than life itself.

Confronted with abysmal disgrace; faced with losing a reputation nurtured over a lifetime, Gilvary found an honorable way out. He accepted a self-imposed death sentence.

I had tried to caution him of his peril, via a parable about a man and his faithful dog *Spot*. Anything more explicit would have been construed as a threat by an inmate.

Fate is a funny thing. A memorial stone was placed at Dayton's RiverScape in Judge Gilvary's honor – next to the *Flying Dog* concession stand.

Memorial stone at RiverScape

Following release from prison, I'm standing at Judge Gilvary's
memorial stone – next to the *Flying Dog* concession stand.

Mythology about my former prisoner lives on. During
the year he died, the University Of Dayton School Of
Law, under the auspices of colleagues, friends and
family; founded The Honorable James J. Gilvary Sym-
posium on Law, Religion & Social Justice.

Quoting from *Flyer News,* the University of Dayton's
independent student newspaper, Vol. 51, Number 10:

> The Gilvary Symposium is in memory of the late Judge James
> J. Gilvary who affirmed that people's religious beliefs should
> coincide with the laws of the judicial system.

The fallacy of this synopsis is self-evident; especially so when found within a Catholic university. American law has legalized abortion. Many peoples' religious beliefs do not coincide with the law; in this or other areas. And never will.

However, the synopsis accurately depicts Gilvary's views. This was the perception of one who thought of himself as *god* in the courtroom. Accolades from peers and those within the Catholic Church supported the misimpression.

It legitimized his *legislating from the bench.* The law became whimsical; vacillating erratically from case to case. In *Ohio v. Metz,* the 1st, 4th, 5th, 6th, 8th, and 14th Amendments to the Constitution were superfluous. A culture of corruption became the ancestor of anarchy.

Still, Judge Gilvary affirmed important spiritual dynamics; via blatant hypocrisy. Though religious beliefs failed abysmally, to "coincide" with the oath taken to uphold the laws of the judicial system; there is something to be learned from his ethical and moral failings.

He affirms *in absentia,* the sanctity of the oath.

He affirms *in absentia,* reputation is often an illusion, carefully cultivated for others to see.

He affirms *in absentia,* practitioners of the laws of the judicial system are to conduct themselves in accordance to *Universal Laws of Life,* as governed by the *Universal Supreme Court* wherein God reigns as *Universal Supreme Court Justice.* In ancient Roman days, Cicero proclaimed as much.

He affirms *in absentia,* ignorance – or even pretense of ignorance – of those laws is no defense.

And he affirms *in absentia,* the ultimate price paid for blasphemy; defined by Webster as: *Theol. the crime of assuming to oneself the rights and qualities of God.*

Fate is a funny thing. While in prison, I wrote a parable about a man and his dog, *Spot.* In life, a man went to the grave, and a dog went to the White House.

Spot on White House lawn
Photo: Paul Morse/White House

When George H. W. Bush was president, George W. and Laura were given a puppy. *Spot* was the only dog born in the White House that left; and then returned to live there.

The mythological story of how she earned this distinction is remarkable. It is a story that will keep for another day.

Epilogue

Unlike Youngstown, there would be no FBI investigation in Dayton. Pursuant to the instructions from Washington; my sister, Karen took my evidence to the Cincinnati FBI office. They simply sent it to Dayton.

Karen followed up and Special Agent Timothy Shaw, from the Dayton FBI office, asserted the information was "lost" – until she told Shaw we possessed copies. Later, Washington notified me the FBI found no criminal activity in Dayton, within federal jurisdiction.

So I served the remaining twenty-two months of my sentence. But my real objective had been achieved.

Gilvary died on May 21, 1999. Just as the quality of his life disintegrated; mine improved. My last day as a security office clerk was January 10, 1999. The reason for this was amusing, at the time.

Inmates ran the institution, in large measure. And a few adventurous ones were caught up in a gambling scandal, in the prison administration building. Someone had created a gambling site on the prison's computer system!

How this was accomplished was secretive; and those who participated went to the Hole until transferred. But inmates no longer ran the institution; and all of us who worked as clerks were out of a job. I was finally permitted to work in the library.

But this was no longer good enough for me. I was on a waiting list for a computer class. Each time I asked where I stood on the pecking order for admission, an annoyed instructor informed me to be patient; my turn would come.

On my last day as a security office clerk, I managed to slip a confidential roster of the prison's inmates out of the office. An inspection of the roster revealed I had been on the "waiting list" for the computer program; longer than two inmates - in the class - had been in the institution!

Our prison operated as its own society; with griev-ance procedures. I sent a Kite requesting a meeting with the institution's Inspector. Upon meeting with him, and after presenting my case; I was informed that prison rules had been broken – by me. Stealing the confidential prison roster was a flagrant violation.

I suggested he did not want to go there, with me; and reminded him of his presence when an Ohio State Patrol trooper had looked at evidence I had, concern-ing the judicial system in Dayton. Perhaps I should publicize prison protocol? And shazam! February 26, 1999 was the day I entered the elitist classroom.

I was one of seventeen inmates enrolled in the com-puter course. Soon after my admission, inmates were supposed to overcome inhibitions by performing skits in class. Two of us performed together. I wrote a skit.

"I ain't doin' it, Metz. No way in hell! Why don't *you* play the woman?"

"I would, but I'm thinking of you."

"What the hell does that mean? You want me to put on a fuckin' *scarf.*"

"I know, I know. But look at the other choice."

"What other choice?"

"You'd look funnier 'n hell with a white man's nose!"

Prison's Odd Couple - Sinbad and Abigail

Following Gilvary's death, appellate judges could attempt to deny participating in *The Perfect Crime*. After all; they had no chance to "correct" trial court errors.

I reluctantly filed a motion for leave to file a delayed appeal on February 2, 2000. A prayer was included for those who had ensnared Gilvary: Prosecuting Attorney Mathias H. Heck, Jr., and appellate judges - Brogan, Wolff, and Fain (a.k.a. FAKE). From the motion:

> "The normalization of deviance is common to organizations and individuals alike, resulting in mistake, mishap, and misconduct, too often with disastrous results."

So it was that teacher Christa McAuliffe lost her life January 28, 1986; concluded ethnographer Diane Vaughn in her definitive book, *The Challenger Launch Decisions – Risky Technology, Culture and Deviance at NASA.*

So it was when I ventured into the courts as a pro se, voluntarily in civil cases, and then by coercion in the instant case, wherein I was sentenced to six years in prison: mistake, mishap, and misconduct. On March 11, 1997 the "normalization of deviance" resulted in...

A darker side of Judge Gilvary was exposed in the instant case, diametrical to the reputation he enjoyed amongst his peers, and in the community at large. He exhibited a willingness to violate everything he seemingly stood for. The judge I experienced emptied the Canons at me, in a charade wherein an entire trial was *faked*.

Judge Gilvary had lost his soul in defying his oath, for the benefit of others. So long as he was not disqualified, those whom he protected had an obligation to protect him....

John Donne wrote of the brotherhood of man and his views of the dependence of each man on all others, in *Devotions* in 1624. Ernest Hemmingway took the title of *For Whom the Bell Tolls* from Donne's works.

It wasn't until his death that I learned that Judge Gilvary was practically Prosecutor Heck's godfather... To Mr. Heck, I would offer: How much he must have loved you!

Vengeance is God's province.... A prayer from prison:

> May there be **peace** in the valley; a **peace** tempered to perfection in the light of *universal laws of life* that transcend any particular race, religion, national origin or sexual orientation, before one

God

> Who reigns supreme over the rich and the poor; a **peace** that shines as a beacon of hope for the world to emulate. May that **peace** begin in my heart, in my soul; may that **peace** begin in yours.

... With the death of Judge Gilvary, and with his absolution by the FBI, I am...presently able to have confidence in the Court to review said appeal on its merit.

And so it is that you are being offered redemption. The bell tolls for thee. WHEREFORE, I humbly seek leave of the Court to file a Delayed Appeal.

The prosecutor's office objected February 15, 2000:

> [Metz] now claims that with [Judge Gilvary's] demise, he now has the confidence in the justice system to allow this Court to review his case. This is not reasonable.

The appellate court ruled on March 21, 2000:

> PER CURIAM:
> ... Due to appellant's previous abandonment of his direct appeal, this court finds no reason for permitting a second delayed direct appeal. Accordingly, IT IS HEREBY ORDERED that appellant's motion for a delayed appeal is **overruled.** This matter is **dismissed.**
> IT IS SO ORDERED.
> James A. Brogan, Judge
> Mike Fain, Judge
> Frederick N. Young, Judge

Matters between me and the judicial system had never been simple. And they were not about to become so. An outreach from prison - for *peace in the valley* - was spurned. My captors had another dishonorable scheme in mind, to free themselves from accountability; involving the infamous Warren County detainer.

The 2000 Summer Olympic Games took place in Sydney, from September 13th to October 1st. Pickaway Correctional Institution school officials came up with a novel idea. We would have our own Olympics. The warden approved.

The concept was to overcome the isolation and lack of identity commonplace in prison; and get inmates connected with outside events. The response was incredible, as inmates enthusiastically participated.

A committee was formed to structure things. Games were selected. They included sports activities such as basketball, football toss, weight lifting, horseshoes, miniature golf, and volleyball. Other events included checkers, chess and the card game, Spades.

Every class had to choose a country to represent. Each inmate could enter as many events as he wanted. But each of us entered at least one competition.

Acceding to wishes of black inmates wanting an African nation, our computer class selected Egypt. We created an Egyptian display. As my contribution to the activity, I found a picture of a camel, and typed underneath it:

Did you ever see a camel hump?
Verb or noun?

Dates for the games were decided. Opening ceremonies were held in the prison yard, with government dignitaries from Columbus in attendance.

Another inmate and I decided to partner-up in Spades. We had become friends in the computer class.

I lived in A-Unit and he lived in C-Unit; we had never played cards together.

As the day approached to begin playing, he told me other inmates planned on cheating. We needed to devise a set of signals, to remain competitive.

"Oh no, we don't," I responded emphatically.

"Then we don't stand a chance," he complained.

"Oh yes, we do!" I exclaimed patiently.

"How?"

"The whole idea of the Olympic Games is to learn another way of thinking and living. Integrity is a key."

"But those other guys..."

"To hell with the other guys. Why do you think I asked you to be my partner? Do you think a one of the cheaters can teach you anything about winning in the game called *life?* No way in hell. And they won't win at Spades either."

"What are we going to do then?" he asked.

"It's very, very simple. I know you are a Christian. I will tell you what I've told my wife from the beginning: *We walk by faith, not by sight.*"

He asked with a grin, "Do you think that will work?"

"It works for me," I ended with a shrug.

Armed with that, my friend and I won round after round; winning the Gold Medal.

Olympic Games opening ceremonies in prison yard

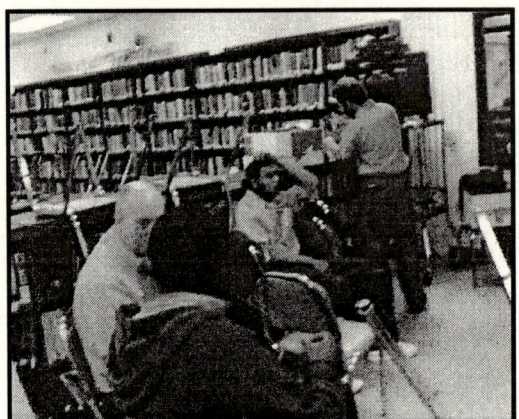

Preparing Egyptian exhibit in prison library

Watching Olympic events in prison gymnasium

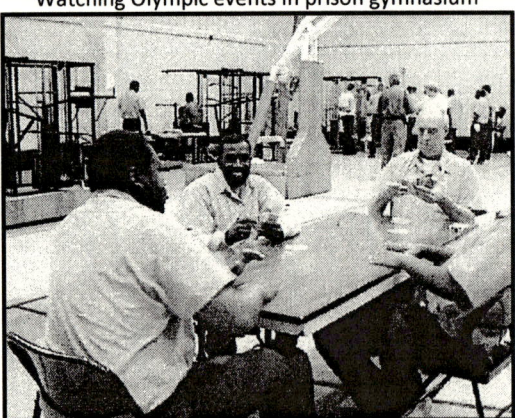

In action – one of six rounds to Olympic Gold

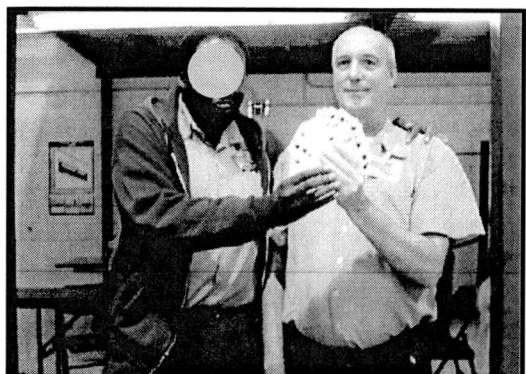

Posing for the camera, after winning a Gold Medal.

Receiving a Gold Medal - at Award Ceremonies

My partner said to me, "I never thought we'd win."

"I did. You see, it was a spiritual matter with me. And it provides an omen for very important things to come. Thank you for being such a significant part of my life."

After the Olympics ended, many inmates wanted the opportunity to *take down* the old white man, referred too as Judge Killer. But my friend and I agreed; we never played again. Let the mystic of victory live on!

I prepared for another legal debacle, from my foes – who never gave up – involving the Warren County detainer. August 20, 2000, I wrote the victim, beginning:

"Enclosed please find a money order of $700 for the $600 collected from you in the summer of 1995 for a water softener....If this is insufficient for the problems caused you, please advise me of a sufficient amount, and it shall be promptly forwarded too you."

My analysis had been correct. November 14, 2000, an Indictment was created in Warren County; charging me with theft by deception. The grand jury indictment alleged the victim had never been reimbursed.

Following a video arraignment, I was transported to the Warren County jail on December 27, 2000. A trial was set for February 20, 2001, by Judge P. Daniel Fedders; *the same day I was scheduled to be released from prison.*

Again, I was ready for an abusive State and unconscionable judges, involving another conspiracy. I had learned about Jack Quinn prior to going to prison, from a local newspaper; alluding to his political clout.

The Western Star—January 8, 1997—Page 5-A

Rep. Strickland takes oath

Contributed photo

As some 50 Warren County officials; commissioners, mayors and township trustees, friends and well-wishers looked on, Common Pleas Judge Neal Bronson administered the oath of office to Ohio 6th District Congressman-elect Ted Strickland. The ceremony was held Dec. 28 in the county common pleas court building on Justice Drive in Lebanon. A reception was held at the home of Lebanon attorney Jack Quinn after the ceremony.

Prior to going to prison, I knew who my attorney would be — should I ever need one in Warren County. "A reception... at the home of Lebanon attorney Jack Quinn..."

Just before I was taken to Lebanon, Quinn was the defense attorney in a murder case that quantified his abilities. Jeffrey Bornhoeft slipped into his ex-wife, Shawn Johnson's apartment, and shot her husband, James Johnson three times in the head as he slept. Bornhoedt had telephoned Mrs. Johnson; and too her horror, she listened as the murder took place.

Quinn used an insanity defense. Bornhoeft suffered from depression, schizophrenia and paranoia. Ohio Revised Code provided for such a defense.

It was described by Quinn as one that worked about once a century. On Election Day, November 7, 2000, Quinn won! Against long odds, a jury found his client was insane.

Judge Fedders set an initial sentence at six months in a locked-down mental institution. Bornhoeft could be freed, should he ever be found to be sane.

Attorney Jack Quinn had the wherewithal to make things happen in the courtroom! From my limited perspective, he was *the consummate attorney.*

Supposedly held helpless in jail, without the ability to defend; I retained Quinn via a telephone conversation. Upon receipt of a $1,500 fee; he visited me in jail.

Told I was sent to prison for six years, over $7,040; Quinn responded, "You must have done something else – something very, very bad!"

"Someone did," I acknowledged.

Quinn asked what I expected. He was told: Warren County lacked jurisdiction, since a similar Greene County count had been taken to Montgomery County; this was 2001 – the event took place in 1995; and I repaid the victim prior to grand jury indictment. The "crime" required the intent to permanently deprive. I expected a dismissal.

The veteran defense attorney, who had clout in Warren County; came back to me with a plea bargain: plead guilty to a felony and be granted probation.

I refused. Quinn told me that unless I pled guilty to a felony, Fedders was sending me back to prison for another year. And I told Quinn *I had another year in me!* I informed Quinn there was $10,000 available, for my defense. Quinn responded quickly: Money was not the issue. A deal was a deal; his fee was $1,500 and another $1,000 if we went to trial.

But supposing we won at trial? Then what? Quinn wanted to know. I answered with a, *this ain't my first rodeo* stare of disdain. And he informed me he would see what else could be done; and get back to me.

Weeks passed, and I heard nothing further from Quinn. I waited out the uncertainty in a serene state of mind. I tossed the ball to Quinn; and he accepted.

Quinn held a position of stature within the local legal fraternity. He could not be intimidated by retaliation tactics. He would work things out for me.

The clock kept ticking. The Tuesday, February 20th trial date kept getting closer. And closer. The Tuesday, February 20th out-date from prison kept getting closer. And closer. Still, I heard nothing from Quinn; and he heard nothing from me.

Finally, on Wednesday, February 14th, I was summoned from jail to a juror's seat in Fedders' empty courtroom. (Quinn's stature was apparent. After our initial meeting, I was taken to Fedders' empty courtroom – and left in the jury box.) Quinn approached in what appeared a less than joyous manner. Fedders had agreed to accept a *guilty* plea to a misdemeanor.

I would serve no more time. Quinn did not appear to be thrilled with the offer. Superficially, it appeared he had failed me. As he waited for a reaction; I believed I understood the realities. The need to discredit me remained. Quinn understood; for he was in the clique.

He had learned of the *sincerity* behind the efforts to extort a guilty plea from me. He had seen my letter to Ted Stark, giving rudimentary details of reasons for my imprisonment. He saw my references of turning to the FBI – to no avail. Yes, the *fix* was in again.

But instincts told me Jack Quinn really represented *my best interests.* This would have been an easy case to get dismissed — under most circumstances. One motion would have accomplished it. But had it been simple; Quinn could have done so weeks ago. Implicit caution was demonstrated, by his failure to do so.

Choosing words carefully, I asked, "Jack, compared to other cases, other felony fours; have you earned your fee?"

"I have," came Quinn's unhesitant response.

"And you think I should accept this deal?"

"As your attorney, I advise you to accept this plea."

"I agree. But I want to know something else, if you'll tell me. Am I hearing correctly; what you are saying to me, without saying it? That there may be *other reasons;* very significant *other reasons* for me to accept this plea?"

Quinn looked me directly in the eyes, "Sometimes it is important to know when to hold 'em, and when to fold 'em, Ray. *I earnestly implore you to accept this plea."*

"It's done. And Jack, I want to thank you for your fine representation. I, and my wife and my family thank you.

"But you know what, Jack? It would almost be worth $10,000 to force prosecutors to bring Ted Stark into court to testify. Here's a man who owns a $350,000 home; who complained in 1995 his water softener was not installed, and that he was out $600. Lo and behold, after he was repaid $700 almost six years later; the clowns decided it was time to prosecute me!

"I wish the assholes had to explain their version of justice to him; especially since he knew I had requested an FBI investigation into the justice system in Dayton. However, it's very apparent; it's time to fold 'em."

At that, the gregarious smile lit Quinn's face again. We parted with a clear understanding of the realities; and the mutual respect that only such intimate insight invites.

On the morning of February 16, 2001, I stood at a podium in Warren County Common Pleas Court in Lebanon, Ohio; in an orange jump suit, in shackles. Attorney Jack Quinn stood at my side.

The bailiff announced, "All rise."

Judge P. Daniel Fedders entered and took his seat. I glanced to my right and saw Warren County Assistant Prosecuting Attorney Keith Anderson had stood up, as Quinn and I did. Other than the court stenographer, no one else was present.

"Don't screw this up, and we'll be out of here in a few minutes, Quinn whispered to me. "It's all been arranged; plead guilty this morning and you'll be back in prison this afternoon."

"I understand the drill," I whispered back.

With a shallow look of a worn out undertaker, Judge Fedders began:[46]

"Please be seated. This is the case of the State of Ohio versus Metz, case number 19002. Let the record show the defendant is present and represented by Mr. Quinn. Is there something to come to the attention of the court now, Mr. Anderson?"

Anderson solemnly played his role, "Your Honor, the State would request to amend this charge to reflect a theft as a misdemeanor of the first degree. I think the defendant would then plead guilty.

"We have further represented to the court that restitution has been paid and we do not request and would agree that there be no more jail time, considering what the defendant has served for this and similar offenses in prison. He's been in prison for similar offenses out of Montgomery County."

Judge Fedders looked at me, "Mr. Metz, they tell me that you may wish to plead guilty to this charge as a misdemeanor. Do you understand that you're presumed to be innocent of any wrongdoing here and you're entitled to a trial first? You're entitled to make

---

[46] Conversation is taken from the official transcript.

the State prove you're guilty; do you understand that?"

"Yes, Your Honor."

Judge Fedders continued to create the appearance of propriety for the record. "Do you understand that at a trial like that the State's witnesses have to come in and testify under oath, the attorney gets to cross-examine them? You can bring witnesses to the trial to testify on your side and even testify yourself if you want to; do you understand that?"

"Yes, Your Honor."

Fedders was on a roll. "Any verdict of the jury has to be unanimous. And if it's not unanimous, the jury cannot find you guilty. You could waive a jury and I'll try the case myself, and you won't be found guilty by me unless the State proves beyond a reasonable doubt that you're guilty."

"I understand, Your Honor."

"If you plead guilty to this today, I'm going to sentence you to thirty days in the county jail; do you understand?"

"Yes, Your Honor."

"Considering everything I've just told you, do you still want to plead guilty?"

"Yes, Your Honor."

"Mr. Anderson?"

Anderson again played his cleverly rehearsed role, "Count one [there was only one count] alleges that in June through October, sometime during that period, in – I'm sorry, let me get this date right – in the year 1995, the defendant did with purpose to deprive Ted Stark of property or services, this being cash, knowingly obtained control without the express or implied consent of the owner. It's a violation of 2913.02(A)(2).

"This involved a dealership, a water softener dealership. The defendant took the victim's at that time six hundred dollars. I believe nothing was ever provided in return. Restitution has been made I think this past fall sometime, judge."

Fedders addressed my counsel, "Mr. Quinn, does your client acknowledge that those facts are true?"

The polished Quinn said, "We do, Your Honor."

Judge Fedders continued, "You just signed a form, Mr. Metz. When you signed this form you understand you were telling me in writing that you're aware of your rights, but you want to plead guilty anyway?"

"Yes, Your Honor."

"The Court finds that the plea of guilty to one count of theft as a misdemeanor of the first degree is being made knowingly, voluntarily, and intelligently and therefore, it's accepted.

"I propose to proceed with the matter of the sentence now. Is there any reason you can give me, Mr. Prosecutor, as to why we shouldn't proceed with the sentence?"

Anderson replied, "No, Your Honor."

Fedders pressed, "Do you have anything you want to say about the sentence?"

Anderson again said, "No, Your Honor."

Attorney Quinn interjected, "Your Honor, I'd just like to read one sentence into the record. The defendant has made full restitution, actually overpaid the restitution, but we're not complaining about that. But he did write to the victim in this case, and I'd just like to read from the last paragraph of that letter which says, 'I was invited into the sanctity of your home and was honored with your trust. I express my profound sorrow for having failed you and I humbly ask for your forgiveness.' A money order for seven hundred dollars was enclosed which exceeded the amount of restitution."

Judge Fedders said to me, "All right. I'm sentencing you to thirty days in the county jail. You'll receive credit for any time served in the county jail awaiting this particular case. You can also appeal this if you want to, but you have to file a notice of appeal within thirty days from today.

"Officer, you may take the defendant."

Quinn reached out to shake my shackled hand, "Good luck to you." He hesitated and then added, "If you want too, you may call me next week after you get home."

I looked at him calmly and thanked him for his services, without further commitment. He had earned his fee. Before retaining him I had faced another year in prison unless I pled *guilty* to a felony. Quinn's influence and my money got the charge reduced to a misdemeanor. We owed each other nothing further.

That afternoon, a deputy sheriff taking me back to Pickaway Correctional Institution glanced at me in his rearview mirror, "It's very unusual for there to be such a rush for us to return an inmate to prison. You're getting V.I.P. treatment, Mr. Metz."

"I suppose so," I responded with a laugh. "I have enjoyed Warren County's hospitality since two days after Christmas. Monday is President's Day. I am going to be released from prison on Tuesday."

"How long you been in prison?" the deputy asked.

"Four years, come Tuesday," I replied.

"That's a long time to be locked up."

"1,461 days," I acknowledged.

Riding in the back seat of the Warren County Sheriff cruiser in shackles, from Lebanon for the hour or so journey back to prison in Orient; the mood became melancholy. This legal skirmish had begun on June, 13, 1994, the dreadful day the O.J. Simpson murders were discovered. The psyche reacted to a kind of post-traumatic stress; exacerbated by the abuse of power.

The first phase of a long journey ended on the 985th day, with my conviction in Judge Gilvary's courtroom. Though I lived though each day; and every event, it seemed unbelievable.

I had no regrets for the choices I made throughout. But there was a nagging sense of failure; and a lingering feeling of remorse, until I came to terms with it.

They broke me! Much like other prisoners of war, I was subjected to what my captors used as psychological torture.

Kidnapped by the gavel, in lieu of the gun, and after enduring all my oppressors could hand out; in the end, after heeding the sound advice of counsel, they broke me. And I *confessed* to a crime that could not possibly exist.

There was one more reality to embrace. And I struggled with it. What might have happened, had I not pled *guilty?*

What if I had served the extra year in prison that Fedders threatened? Then what? Would I have been killed, to silence me? I simply could not know.

A fear of death did not break me. My love of Ann was the extortion used to break me. The thought of Ann alone and destitute, became a ransom I had to pay.

Having spent 1,457 days locked up to date, this was the 2,442nd day since the odyssey had begun. There were four days left, to say goodbye to my friends.

Riding in the back of the cruiser, my mind wandered to other times. From "Casey at the Bat" written by Ernest Lawrence Thayer in 1888; and published in the *San Francisco Examiner:*

> Oh somewhere in this favored land the sun is shining bright,
> The band is playing somewhere, and somewhere hearts are light,
> And somewhere men are laughing, and little children shout;
> But there is no joy in Mudville – mighty Casey has struck out.

The spring of 1961 was a good one in Cincinnati, for so many. This was especially true for sports fans. The Bearcats had won the NCAA basketball championship.

The Reds were beginning a season under Manager Fred Hutchinson that would culminate in a 93-61 record, and a National League championship. They lost to the mighty Yankees (109-53) in the World Series (4-1). But it was the Red's first pennant since 1940. Yes, it was a very happy time for many in the Queen City!

Daniel Fedders graduated from University of Cincinnati's School of Law that spring of 1961. Like many young attorneys in private practice, Fedders had occasions to work as the law director for the cities of Franklin and Springboro, and then as an assistant prosecutor for Lebanon.

Governor James Rhodes appointed Fedders to the Warren County Common Pleas Court in 1971. It was a position he held until retirement in February 2003, after a forty-one year legal career.

But for me, there was *no joy in Mudville,* that spring of 1961. I was alone and disenfranchised at the University of Cincinnati; a sexual abuse victim, soon to be another statistic – a college dropout, with lost hopes and broken dreams; carrying a secret buried deep within the soul.

Fate is a funny thing. Four decades after that spring of 1961, the UC graduate and the UC dropout met in a courtroom. And it all ended unceremoniously in Lebanon, Ohio, twelve miles from where it began for the dropout; in the darkness of night next to the Voice of America facility. *Four decades later; and twelve miles!*

It ended with an attempted rape of the psyche; just as such a rape had occurred those decades before; via the sexual assault by UC Professor Sherrill Wilkes, and an inevitable cover-up. It ended with one abusing power; demonstrating by word and deed, the life of the other did not matter - and counted for nothing.

Mine eyes have seen the glory! As I rode in the back of the sheriff's cruiser; I felt so humbly blessed to have been given the life fate handed me. And I remembered a legend's remarkable farewell speech on July 4, 1939; Lou Gehrig Appreciation Day at Yankee Stadium.

Fans, for the past two weeks you have been reading about a bad break I got. Yet today, I consider myself the luckiest man on the face of the earth. I have been in ballparks for seventeen years and I have never received anything but kindness and encouragement from you fans. Look at these grand men. Which of you wouldn't consider it the highlight of his career just to associate with them for even one day? Sure I'm lucky....When you have a father and mother work all their lives so that you can have an education and build your body, it's a blessing.

When you have a wife who has been a tower of strength and shown more courage than you ever dreamed existed, that's the finest I know. I consider myself the luckiest man on the face of the earth. And I might have been given a bad break, but I've got an awful lot to live for.

Lou Gehrig drank deeply, from the cup of life. He was a fierce competitor, but played the game he loved with a sense of humble gratitude. He accepted the hand fate gave him with the same grace.

Thinking of Lou Gehrig brought to mind another good and decent man; United States Magistrate Judge Michael R. Merz. And I thought of life's many twists and turns that gives it its special flavor. I thought of *Merz to Metz,* and the significance of each life.

In a federal court ruling on January 23, 1995, Merz wrote concerning use of a judge's signature stamp:

> One can imagine a judge suffering from, for example, Lou Gehrig's disease, who would be perfectly capable of deciding matters but not capable of writing her name.

A month prior to Merz's decision, on December 27, 1994, Miamisburg Municipal Court Judge Robert E. Messham, Jr. scrawled an eviction order in his own hand, while sitting on the bench; and sent it to Maria Lowman to affix his signature stamp. No one had appeared in court. A lot of water had passed under the bridge since that day; too much of it muddied.

For prison personnel, convicts entering and leaving the institution was a routine matter. There were procedures in place to handle the flow of human misery.

Inmates were not processed into or out of the institution after 4:00 p.m. weekdays, or on weekends and holidays. We barely made the cutoff time, that Friday afternoon.

To an outsider, what happened next would seem strange. I was given what equated to a hero's welcome back, by my prison friends and acquaintances.

It humbled me to have inmate after inmate come to me, and offer to prepare a final meal to share, with commissary; or tell me what it meant to him, having had me in his life. The feelings were mutual, I assured again and again.

There were goodbyes involving prison guards I respected. And a special goodbye was in order for Mr. Sexton, the prison librarian.

"Well, Metz, what are you and your wife planning to do, once you get home?" Ms. Gossett wanted to know.

I grinned at my favorite officer and said as innocently as a soon-to-be-ex-con could muster, "First thing, we're gonna try and have a baby."

"A baby! At your age? What would you want a baby for?"

"Oh, I didn't say we *wanted* one. I just said we wanted to *try* to have one."

"Metz, you're something else," Gossett said with a laugh. She turned reflective, as she said with kind concern, "Watch yourself, Metz. Don't you go pissing anyone off again. I don't want to see your ass back in here!"

"I lost the right to own a gun. But they did not take away my pen. The pen remains both the scalpel, and the balm."

Prison officials knew I was going to be in court on Friday, February 16th. Never imaging I would get V.I.P.

treatment, and a special ride back to prison that afternoon; meant I would have to be transported on the day of my scheduled release.

Officials had prepared for me to leave prison one day late. Surprised by my return on the 16th, the Expiration of Sentence was corrected with a red marker, changing the red ink stamped "1" to "0."

EXPIRATION OF SENTENCE

FEB 2 0 2001
Effective Date

TO: HORACE METZ   OFFENDER NUMBER: 346-086

Having served the definite sentence imposed by the Court or the maximum sentence for the offense(s) for which you were convicted, the rights forfeited by your conviction pursuant to Section 2961.01 of the Ohio Revised Code are restored. These include your right to vote, to serve on juries, and, unless precluded by Sections 2921.02, 2921.41 and 2921.43 or other Sections of the Revised Code, to hold any office of honor, trust or profit.

The expiration of your sentence <u>does</u> <u>not</u> relieve you of any disability prohibiting you from possessing a firearm under Section 2923.13 of the Revised Code.

We offer our best wishes for your success in the future.

                              Warden or Chief of the APA

Date: FEB 2 0

I have this date received from   PICKAWAY CORRECTIONAL INSTITUTION

my Certificate of Expiration of Sentence on Docket Number(s):   95CR2317

Signed: Horace Metz

The four days passed quickly. I went to the salley port on Tuesday morning, February 20, 2001. And as I stood there, being processed out, I could see my sister, Karen's van in the parking lot.

Dressed in a red jumpsuit, carrying a grocery sack with my personal belongings, including the Bible provided me by The Gideons; I walked through the salley port gate.

Getting into Karen's van, I saw Ann and Mother. Looking to the rear; were Karen's two grandchildren, Matthew and Elizabeth. There sat Jeff. My son had come all the way from Denver, to see his dad get out of prison. What a surprise!

I choked with emotion, as Jeff said, "Hi dad. What a nice outfit you have on. Did you get to pick the color?"

"No, but there's a reason for the red. A lot of dumb-assed inmates change clothes in the car after getting out, and throw the prison garb out the window. People used to see it, and think someone escaped. Now law enforcement can tell it's just another idiot, whose first crime back on the streets was littering.

"Are you hungry?" Karen wanted to know.

"Of course, favorite sister," I answered my only one.

"Where would you like to eat?"

"Turn towards Columbus. There's a Cracker Barrel at the next exit."

After everyone else left the van, I changed into civilian clothes Ann had brought for me. For the first time in four years, I was not dressed in the State's clothes.

Walking around in the Cracker Barrel store was surreal. I could move about; pick things up at will to look at; and put them back without wondering if everyone watched me. I could stand next to someone, or smile at a child, without wondering if they thought of me.

And the food. Oh, what a meal, The Sampler breakfast was; with eggs over easy – *over easy, I ordered* – and country ham – *cured and salty* – smoked sausage, and bacon; biscuits and gravy, and grits; and apple butter jam, and marinated sliced apples, with all the coffee I wanted.

As I ate and enjoyed the fellowship with family members I loved, and who loved me, I was free! I really, truly was free!

*   *   *   *   *

Marcus Tullius Cicero (106-43 B.C.) wrote of duty:

> [W]ho would presume to call himself a philosopher if he did not inculcate any lessons of duty? But there are some schools that distort all notions of duty by the theories they propose, teaching the supreme good and the supreme evil. For he who posits the supreme good as having no connection with virtue and measures it not by a moral standard but by his own interests — if he should be consistent and not rather at times over-ruled by his better nature, he could value neither friendship nor justice nor generosity; and brave he surely cannot possibly be that counts pain the supreme evil, nor temperate he that holds pleasure to be the supreme good.

The lawyer, politician and philosopher further wrote incisively, about power and law:

> Power and law are not synonymous. In truth they are frequently in opposition and irreconcilable. There is God's Law from which all Equitable laws of man emerge and by which men must live if they are not to die in oppression, chaos and despair. Divorced from God's eternal and immutable Law, established before the founding of the suns, man's power is evil no matter the noble words with which it is employed or the motives urged when enforcing it. Men of good will, mindful therefore of the Law laid down by God, will oppose governments whose rule is by men, and if they wish to survive as a nation they will destroy the government which attempts to adjudicate by the whim of venal judges.

Lingering in the psyche was my pledge of allegiance, created January 23, 1995. I made a commitment in a letter; to appellate judges, Jim Brogan and Mike Fain:

> And what were those words from the bench? In the beginning of the hearing? "God save the United States of America...and the State of Ohio..." God has a heap of work to do, in the legal profession and in the court system. As *His* employee, I'll do my part.

I believe I did my part; and have been rewarded. But another task remained, before this ol' Casey takes his final turn at bat. In a continuing quest for *peace in the valley,* my story needed to be shared.

To each of you who yearns to escape a prison of the psyche, *from all of me,* may God bless your life as He has mine. And, may God bless America again.

Horace Ray Metz
Summer of 2012

raymetz@live.com

CPSIA information can be obtained at www.ICGtesting.com
Printed in the USA
LVOW060812071012

301782LV00002B/150/P